Trading on Art

Trading on Art

Cultural Diplomacy and Free Trade in North America

SARAH E.K. SMITH

UBCPress · Vancouver

Printed in Canada on FSC-certified ancient-forest-free paper (100% post-consumer recycled) that is processed chlorine- and acid-free.

UBC Press is a Benetech Global Certified Accessible™ publisher. The epub version of this book meets stringent accessibility standards, ensuring it is available to people with diverse needs.

Library and Archives Canada Cataloguing in Publication

Title: Trading on art : cultural diplomacy and free trade in North America / Sarah E.K. Smith.

Names: Smith, Sarah E. K., author

Description: Softcover edition. | Includes bibliographical references and index.

Identifiers: Canadiana 20250134063 | ISBN 9780774868921 (softcover)

Subjects: LCSH: Cultural diplomacy – Canada – History – 20th century. | LCSH: Cultural diplomacy – Canada – History – 21st century. | LCSH: Traveling exhibitions – Political aspects – North America – History – 20th century. | LCSH: Traveling exhibitions – Political aspects – North America – History – 21st century. | LCSH: Canada – Foreign relations – 1945-

Classification: LCC FC242 .S65 2025b | DDC 327.71009/04—dc23

Canada Council for the Arts Conseil des arts du Canada

Canada

BRITISH COLUMBIA ARTS COUNCIL

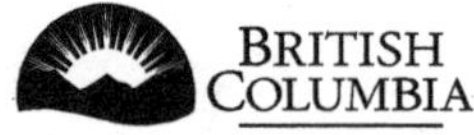

UBC Press gratefully acknowledges the financial support for our publishing program of the Government of Canada, the Canada Council for the Arts, and the British Columbia Arts Council.

This book has been published with the help of a grant from the Canadian Federation for the Humanities and Social Sciences, through the Scholarly Book Awards, using funds provided by the Social Sciences and Humanities Research Council of Canada.

UBC Press is situated on the traditional, ancestral, and unceded territory of the xʷməθkʷəy̓əm (Musqueam) people. This land has always been a place of learning for the xʷməθkʷəy̓əm, who have passed on their culture, history, and traditions for millennia, from one generation to the next.

UBC Press
The University of British Columbia
www.ubcpress.ca

For Kim, Kathy, and Kay

Contents

Figures and Tables

Figures

Table

Acknowledgments

I am grateful to the anonymous reviewers of this book for the time and care they took in providing feedback. Their thoughtful responses allowed me to better understand my research and how it sits within the field, and their guidance was essential to refining the text to best present these ideas.

This book was made possible, in part, by funding at various stages from the Social Sciences and Humanities Research Council, the Fulbright Foundation, the Canada Research Chairs program, Carleton University, and Western University. I am also grateful to the Faculty of Information and Media Studies at Western University for a grant in support of the images reproduced here. I was able to work with talented research assistants, and I thank them for their efforts: Bethany Berard, Eduardo Luciano Tadeo Hernández, Sarah MacLean, and Francisco Zepeda Trujillo.

While conducting my research, I interviewed artists and curators, all of whom gave generously of their time in conversations that greatly aided my thinking. I give my sincere thanks to them for the work that they do and for their willingness to share their practices with me. I am also deeply indebted to the many librarians and archivists who facilitated my research at numerous institutions. Here, I would like to single out Cyndie Campbell, Philip Dombowsky, and Heather Home.

The chapters in this book were informed by the generous intellectual communities in Communication and Media Studies at Carleton University and the Faculty of Information and Media Studies at Western University. At Carleton, the Belcher writing groups (especially Merridee Bujaki's mentorship) and the CRIW writing retreats were a lifeline. They provided camaraderie and counsel, as well as feedback from participants Meredith Lily and Sandra Robinson.

This project is informed by the teaching and mentorship of Lynda Jessup and Kirsty Robertson, as well as Jan Allen, Jeffrey Brison, Susan Lord, and Clive Robertson. It is also shaped by Louis Hock, who offered mentorship during a semester at the University of California San Diego (UCSD). My time at UCSD was an invaluable opportunity to consult the inSite Archive and to connect with artists and organizers in the region involved in inSite, many of whom generously agreed to interviews, including Louis, Jordan Crandall, Carmen Cuenca, Ricardo Dominguez, Eloisa Haudenschild, Michael Krichman, and Mark Quint. Another formative experience was my connection with the Culture and the Canada-US Border research network led by Gillian Roberts and David Stirrup – a group that provided feedback at a key moment in the project's development. Later, I was lucky to meet Maria del Carmen Suescun Pozas and Alena Robin, who were collaborating on an initiative addressing the relationship between Latin America and Canada. Maria and Alena built an engaged community around this topic. I benefited from participating in this group, and I give my thanks to Maria and Alena for their encouragement and vital feedback. This project also reflects the generosity and guidance of Jennifer Hyndman, Peggy Levitt, Alison Mountz, and Imre Szeman, who shared disciplinary perspectives that allowed me to reflect on my methods and the relationship of my work to studies across the social sciences and humanities. I am also incredibly indebted to Nicholas J. Cull, Jay Wang, and the community at the University of Southern California Center on Public Diplomacy, who welcomed me into the field of public diplomacy during my tenure as a Fulbright Visiting Research Chair and gave me a new language with which to discuss my work, along with a cadre of interlocutors.

As I worked on the manuscript, my thinking about art and cultural diplomacy was transformed through the North American Cultural Diplomacy Initiative (NACDI), a research network I established with Jeffrey Brison, Lynda Jessup, and Sascha Priewe. I was fortunate to find such critical and engaged collaborators in these three and across the larger NACDI community, which has grown considerably since 2017. The network has pushed me to think about how we might conceive of and understand a critical cultural diplomacy and to reflect on the narrow ways in which culture and diplomacy have long been defined. *Trading on Art* reflects ideas exchanged with NACDI members, as well as specific insights from Nicholas Cull, Patricia Goff (whose work is central to my understanding of the cultural exemption and cultural diplomacy), Simge Erdogan-O'Connor, Bronwyn Jaques, María Montemayor de Teresa, Guadalupe Moreno Toscano, Amy Parks, Amanda Rodríguez Espínola, Ben Schnitzer, Eduardo Luciano Tadeo Hernández, César Villanueva Rivas, and Francisco Zepeda Trujillo.

This book also connected in unexpected ways with my research on visual art and labour. I am pleased to address some of the links between free trade and the Ontario-based Independent Artists' Union and thank Greig de Peuter for our ongoing collaboration on the union's work and impact, his willingness to let me draw connections between my two projects, and his patience as I completed the book. Finally, as a project invested in contemporary art and art that is framed in relation to the Canadian state, this research reflects my discussions with the Open Art History collective, where I was an active member between 2020 and 2023. I thank Johanna Amos, Alena Buis, Elizabeth Cavaliere, Jennifer Kennedy, and Devon Smither for providing a vibrant community in which to think about visual culture and Canadian art.

I am grateful to editor James MacNevin for his guidance and to Ann Macklem and the larger team at UBC Press for their help. Working with Tim Pearson, whose careful reading of the manuscript helped me to realize my goals for the book, has also been a pleasure. I am indebted to his skilful editing and constructive suggestions. Completing this volume was a long journey, and the fact that I finished it at all is due in no small part to the incredible support of my friends and family. I thank Alena Buis, Maria-Carolina Cambre, Tonya Davidson, Sean Graham, Paul Kershaw, Erica Mitchell, Sam Mogelonsky, Tracy Neumann, Nicole Nolette, Melissa Redmond, Kirsty Robertson, Taryn Sirove, and Carla Taunton. Most importantly, I thank my family: Kathy, Kim, Alex, Tannys, Oakley, Kath, Dale, and Don – and Craig, who never tired of asking when the book would be done.

Trading on Art

Introduction

In 1989, Toronto-based activist artists Carole Condé + Karl Beveridge created a photographic work that frankly addressed free trade between Canada and the United States. Titled *Free Expression* (Figure 1), it renders free trade as a visible force – it dominates – pulsating through the world in the form of a signal from a radio tower perched atop the planet. In the foreground, a man and a woman interrupted sit at a desk piled with Canadian publications. The perspective is skewed to provide an aerial view of their desk, revealing a slew of alternative periodicals, including *Tiger Lily, Fireweed,* and *Fuse* – a literary magazine for women of colour, a feminist quarterly of writing, politics, art, and culture, and a politically oriented visual art magazine, respectively.[1] This selection makes clear reference to the vitality and diversity of the Canadian arts scene at the time.

The scene is set for confrontation. While the older man looks over his shoulder apprehensively, the seated woman gazes directly at viewers, drawing them in. Behind her, another woman stands with arm outstretched and hand raised to stop a column of men from marching into the room. *Free Expression* depicts an impending conflict between cultural producers. Three of the intruders wear business attire, their heads replaced by media images including *Fortune* and *Time* magazines, as well as a television set showing George H.W. Bush, then president of the United States. The floor behind them tilts radically, disrupting the perspective of the image. A framed photo of Prime Minister Brian Mulroney hangs on the wall, slightly askew, a ghostly glow illuminating his face.

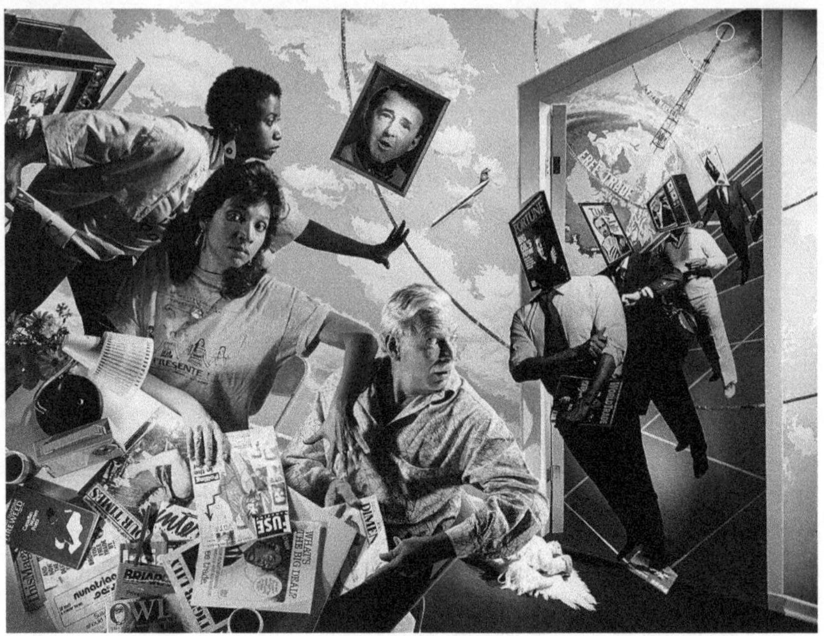

FIGURE 1 Carole Condé + Karl Beveridge, *Free Expression,* 1989, photograph. Courtesy Carole Condé + Karl Beveridge.

Produced as a postcard, *Free Expression* circulated widely as a low-cost multiple enclosed in an issue of *Fuse.* It is one example of how free trade inspired the production of art that reflected the new trade agreements, as well as changing ideas about North America. In the face of US economic power, the photo depicts a nation-based struggle. It affirms the category of Canada, naturalizing Canadian culture and depicting Canadian cultural production as pitted against US cultural hegemony. Many other artworks about free trade produced during this period took this stance. What lends them continuing interest today, however, is the access they give to cultural representations of histories of free trade in Canada, which have been neglected despite a great deal of research on free trade, culture, and the US-Mexico border region.[2] In fact, a substantial body of Canadian art addresses free trade. Like *Free Expression,* the works I examine in this book tackle and reveal the debates over trade that polarized Canadian and North American society near the end of the twentieth century. Bearing explicit and sometimes more covert political messages, they sprang from artists' engagement with the changes brought by free trade. They demonstrate the cultural dimensions of free trade, a mechanism typically assessed only from economic perspectives in academic literature.

In many ways, North America in the early twenty-first century appeared as a natural transnational regional unit consisting of three geographically proximate nations linked by economic, political, and cultural ties. In fact, this unit had to be created because prior to the late twentieth century North America was not conceived of in this way. In the twentieth century, it did not exist as a cultural entity: instead, the Americas were understood as divided between Anglo and Latin America.[3] Canada and Mexico were each preoccupied with the United States and did not develop strong ties to each other, a situation described by political economist Pablo Heidrich and political scientist Laura Macdonald as "dual bilateralism."[4] Therefore, a great deal of ambiguity surrounded the relationships between the three North American countries, with Canada's efforts vis-à-vis Mexico characterized as indifferent and Mexico's ties divided between Anglo-America and Latin America.[5] In the context of free trade at the end of the twentieth century, a new understanding of the continent meant significant changes in how each country perceived its relationships with its neighbours. Given the breadth of these changes, political scientist Guy Poitras argues that North America was invented as a region at this time.[6] Indeed, a longer examination of the continent's history reveals the impact of late-twentieth-century free trade agreements on regional integration. The 1989 Canada-US Free Trade Agreement (CUSFTA) advanced trade liberalization, bringing the Canadian and the US economies together through the reduction of tariff and non-tariff barriers, as well as offering a mechanism for dispute resolution.[7] In 1994, the North American Free Trade Agreement (NAFTA) expanded the free trade zone to include Mexico. It affirmed an understanding of North America as a transnational region comprising three states with interconnected economies.

Although I present this new North America as a hegemonic narrative advanced by the three state governments, it must also be understood in historical context as a moment in an ongoing story about the continent. North America is a concept that has long been in flux.[8] In examining the government use of culture in service of the reimagined continent, this book engages with methodological nationalism. However, it does not reproduce the nation-state as a natural site of inquiry, showing instead that it fabricates itself through cultural goods (specifically visual art) and that it employs certain narratives to achieve its political ends. In all, this project acknowledges that the nation is not a given but rather, as Benedict Anderson explains, an "imagined community," built and carefully cultivated in a manner that obscures its very construction.[9]

The cultural invention of North America is complicated by the fact that culture was explicitly exempt from CUSFTA and later trade agreements. The CUSFTA exemption was significant – as political scientist Patricia Goff argues, it was new to the multilateral system and it sparked similar exclusions in preferential free trade agreements.[10] Specific to the cultural industries, the exemption is defined in article 2005 of CUSFTA, which records Ottawa's ongoing anxiety over its capacity to "encourage and help Canada's cultural industries," defined as "film and video, music and sound recording, publishing, cable transmission and broadcasting." CUSFTA acknowledges "Canada's unique cultural identity" and states explicitly that it remains untouched by the trade agreement. It further highlights that each country can pursue cultural policies according to its own interests.[11]

The definition of the cultural exemption in CUSFTA – limited to the cultural industries – raises the obvious question of how to define culture. One way of doing so is to understand it within a three-part framework.[12] First, culture is a way of life or expression of values. Second, it is evidenced in visual and material production, such as the fine arts. And third, it consists of the cultural industries, also known as the creative industries, encompassing commercial production of film and music. This book concerns itself with the second category, exploring works of art and exhibitions to illuminate the ways that culture responded to and engaged with trade rather than the way that trade agreements defined and interacted with culture, which falls mainly under the third category. Thus, my focus differs from other analyses of trade agreements that address commodity exchange and culture as a commodity (though it is worth noting that the second and third categories often overlap).[13]

Culture may have been omitted from the purview of CUSFTA, but it was an important issue for Canada in negotiating the agreement in 1986 and 1987. The cultural exemption was the result of Canadian advocacy, and at Ottawa's insistence it carried over into NAFTA (which superseded CUSFTA). Its endurance – albeit as a limited provision – demonstrates the significant value that the Canadian government accorded to culture. Goff explains, "Government efforts to protect these [cultural] industries go beyond economic concerns to a desire to uphold the distinctiveness of their respective cultures and to maintain control of what is perceived to be an instrument of power in the (re)production of political community."[14] Cultural exemptions are often understood as a binary between protectionists (who support measures to promote domestic cultural industries) and free traders (who oppose such measures). Goff, however, notes the complexity of cultural industries debates, suggesting that a dualistic approach does not hold up, given "non-commercial, sociocultural concerns – a desire to promote and preserve cultural diversity and collective identity."[15] This recognition of the non-monetary value of culture is reflected in other policy agreements, most notably the UNESCO Convention on the Protection and Promotion of the Diversity of Cultural Expressions, which was signed in 2005 and implemented in 2007. It emphasizes the "dual nature, *both cultural and economic,* of contemporary cultural expressions produced by artists and cultural professionals."[16] Goff, however, points out that it does not supersede existing treaties; rather, she characterizes it as a "normative" influence.[17]

Goff perceives Canada's cultural exemption as a static clause, unchanged since CUSFTA, which acts "to nurture and uphold Canadian culture."[18] Nonetheless, as Goff reveals, Canada's cultural exemption strategy differed significantly across preferential free trade agreements.[19] She notes, "With smaller partners, Canada was always able to maintain a relatively strong, blanket exemption. With larger and more powerful partners, the Government of Canada pursued a cultural exemption strategy, but the outcomes varied."[20] This variety was made possible by the emergence of free trade agreements that were external to the multilateral system.[21] Whereas CUSFTA stands out for its initial use of the exemption, the idea to protect (to various degrees) culture (defined in various ways) in free trade agreements is not unique to Canada. In fact, the long-standing tension between trade liberalization and cultural policy has played out in trade negotiations globally over the last three decades. In addition to Canada, France, the European Union, and South Korea have all grappled with cultural protections in trade deals.[22]

In this book, I resist the conventional reading of free trade agreements, which is through an economic lens. Instead, I focus on visual art, exploring specific works, exhibitions, programming, institutions, and other initiatives to argue that art was vital to naturalizing the North American economic unity achieved in the free trade deals.[23] To be clear, not all art shows of the period speak to the dynamics of North American free trade that I address here. Rather, I have selected certain major exhibitions that received government support and that conveyed similar messages about North America, which evidence a specific approach and had significant impact. Exhibitions and cultural initiatives were key means by which new ideas of North America were messaged to the public. The Canadian, Mexican, and American governments employed art shows as a means to demonstrate their shared interests. In the case of *Panoramas: The North American Landscape in Art*, a 2001 online exhibition, works by Canadian, Mexican, and American artists were used to depict the commonalities of North American landscapes. Exhibitions such as these demonstrate how art helped to naturalize the integration of the three NAFTA countries.

Paradoxically, art also offered a venue for dissent against this same economic unity. Works such as *Free Expression* by Condé + Beveridge frankly express apprehension regarding free trade and visualize its potential impact on the art community, revealing concerns about American cultural imperialism. The artists revisited these issues in subsequent works, including *Shutdown* (1991), which depicts the impact of CUSFTA on Canadian labour (Figure 2). *Shutdown* centres on the frustrations of a worker who has lost her job due to free trade. At the left, a fractured domestic interior alludes to financial hardship, and a black-and-white image of an empty factory fills the right side of the picture. Explaining that the rhetoric around free trade obscured its impact on Canadian labour, Condé + Beveridge note, "We have been too easily convinced that

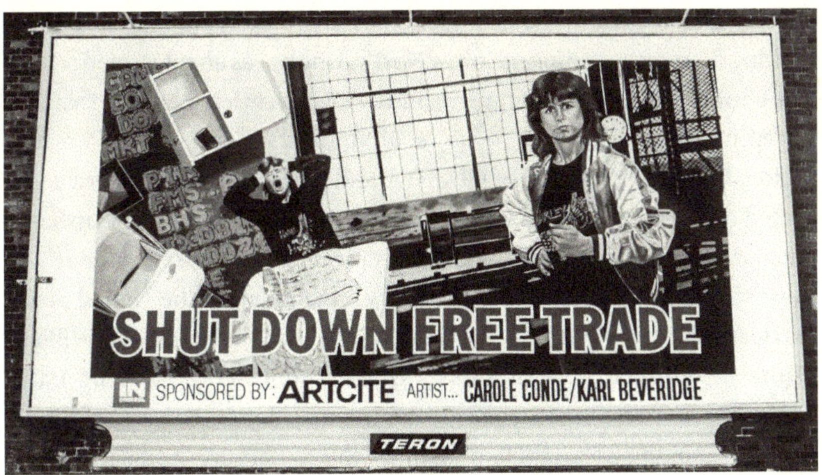

FIGURE 2 Carole Condé + Karl Beveridge, *Shutdown,* 1991, painted billboard commissioned by artcite, Windsor, Ontario (originally a photographic image). Courtesy Carole Condé + Karl Beveridge.

the jobs are simply the abstract and flexible components of corporate bottom lines. There is little sense that jobs not only provide basic living needs but are the means by which people maintain a social sense of self and community."[24] Underscoring the stakes for workers, the artists personalize the impact of free trade, pointing to the struggles of an individual. The photograph was installed as a painted billboard in Windsor, Ontario, where it was viewed against the Detroit skyline. This placement brought it into the public sphere, where it explicitly commented on those who were directly affected by free trade, enhanced by the Windsor region's close ties to the North American auto industry. The work's execution in Condé + Beveridge's characteristically explicit and comprehensible style further contributed to its legibility.

Panoramas and *Shutdown* speak to congruent aspects of the larger issue that lies at the heart of this book – art's role in creating North America, whether as an integrated whole (as envisioned under NAFTA) or as separate national domains (realized through works that resisted the dominance of the North American imaginary). The art, exhibitions, and cultural initiatives explored here provide evidence of art as a venue for questioning a specific set of political and economic developments, a vehicle for the state to manufacture consent and for cultural producers to express dissent. Seeking to unsettle the invention of North America as an integrated whole, this book addresses developments in the late twentieth century that saw sweeping economic agreements reconfigure the continent into a new regional unit.[25] As a result of CUSFTA and NAFTA, North America was united under trade liberalization that went beyond the industry-specific, auto-pact-type agreements of the early twentieth century.[26] One of the most striking changes was Mexico's new attachment to the United States and Canada. Under NAFTA, the rhetoric was such that journalist William Orme Jr. quipped, "Mexico has switched continents," leaving Latin America.[27] Popular and scholarly attention has focused overwhelmingly on this changing Mexico-US dynamic, which, I argue, overshadows the implications of free trade for Canada and its relationships with its continental trading partners.

CUSFTA and NAFTA had important effects on Canada beyond trade, buttressing its so-called special relationship with the United States and drawing increased attention to its previously marginal ties with Mexico. My emphasis is on Canadian cultural production, exploring how art was used to demonstrate Canada's links to North America and to build new connections with Mexico. I also discuss exhibitions that were initiated or toured in Canada, as well as those with significant Canadian content that were staged in other NAFTA countries. Culture's contradictory association with free trade is further revealed through its prominent use as a form of diplomacy to advance trade relations between nations and to promote specific versions of national culture. Through the examination of artworks and exhibitions, I push back on the seeming inevitability of neoliberal North America by showing how art mediated the integration of the continent.

Thus, this book revises the dominant perception that culture has been absent from free trade histories. Despite its categorical exclusion as an exchange commodity from the trade deals of the 1980s and 1990s, culture played a large role in the negotiation of the agreements and in their aftermath. In fact, as Susan Crean, Laurie Edwards, and Maria D. Hebb note, the cultural exemptions in CUSFTA and NAFTA do not fully take all forms of cultural production into account. The "sectoral exemptions do not address the circumstances of most Canadian cultural producers as protecting the sector does not necessarily entail protecting the small business environment in which they operate. Nor do exemptions address the question of where culture intersects with intellectual property law."[28] In discussing the audiovisual industries, communication scholar Hernan Galperin characterizes the paradox of culture and free trade by suggesting that culture lies at the intersection of numerous policy and intellectual theories. Given this, the "trade in cultural goods brings to light different conceptions about the nature of economic development, cultural artifacts, and issues of collective identity."[29] More specifically, the complex relationship of culture and free trade can be seen as a "double narrative." According to art historian Kirsty Robertson, this narrative "consistently places Canadian culture as metonymic representation of Canadian identity." It is "always 'off the table' at trade negotiations, while simultaneously being highlighted as a vehicle for encouraging new economies and investment in Canada."[30] It is precisely these contradictions that are examined here. I reveal the conflicting narratives of culture and free trade, identifying a central paradox – that while art was employed to promote a new vision of North America, cultural industries were specifically excluded from the very trade agreements that necessitated such a vision.

Thus, the book foregrounds the Canadian government's instrumentalization of culture to advance free trade. The case studies presented here show that the Canadian government espoused an ambiguous position: even as it insisted that cultural products be excluded from free trade negotiations, it simultaneously mobilized cultural products (including visual art) to project nationalism, strengthen ties with the United States and Mexico, and communicate trade relationships to the public. This contradiction speaks to the complexity of how culture is utilized by governments for differing ends and opens up the varying perspectives from which we can understand cultural production and its circulation. Further, I argue that the Canadian government invested heavily in exhibitions, sometimes to a greater extent than its American and Mexican counterparts, revealing the stock it placed in culture to advance its foreign policy agenda. Such investment makes clear that the Canadian government viewed cultural initiatives as an important tool in achieving its economic and political goals. This dynamic exposes the ease with which cultural initiatives can be used in service of the state, but also, as discussed in Chapter 3, speaks to the Canadian government's keen interest in securing its own position within the continent.

An important element of narratives around culture, free trade, and North America is the perception of cultural standing, or the conventional understanding of a particular national culture's value in relation to others on the world stage. During the late twentieth century, the popular imaginary held that Canadian culture was at a disadvantage in comparison to that of the United States, which was perceived as dominant. Mexico, however, was in an entirely different position. In a well-publicized response to a reporter's question about the impact of free trade on Mexican culture, Mexico's secretary of trade and industrial development Jaime Serra Puche was dismissive.[31] "This has little relevance for Mexico," he stated. "If you have time you should see the exhibition 'Mexico, Thirty Centuries of Splendor' and you will realize there is no cause for concern."[32] Serra's cheeky reference to *Mexico: Splendors of Thirty Centuries* stands out as another way that exhibitions were discussed in relation to free trade.[33] Encompassing over three hundred and fifty objects, paintings, and sculptures, the show was a substantial presentation of Mexican culture. It surveyed an immense period – locating Mexico's history (which can arguably be dated to the War of Independence in 1810) within a much longer narrative and highlighting cultural production through the mid-twentieth century.[34] Curator Brian Wallis, however, pinpoints the problem with addressing such issues through the sweeping and simplistic narratives provided by blockbuster shows: "These shows narrow our view of a country to a benign, if exotic, fairy tale." He also calls out the mix of sponsors who employ culture to achieve specific ends. Noting the misleading quality of such exhibitions, he explains that they "are far from the disinterested scholarship most museums claim to provide. Though scrupulously researched and painstakingly displayed, nationalist exhibitions are, in the end, a blatant, self-admitted form of propaganda."[35] Although the art shows and initiatives addressed in this book do not rise to the level of propaganda (which is predominantly linked to a specific call to political action), their clear purpose was to disseminate specific perspectives and information that shaped a particular narrative about a nation.

In contrast with such nationalistic exhibitions, post-NAFTA shows tended to include more overt gestures toward cultural diplomacy between Canada, Mexico, and the United States. For instance, *Panoramas: The North American Landscape in Art* is notable as the first online exhibition supported by the governments of the three countries. It was also the first exhibition hosted online through the Department of Canadian Heritage's special operating agency, the Canadian Heritage Information Network, which advances digital collections management resources in Canadian museums. At the same time, other shows provided alternative paradigms for understanding national culture in North America. One of these was *Remix: New Modernities in a Post-Indian World,* which employed an Indigenous perspective to highlight the artificiality of national associations in North America – pointing to the naturalization of settler-colonial frameworks. *Trading on Art* brings together these and other understudied exhibitions to show how art was used to bolster the seeming inevitability of North American unity.

Exploring art as a form of resistance, this book also argues for the significance of art production in the period, identifying it as a space of dissent. To this end, I chart a range of works produced by Canadian artists about free trade, showing how they debated and reflected on the subject. Their work exposes the uneven implementation of free trade and speaks to its widespread contestation, evidenced most prominently in the alter-globalization protests that swept the world at the turn of the millennium – many of which are chronicled in video art production.[36] I focus on video art as a means of tracing some of the protests against free trade, as well as discussing changing tropes of North America. Acknowledging the medium's activist roots and its ease of dissemination, I show how video works engaged with free trade and the complexities of grappling with a transnational regional identity, as well as national identity.

I also examine contemporary art projects in other media that rejected free trade. In Chapter 5, I address the binational art festival inSite, which took place in the Tijuana–San Diego region through five iterations between 1992 and 2005. It spoke to art production in North America during a period of increasing economic integration that witnessed the free trade agreements of 1989 and 1994. Contemporary art also comes to the fore in Chapter 2, which discusses 49th Parallel: Centre for Contemporary Canadian Art/49e Parallèle: Centre d'art Canadien contemporain, a New York City gallery that was sponsored by Ottawa. This chapter, however, deals with cultural diplomacy and thus provides a case study for a theme that lurks just below the surface of the entire book.

Trading on Art raises issues of competing nationalisms, transnational movements, the efficacy of state-sponsored cultural initiatives, and the agency of artists and cultural practitioners in the face of significant government investment in diplomatic, economic, and cultural projects. It directs attention to the cultural dimensions of free trade, assessing the use of art to invent a new transnational regional imaginary. Although "regional" is often assumed to mean subnational, especially in Canada, I employ the word to refer to North America as a region that was constructed by the trade agreements that linked Canada, Mexico, and the United States. I argue for art as a central means of debating, mobilizing, and naturalizing free trade and also contend that considering what is excluded from free trade agreements is as essential as understanding what is in them if we wish to fully assess the history of North American economic (and cultural) integration.

The book is organized in three parts, each containing two chapters on a particular aspect of visual art in relation to free trade. The first, Exhibiting Diplomacy, examines exhibitions and institutions as a form of cultural diplomacy prior to the period of free trade at the end of the twentieth century. Part 2, Picturing North America, delves into how art shows worked to construct narratives about the continent amid and following economic integration under free trade. The final section, Creating Resistance, focuses on art that was critical of free trade. The three parts are loosely chronological, beginning with the cultural diplomacy initiatives that set the groundwork for the harnessing of culture that promoted continental integration in free trade's wake.

Chapter 1 discusses the relationship between Canada and Mexico. Prior to 1994, these two countries emphasized their respective bilateral relations with the United States rather than with each other. Under NAFTA, however, they began to build a dialogue that was facilitated by art shows and cultural exchange. I outline the exhibition history of Mexican modern art in Canada to demonstrate what changed and what remained the same under free trade. Concentrating on an exhibition titled *Mexican Modern Art: 1900–1950*, I specify how it related to NAFTA and explore the persistence of apolitical and exotic frameworks in the display of Mexican art in Canada. The analysis underscores the significant expectations and motivations shaping the use of art shows in the service of cultural diplomacy, stressing the role of state actors in mobilizing exchanges of cultural goods.

The second chapter turns to the Canada-US relationship and the Canadian government's investment in the creation of 49th Parallel, a gallery in New York City. A forgotten enterprise, the gallery used experimental art to present Canada as a trade partner during a key period that corresponded with CUSFTA and NAFTA. I identify three approaches in its promotion of Canadian art between 1981 and 1992, when it closed its doors. It encouraged trade, both in the wider sense and specifically within the art market, and I document how officials used cultural display to soften the ground for bilateral cooperation between Canada and the United States. This case study demonstrates Canada's emphasis on US relations during the lead-up to CUSFTA. Many of the assumptions about Canadian culture and its role abroad – which characterized the tenure of 49th Parallel – endured in the NAFTA period. As such, this case study serves as a counterpoint to the preceding discussion of Mexican art, as well as provides the background to the cultural diplomacy exhibition initiated in NAFTA's wake that I discuss in the third chapter.

Chapter 3 looks at three exhibitions that were central to advancing connections between Canada, Mexico, and the United States in the wake of NAFTA. They played a significant role in laying the groundwork for envisioning the *new* North America, inventing and depicting a novel history for the region. The exhibitions were titled *Panoramas: The North American Landscape in Art; Carr, O'Keeffe, Kahlo: Places of Their Own;* and *Baja to Vancouver: The West Coast and Contemporary Art*. This chapter addresses the importance of art in creating and sustaining the nation, noting that national narratives have historically drawn on the landscape genre and engaged with regionalism in various ways. I argue that the governments of Canada, Mexico, and the United States employed art to promote intra–North American ties. Their framework was then picked up in subsequent projects that did not receive state support, thus revealing the spread of new readings of the continent that prioritized transnational links.

Chapter 4 focuses on art shows that featured Indigenous visual and material culture. Canada, Mexico, and the United States have long used exhibitions of Indigenous art to advance their respective national projects. After NAFTA, however, Canada began to employ these shows to speak about the shared histories of the NAFTA countries – particularly between itself and Mexico. My analysis draws on the exhibitions *First Peoples of Canada: Masterworks from the Canadian Museum of Civilization,* and *Remix: New Modernities in a Post-Indian World.* The former erased Indigenous claims to land while simultaneously seizing on Indigenous culture as emblematic of the settler nation-state, whereas the latter used an innovative exhibition structure to problematize contradictions of identity for Indigenous artists.

Part 3 of the book reveals how art opposed free trade. Chapter 5 focuses on border zones as spaces of art production and sites where the fractures between states remained visible despite expanded economic integration under free trade. The chapter discusses inSite, often referred to as the "border biennial," which commissioned art interventions in the Tijuana–San Diego region from 1992 to 2005. My assessment of inSite addresses artistic treatments of the border zone that focused on physicality, contrasting them with works pertaining to the Canada-US border, which was largely perceived as a conceptual divide. This difference was especially marked before 9/11 prompted a "re-bordering" between Canada and the United States.[37] Chapter 6 moves on to art production in Canada and its rejection of free trade, concentrating on video, an easily disseminated medium with activist leanings. Canadian video artists critically engaged with free trade discourses from the late 1980s to 2010. Using diverse strategies, from media talkback to performative investigations of nationalism, they destabilized the reimagining of a North American region united by free trade.

North American unity returned to the forefront of public discourse as a result of the 2017 renegotiation of NAFTA.[38] Replacing NAFTA, the Canada-United States-Mexico Agreement (CUSMA) was announced on 30 September 2018 and was publicly signed at the G20 summit in Buenos

Aires on 30 November 2018.[39] The reopening of the deal ignited new debates over labour standards, dispute-settlement mechanisms (laid out in the contentious Chapter 19 of NAFTA), and how exactly free trade benefited the countries involved.[40] During the negotiations, Canada affirmed its long-standing commitment to the cultural exemption. As Prime Minister Justin Trudeau explained in September 2018, "Defending that cultural exemption is something that is fundamental to Canadians."[41] However, the CUSMA talks were not accompanied by the charged debates regarding national culture that had played such a key role in CUSFTA and NAFTA.[42] Only when the text of the agreement was released in October 2018 did greater discussion of the exemption arise, particularly about what it would not cover, such as the extension of copyright for intellectual property.[43]

This book questions our understanding of North America as a region. It also asks readers to consider the role of art in trade, reflecting rhetoric around new economic agreements, conveying dissent, and carrying dominant messages from governments. *Trading on Art* should be seen as a counterpoint to studies that focus exclusively on economics. It shows how art is wrapped up in international affairs and political-economic situations. Culture played a paradoxical role in CUSFTA and NAFTA. Excluded from both agreements, it was nevertheless used by governments to reinforce their messages about continental unity and to advance a North American imaginary. For their part, many artists spoke back to free trade and the dominant message of a unified North America. Art also documented the direct activism happening around free trade, including alterglobalization protests.

In this book I illuminate the overt and covert use of culture to support state aims, arguing that it is noteworthy but often unrecognized. To be clear, the Canadian government was largely upfront about its instrumentalization of art, with the exception of 49th Parallel (which became a point of tension). Nevertheless, the underpinnings of many of the projects discussed here – including their creation, funding, and how their narratives slotted into government priorities – were not always transparent to the public. Thus, *Trading on Art* aims to shine a light on the economic and political context of these exhibitions related to free trade. The book also brings a multitude of initiatives together to speak to the government's broader use of culture, not to pass judgment on this instrumentalization of culture but to identify the artworks, institutions, and policies shaping the larger field in which it played out.

The complex history of art and free trade is important to acknowledge, especially in light of the new CUSMA, where a reading of free trade in relation to culture has been conspicuously absent. Only by revisiting the earlier moments of free trade history do the contributions of art, exhibitions, and cultural initiatives to discourses of free trade and geopolitical change become apparent. Thus, a reconsideration of the significance of culture to free trade attunes us to the many ways in which new narratives about North America and Canada and its free trade relationships might be messaged going forward. Our recent conversations about CUSMA trouble the perception of North American integration that was developed over many years and emphasize the need for a critical examination of its origins.

PART 1

Exhibiting Diplomacy

1

Mexican Art in Canada

When Mexico's secretary of trade and industrial development Jaime Serra Puche publicly invoked the US blockbuster exhibition *Mexico: Splendors of Thirty Centuries* during NAFTA negotiations in the early 1990s (as mentioned in the introduction), he pointed to the role of Mexican art in both promoting national narratives and advancing Mexico's standing in the world. Laying bare North American realities (specifically around the contentious issue of cultural protections), his comments spoke to the close networks of cultural exchange between Mexico and the United States. In contrast, a key element of the NAFTA dynamic was the perceived distance between Mexico and Canada. Consequently, following completion of the agreement, the two states devoted attention to forging greater bilateral ties through cultural exchange. To understand these developments, this chapter considers the history of art exchange between Mexico and Canada from 1943 to the turn of the millennium. I focus my examination on representative exhibitions, the standard in cultural diplomacy, which have elsewhere been labelled blockbuster exhibitions, treasures shows, and prestige exhibitions, amongst other descriptors.

Canada's first exhibition of Mexican art, held in 1943, was titled *Mexican Art Today.* At the time, the prevailing attitude among government officials and cultural practitioners was that art both possessed universal qualities and contained and conveyed national attributes. Thus, it was perfectly positioned to help forge relationships between countries. This view was exemplified in the Introduction to the catalogue for *Mexican Art*

Today, where curator Henry Clifford stated that "the pictures will speak for themselves."[1] The story they told was one of Mexico's place in the world and its relationship to Canada. Interestingly, almost sixty years later, many of the same pictures would reappear in *Mexican Modern Art: 1900–1950,* but this time they told a different story, one that articulated a free trade alliance between the two countries. Throughout the half-century that elapsed between the two exhibitions, state alliances provided the main impetus for displays of Mexican modern art in Canada. However, the shows consistently reinforced particular attitudes and approaches to Mexico. Foremost among them was a depoliticization of the art that divorced it from its contexts and immersed it in exoticism, commonly signalled by words such as "passion" and "colour."

Exhibiting Mexican Art in Canada

To contextualize *Mexican Modern Art,* it is necessary to examine the history of exhibiting Mexican art in Canada, which provides insight into the changing relationship between Canada and Mexico. Until lately, this relationship has not been subject to much critical attention. In 1996, curator and art critic José Springer noted that "the Canada-Mexico link lies virtually unexplored," suggesting that connections between the two countries were understudied due to the dominance of the United States in North America.[2] Sociologist Victor Armony wrote in 2014 that in comparison to US Latino populations, "much less consideration has been given to Canada's comparatively small, but rapidly growing population of Latin American origin."[3] In the visual arts, recent attention has been paid by scholars to deficits in the study of Latin American art in Canada.[4] Drawing on data from art historian Evonne Levy's project "Art History in Canada: 1933–Present," art historian Alena Robin notes that Latin American, African, and Islamic art is the "least represented among [Canadian] art history departments."[5] In fact, Robin's survey indicates that Canadian museums are more supportive of Latin American art than are their university counterparts.[6]

This chapter focuses on the National Gallery of Canada (NGC), as that institution played a fundamental role in bringing Mexican art to Canada during the twentieth century, coordinating and hosting exhibitions that subsequently moved on to other Canadian museums, predominantly in large urban centres such as Toronto and Montreal. Additionally, the NGC has long been involved – to varying degrees – with government cultural diplomacy efforts. As a federal institution, it is a natural hub for government projects, which have included partnerships with the Department of External Affairs (now Global Affairs Canada).[7] The gallery has also built relationships with various Canadian embassies worldwide.[8] Notably, these were central not only to the circulation of foreign art in Canada but also to the placing of exhibitions of Canadian art abroad (a priority for the Canadian government). Often, reciprocity was a condition for the exchange of blockbuster exhibitions of national patrimony. It could also apply to shows organized by other Canadian museums. For example, in 2008 the Canadian Museum of Civilization sent a touring exhibition titled *First Peoples of Canada* to China (discussed in Chapter 4). Consisting of Indigenous visual and material culture, it had been preceded by *Treasures from China*, sent by the Beijing government to Canada in 2007. *First Peoples of Canada*'s later appearance in Mexico was also tied to a subsequent reciprocal show from that country, which was titled *Maya: Secrets of Their Ancient World.*

The NGC's role as facilitator of Mexican art in Canada necessitates an examination of its activities, albeit with the recognition that other individuals and institutions also engaged with Mexican art in the period.[9] The National Gallery of Canada Archives possesses records for the Mexican art shows that were held at the gallery, including documents regarding their organization (including partners and funding), as well as press coverage, which speaks to their reception and curatorial approach. The NGC staged four such shows between 1943 and 1999 (Table 1); others did not come to fruition, dating from as early as 1930.[10] Overall, the files at the archives reveal that Canada paid scant attention to Mexican art during the period.

Of the exhibitions listed in Table 1, those of 1943, 1960, and 1999 were of major importance.[11] The 1946 show was modest in both size and the calibre of works displayed, and will not be discussed. The other three were similar in several respects: they concentrated on two-dimensional work (painting, drawing), they were large-scale and comprehensive, and

TABLE 1
National Gallery of Canada exhibitions of Mexican art

Date	Title and description	Curator(s)	Organizing institution(s)	Canadian venues
1943	*Mexican Art Today* Over two hundred oil paintings, watercolours, drawings, woodcuts, lithographs, and photographs by roughly sixty artists, including Frida Kahlo, José Clemente Orozco, Diego Rivera, David Alfaro Siqueiros, and Rufino Tamayo	Henry Clifford, in collaboration with Inés Amor	The Philadelphia Museum of Art, in collaboration with the Dirección General de Educación Extraescolar y Estética in Mexico	The NGC, which coordinated the exhibit's tour to the Art Association of Montreal (AAM) and the Art Gallery of Toronto (AGT)
1946	*Contemporary Mexican Painting* Twenty-six wall-based works in a range of media (oil, gouache, watercolour, tempera, charcoal, pencil drawing, ink drawing). Also featured several pieces of furniture (chairs, tables, a loveseat, and a screen). Artists included Rivera, Siqueiros, and Tamayo	Inés Amor	The NGC, in collaboration with the Galería de Arte Mexicano in Mexico	The NGC, which coordinated the exhibit's tour to the AAM, the AGT, and the Willistead Art Gallery in Windsor, Ontario
1960–61	*Mexican Art: From Pre-Columbian Times to the Present Day* More than two hundred works representing over four thousand years, with pre-Columbian sculptures, colonial sculptures and paintings, twentieth-century paintings, prints, photographs of contemporary architecture, and Indigenous crafts	N/A	The NGC, in collaboration with the Instituto Nacional de Bellas Artes, Mexico	The NGC, which coordinated the exhibit's tour to the Vancouver Art Gallery and the Montreal Museum of Fine Art (MMFA)
1999–2000	*Mexican Modern Art: 1900–1950* Over 270 works, including paintings, sculpture, drawings, prints, and photography by Kahlo, Lola and Manuel Álvarez Bravo, Gerardo Murillo (Dr. Atl), Rivera, and Siqueiros	Luis-Martín Lozano	The NGC and the MMFA	The NGC and the MMFA

Note: This table does not list exhibitions that did not progress beyond the proposal stage.

they featured art associated with Mexican nationalism, specifically works by *los tres grandes,* the famed muralists David Alfaro Siqueiros, Diego Rivera, and José Clemente Orozco.[12] Furthermore, each exhibition aligned with significant Canadian and Mexican government priorities. As such, they confirm that the NGC involved itself with Mexican art as a means of facilitating bilateral relations, a form of cultural diplomacy. This aim was overt; discussing *Mexican Art Today,* the *Ottawa Journal* noted, "In showing special collections from other countries, the Gallery hopes to forge friendly links between the nations through the medium of art."[13] At the time, cultural diplomacy was seen as an instrumental activity that was solely under the purview of the state. This corresponds with the dominant understanding of diplomacy as the private preserve of a select club of nation-states. In fact, it was often referred to as "club diplomacy" (distinguished from the "network diplomacy" of the present day, which acknowledges the growing role of myriad non-state actors in international relations).[14]

Audiences in Ottawa, Montreal, and Toronto got their first look at Mexican art in 1943. By comparison, Americans had been introduced to it more than a decade earlier, with major exhibitions in the 1930s.[15] Because Canada lacked expertise with Mexican art, *Mexican Art Today* was organized in the United States – by Philadelphia Museum of Art curator Henry Clifford in collaboration with Inés Amor, a leading gallerist from Mexico City.[16] When the show opened, new formal diplomatic ties were being forged between Canada and Mexico (informal relations dated back to the late nineteenth century), and both nations were embroiled in the Second World War.

This geopolitical context directly affected *Mexican Art Today:* a key impetus for the exhibition came from the Canadian Wartime Information Board (WIB) led by John Grierson. The WIB provided significant financial support and pushed the NGC to take on the project.[17] Established in 1942, the WIB was tasked with domestic communications regarding the war and played an important role in shaping public perception of the conflict. Grierson probably saw the exhibition as a means to stress that Mexico was an ally against fascism. This was noted in press coverage, which also quoted Dr. H.L. Keenleyside, the assistant deputy minister of external affairs, discussing similarities between Canada and Mexico: "both [countries] expend energy in subduing the forces of nature in the same vast continents and in the utilization of natural resources to the betterment of human living."[18] Other articles mentioned the simple fact of the Canadian-Mexican alliance in the war: "Mexico's government encourages creative art, has always been hostile to Fascism and Nazism. Mexican volunteers fought shoulder to shoulder with the forces of the Spanish Republican government."[19] Grierson even spoke at the exhibition opening in Toronto, where he justified it in terms of Canada's nascent role in international affairs, citing its "new force as an international country, at the cross-roads of the modern world."[20] The Second World War provided a key incentive for cultural initiatives that proclaimed Canada's place in the global cultural sphere and enhanced specific bilateral relationships and alliances.

Exhibition openings provide a space for cultural diplomacy, facilitating interaction between diplomatic and government representatives, as well as cultural workers. In 1943, one of these figures was Carlos A. Calderón, the Mexican consul general, who attended the Toronto opening of *Mexican Art Today.*[21] There, he gave a speech in which he praised the developing ties between his country and Canada: "It is with real satisfaction that I can testify to an ever-growing current of mutual sympathy and brotherly understanding between Mexico and Canada."[22] Furthermore, Calderón spoke of an "inter-American spirit," which draws "us still closer as an integral part of the great American family."[23] His comments picked on up on the Canadian government's perception of Mexico as a gateway to South America. The *Ottawa Citizen* referred to Mexico's role in building hemispheric unity by improving Canadian relations with South America: "Mexico is our North American link with the culture of the South – America's millions who live with us in our one-world of today."[24] Although this remark suggests that Canada already saw Mexico as part of North America, this understanding was not widely prevalent. In fact, historian Asa McKercher notes that Canadians were largely Anglocentric in this period, seeing Canada as part of the North Atlantic Triangle with Britain and the United States.[25]

The newspaper coverage also revealed the absence of a close relationship between Canada and Mexico, the differences between the two states, and the fact that viewers could understand Mexico only in contrast with their own country. The *Ottawa Citizen* compared the preferred artistic subject matter of the two countries: "Unlike Canadian artists, whose trend is toward landscape, the Mexicans concentrate on human beings and their problems for their subjects."[26] Nevertheless, throughout the run of *Mexican Art Today,* journalists emphasized the importance of Mexico's art as on a par with its Canadian counterpart, stating that it was "not ... a primitive school but a fully matured school of art" and that it was "advanced in the cultural field."[27] Overall, the newspapers underscored the difference and separateness of Mexican art while holding it up as equal to that of Canada.

In fact, in the mid-twentieth century, Mexican art was highly regarded and circulated widely, including to leading European cities such as London, Paris, and Stockholm.[28] By 1959, the exhibition *Chefs d'œuvre de l'art mexicain* had travelled extensively, stopping at Zurich, Cologne, The Hague, West Berlin, Vienna, Moscow, Leningrad, Warsaw, Paris, Rome, and Los Angeles.[29] Canadian art was not as popular, though it was shown in Europe – notably at the 1924 British Empire Exhibition in Wembley, London. Including Group of Seven works that had not previously been presented internationally, the Canadian submission to Wembley was a "major foreign exhibit."[30] It is revealing that in the mid-twentieth century, the NGC sought to secure Mexican art for display in Canada, whereas Mexican institutions were reluctant to accept a reciprocal show of Canadian art (and ultimately declined it).[31] The Canadian exhibition of *Mexican Art Today* should not be viewed in isolation but rather as springing from the Mexican government's larger interest in cultural exchange and the art world's interest in Mexican art, which did not extend to Canadian art. Thus, Canadian cultural institutions were in step with larger global trends in seeking out Mexican art and reinforcing hierarchies of cultural capital (i.e., the high value placed on Mexican art).

Canadian newspapers also suggested that local audiences lacked the necessary cultural references to connect with Mexican art. In the *Globe and Mail,* Pearl McCarthy wrote that Toronto viewers would need to prepare themselves in advance to understand the show because of their lack of knowledge of Mexican culture, which she described as imbued with Aztec influences, "supernatural" elements, and a preoccupation with death.[32] "Without that attempt," she added, viewers "might see nothing but what [they] would label morbid; and morbid suggest[s] something sickly, which Mexican art certainly is not today, although it has much to do with death. That paradox makes it difficult for plain westerners to understand."[33] Such interpretations framed Mexico and its art as a heady taste of exoticism that might prove too rich for the palates of "plain westerners."[34] Anticipating that its visitors would know little about Mexican art, the Art Association of Montreal announced that it would install an information desk to provide further details on Mexican culture.[35] One report even stated that the desk would be staffed by a "Mexican resident in Montreal," who would be on hand to "explain to gallery visitors the background and surroundings in which these pictures were painted."[36] Thus, the Montreal stop for the exhibition offered opportunities for cultural education.

The messages conveyed by the 1943 exhibition were ultimately complex. Mexico was Canada's ally, joining in the fight against fascism, but the show also spoke to Canadians' ignorance of Mexico, playing up preconceptions that evidence cultural distance and lack of familiarity. As "the most representative showing of Mexican art ever seen in Canada [to that time]," *Mexican Art Today* walked a difficult line between showcasing the significance of Mexican cultural production and exoticizing and depoliticizing it.[37] Through diplomatic overtures, the Canadian government regarded the exhibition as a tool to announce a new formal relationship with Mexico, to create awareness of Mexican culture, and to promote it among the Canadian public. Overall, Canada and Mexico positioned themselves as distinct but aligned sovereign entities. This emphasis on national and cultural difference but shared political interest would also appear in subsequent exhibitions of Mexican art in Canada.

Although the WIB had had to push the NGC to take on *Mexican Art Today,* following the show's success the gallery sought out Mexican art for display. Despite its efforts, however, it failed to secure further exhibitions between 1948 and 1954. Overall, the history of cultural exchange between Canada and Mexico suggests an uneven relationship, one in which Mexico often held the balance of power and seemed largely uninterested in Canada. The gallery's commitment to reciprocal exhibitions may have played into Mexico's response, as the documentation does not indicate that there was a demand in Mexico for Canadian art (whereas Mexican art was recognized internationally).

Not until 1960 did another major touring show of Mexican art appear in Canada: *Mexican Art: From Pre-Columbian Times to the Present Day.* The bilateral political relationship again provided the key for Mexican officials to finally agree to loan an exhibition to Canada. Furthermore, it was linked to a reciprocal show of Canadian art, *Arte Canadiense,* a survey that spanned the eighteenth century to the 1950s, produced by the NGC in collaboration with the National Museum of Canada. *Arte Canadiense* travelled to Mexico City and Guadalajara in 1960 and 1961. It featured French Canadian artworks, Inuit sculpture, Indigenous carvings from the West Coast, paintings, and contemporary graphic art. Funding came equally from Mexican and Canadian partners, with both exhibitions well supported by their respective states and by arts institutions.

New bilateral relationships were forged through the process of organizing exhibitions.[38] Gallery officials in Ottawa and Mexico held face-to-face meetings. For example, Donald W. Buchanan, as associate director of the NGC, travelled to Mexico in October 1959, where he met with several officials, including Celestino Gorostiza, director-general of the Instituto Nacional de Bellas Artes.[39] Held in various Canadian cities, the opening ceremonies for *Mexican Art: From Pre-Columbian Times* once again provided occasions for political engagement. The Mexican ambassador, Rafael de la Colina, opened the show in Vancouver and Ottawa, and the Canadian minister of citizenship and immigration, Ellen Fairclough, was featured at the Ottawa event.[40]

The aim of both the Canadian and Mexican exhibitions in 1960–61 was to establish national prestige, serve as a visual representation of binational relations, and buttress each country's autonomous identity and power. This type of cultural diplomacy was characteristic of the mid-twentieth century in its focus on discrete national narratives. Though it was not directly discussed in the diplomatic correspondence that led to the exchange of exhibitions, the 150th anniversary of Mexican independence, in 1960, ultimately provided context to the shows in both Canada and Mexico.[41] The upcoming centennial of Canadian Confederation in 1967 likewise furnished an opportunity to market both Canada and Mexico as established nations with strong and distinct cultures.[42] The catalogue for *Mexican Art: From Pre-Columbian Times* emphasized the exhibition's importance in building connections, calling it "a landmark in the history of cultural relations between Canada and other countries of this hemisphere."[43] Again, Mexico would be a bridge to Latin America.

Despite the rhetoric of close and growing ties between the two states, as well as Mexico's move to prioritize Canadian trade in 1951, the NGC's numerous failed attempts to secure Mexican art for display reveal challenges in the bilateral relationship. Whereas states may never be as close as they profess to be, the 1943 and 1960 exhibitions demonstrate how the Canadian government, through the NGC, attempted to forge a closer relationship with Mexico and therefore how it sometimes used the NGC as a diplomatic arm. Although exhibitions of Mexican art were few and far between in the twentieth century in Canada, the few that did occur were freighted with political objectives. While the history of exhibiting Mexican art in Canada may be inextricably linked to developing diplomatic relations between the two countries, projects of cultural exchange progressed in fits and spurts depending on political developments. Art was a key to diplomacy – a means of establishing and performing political alliances. In the later twentieth century, the NGC would host group exhibitions that included Mexican artists, such as 1994's milestone *Cartographies: 14 Artists from Latin America.*[44] However, the gallery did not host another show devoted solely to Mexican art until 1999. This was *Mexican Modern Art: 1900–1950.* It featured works similar to those that had toured Canada in the mid-twentieth century, but the messages it conveyed about Mexico and its ties to Canada were significantly different.

Mexican Modern Art: 1900–1950

Mexican Modern Art was shown in Montreal in 1999 and then in Ottawa in 2000. Organized by the Montreal Museum of Fine Art (MMFA) and the NGC, it was a landmark: the largest touring exhibition of Mexican modern art in Canada to date, it comprised approximately 270 paintings, sculptures, photographs, and prints. Many of them had already appeared in earlier exhibitions of Mexican art, but now they were deployed in the service of new messages. The catalogue states that the idea for the show originated in 1990, when discussions of North American integration under free trade began to intensify.[45] New messages were necessary, as Stephen J. Randall and Herman W. Konrad explain, because prior to NAFTA, "Mexico [had] traditionally not considered itself to be part of North America."[46] As mentioned above, the concept of North America has long been in flux, with Mexico maintaining a particularly ambiguous relationship to the continent.

As the first exhibition in Canada to focus on Mexican art since 1960, *Mexican Modern Art* is an important marker in the history of cultural exchange between the two countries. The works dated from the first half of the twentieth century, when Mexico underwent drastic changes, including the Mexican Revolution and the end of the reign of Porfirio Díaz.[47] The show was promoted in terms common to blockbusters of the time, with an emphasis on the unique nature of the art on display. It was marketed as the "largest collection of Mexican modern art ever assembled outside Mexico," and much was made of the fact that it included works that had never toured internationally.[48] Additionally, the inclusion of "cult figure" Frida Kahlo was widely publicized in the press.[49] Works by other notable artists, such as Lola and Manuel Álvarez Bravo, Gerardo Murillo (Dr. Atl), Rivera, and Siqueiros, were also on display. The curator, Luis-Martín Lozano, explained that his aim was "to elucidate Mexico's true contribution to the history of world art." As he put it,

> My intention has been to place the development of modern art in Mexico in a historical perspective by viewing the art of the period 1900 to 1950 as the product of a country's singular artistic drive and ideas, played out against a backdrop of dialogue with the European vanguard; and in doing so, to construct an explanation of what the avant-garde should be, with due consideration for the threads of history that make up the unique fabric of the Mexican nation.[50]

In his assessment of Mexico's artistic contribution in the first half of the twentieth century, Lozano emphasized its interactions with the West. Mexican art was a "cosmopolitan dialogue," he noted: "As the selected works make clear, Mexican artists drank deeply from the well of international modernism."[51] Lozano structured the exhibition around four themes, which were outlined in the catalogue: Early Modernism: Cosmopolitan and Nationalist Trends in Mexican Art; The Mexican Renaissance: Art in Post-Revolutionary Times; Images for a New Era: Modern Photography and the Revival of Mexican Graphic Traditions; and the Many Faces of Mexican Modernism: 1930–1950.

In a press release for the show, NGC director Pierre Théberge stated that the "aesthetic ideas" of Mexican artists "constitute the real history of Mexican modern art."[52] Critics such as Mari Carmen Ramírez argued that this privileging of aesthetic quality reinforced a Western stance. As she wrote, prioritizing quality over culture when curating Latin American art "separates the form from its Latin American meaning."[53] Lozano's choice to employ the concept of a Mexican Renaissance in *Mexican Modern Art* reinforces the point through its allusion to the Italian Renaissance, which is of pivotal importance to the Western art-historical canon. The Mexican Renaissance conveys an understanding of Mexican art that emphasizes the traditions of Mexico and its colonial history.[54] Scholar and curator Olivier Debroise explains that this approach is conventional, presenting a specific "concept of Mexicanness" in which art production is read as a linear narrative of artistic continuity, with Mexico as a "modern nation built on an ancient past."[55] Employing this approach to structure the presentation of Mexican art conflates the artwork with Mexican nationalism and Mexican history, and also tends to prevent a more nuanced reading. The decision to adopt such a conservative curatorial approach was political in that it made room for NAFTA narratives. Trade was at the forefront of the exhibition in many respects: in terms of its larger context, its Canadian and Mexican corporate sponsors, its promotion of Canadian travel and tourism to Mexico, as well as a reciprocal exhibition of Canadian art to encourage Canadian trade in Mexico (discussed later in this chapter). Ironically, the result depoliticized the works, enabling *Mexican Modern Art* to be mobilized in a neoliberal context.

The depoliticization of the exhibition was noted by reviewer Blake Gopnik, who criticized both the show and its catalogue for their lack of attention to Mexican politics, which he saw as key to understanding the history of Mexican identity.[56] Gopnik charged that the exhibition did not adequately address Mexican muralism – central to Mexican art of the period – thus creating a "gaping hole right at the heart of this exhibition."[57] This neglect is significant because these artists were renowned for their alignment with revolutionary politics. Shifra M. Goldman explains that "the majority of muralists espoused left-wing socialist or communist ideas and were antifascist, anti-imperialist, and antimilitaristic."[58] Instead, the exhibition featured a specially created twenty-minute video titled *The Mexican Muralists,* with footage of *in situ* murals in Mexico. However, it covered the Mexican Revolution only superficially, neglecting to clearly situate the murals in their political context. This was not without precedent, as a similar treatment of Mexico's history appeared in *Mexico: Splendors of Thirty Centuries,* whose "essentialist" curatorial approach provided an "absurdly schematized simplification of the country's extremely volatile history."[59] The political neutralization of the muralists' works speaks to how exhibitions can frame specific movements and artists in a heavily decontextualized manner, allowing works of art to be deployed as cultural envoys for very different ends than originally intended.

Lozano's curatorial approach promoted Mexican art within Western frames of reference, highlighting aesthetic quality and modernity while displaying a conservative bias that marginalized the radical politics of the Mexican Revolution. As a result, Mexico appeared analogous to Canada in terms of national art discourse. This message was emphasized in two adjacent exhibitions at the MMFA and the NGC. The one at the MMFA was titled *I and My Circumstance: Mobility in Contemporary Mexican Art (Moi et ma circonstance; Yo y mi circunstancia).* Structured around the theme of mobility, it included fifteen contemporary Mexico City artists, among them Francis Alÿs, Thomas Glassford, Silvia Gruner, Gabriel Orozco, and Miguel Ventura. Curated by Guillermo Santamarina and Paloma Porraz, *I and My Circumstance* was organized by the MMFA and Mexico's national council for culture and the arts (Consejo Nacional para la Cultura y las Artes, also known as Conaculta).[60] It promoted Mexican art production as part of a global discourse, aligning Canada and Mexico within the same cultural sphere.

The catalogue for *I and My Circumstance* hints at a destabilizing role for the show, explaining that through the theme of mobility the "artists subvert the image we had of Mexico by laying bare our common condition."[61] In their contributions to the catalogue, essayists Eduardo Abaroa and Roger Bartra called for an examination of Mexican art beyond the paradigm of national identity. Abaroa detected an "absence of 'national' characteristics" in the artworks. "An artist's nationality is not important," he stated. "In fact, artists may find themselves in exile wherever they go."[62] His comments reference the well-established trope of the avant-garde artist as an outsider. Bartra voiced similar arguments against nationalism: "Mexico no longer exclusively exports objects that are archetypes of national identity, nor do objects imported from abroad today simply represent modernity."[63] These statements seemed incongruous with the presentation of *Mexican Modern Art* in the adjoining galleries.

At the NGC in 2000, *Mexican Modern Art* was complemented by a very different exhibition than *I and My Circumstance,* titled *Mexico as Muse: Photographs 1923–1986.* Curated by the gallery's Ann Thomas, it displayed fifty-seven photographs drawn from the NGC permanent collection, all of which had been inspired by Mexico. The photographers included Americans Edward Weston and Paul Strand, French artist Henri Cartier-Bresson, and Robert Bourdeau, a Canadian. All had undertaken "artistic pilgrimages" to Mexico.[64] The show examined the various ways in which their experiences in Mexico had affected their practices, and their work presented it as a site for art tourism – a wealth of creative inspiration for foreign artists. Making specific reference to the Mexican Revolution, the show's introductory panel mentioned the "special allure" of post-revolutionary Mexico for artists from North America and Europe in the 1920s.[65] This stress on Mexico as a source of creativity significant to global artistic development aligned with *Mexican Modern Art*'s focus on the Mexican Renaissance.

Both *Mexico as Muse* and *I and My Circumstance* complemented *Mexican Modern Art* as a cultural event. They emphasized Mexican visual culture, increasing the breadth of the blockbuster exhibition. In Montreal, *Mexican Modern Art* even seemed to be connected to *I and My Circumstance,* according to one reviewer, who commented that it segued seamlessly into the contemporary works: "We leave the room. There's no end to this exhibition; it also includes a second, separate show of contemporary

Mexican art."[66] Both galleries also put on extensive programs of events and activities to enhance the impact of *Mexican Modern Art.* For instance, as one reviewer reported, the MMFA offered a "program of more than 20 meetings, lectures, concerts, films and guided tours ... called 'A Fiesta of Cultural Activities.'"[67] The intent of these all-encompassing events was clear – to allow viewers to consume Mexico. Reviewing the show for the *Montreal Gazette,* Dorota Kozinska stated,

> Hundreds of paintings, sculptures, prints and photographs have turned the museum into a colourful carnival of dizzying proportions, which may at first be almost too much to take in. And if that weren't enough, numerous lectures, film projections, and activities have been organized by the museum's Cultural Programs Department around the exhibitions. These are meant to immerse the visitor even further in the Mexican psyche.[68]

Not to be outdone, the NGC staged "a series of Mexican-themed cultural events – everything from concerts to a film festival ... to complement the art show."[69] Together, Brian Wallis argues, these exhibitions and programming constitute cultural festivals, the use of which in relation to nationalist projects and "as a form of cultural diplomacy – or, to put it more crudely, public relations – is the latest development in a long history of propagandistic deployments of art exhibitions." Cultural festivals, for Wallis, are an "aggressive assertion of nationalism."[70] They increase the impact and breadth of exhibitions and draw more viewers to the museum. Tourism as a means of public diplomacy can have a significant impact; as historian Dina Berger maintains, it "can actually promote transnational and transcultural understanding and thus improve international relations."[71] Thus, the multifaceted events associated with *Mexican Modern Art* amplified the specific messages about Mexico that were conveyed in and through the exhibition itself.

In both Montreal and Ottawa, the promotional material for *Mexican Modern Art* also framed Mexican culture as exotic, which was essential if the show were to be reinvested with meaning through NAFTA and trade diplomacy. Collaborating with Cossette, an advertising firm, the MMFA created a wide-ranging media campaign.[72] It was visually unified, with an

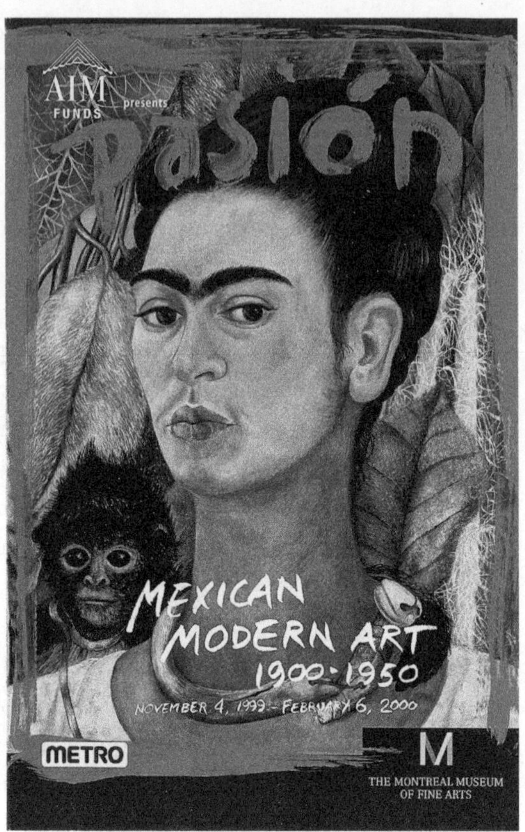

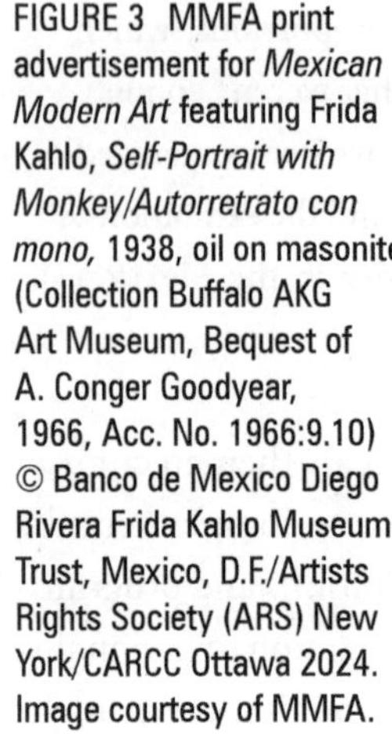
FIGURE 3 MMFA print advertisement for *Mexican Modern Art* featuring Frida Kahlo, *Self-Portrait with Monkey/Autorretrato con mono,* 1938, oil on masonite (Collection Buffalo AKG Art Museum, Bequest of A. Conger Goodyear, 1966, Acc. No. 1966:9.10) © Banco de Mexico Diego Rivera Frida Kahlo Museum Trust, Mexico, D.F./Artists Rights Society (ARS) New York/CARCC Ottawa 2024. Image courtesy of MMFA.

aesthetic that carried over to press kits, stickers, posters, visitors' guides, invitations, and banners.[73] Several print advertisements were created for use in different venues. All were derived from one design, the focus of which was the bright red tagline "pasión," written in a bold, simplified brushstroke. The basis of the design was a 1938 Kahlo painting, *Self-Portrait with Monkey,* which was part of *Mexican Modern Art*. "Pasión" was added to the name of the show in English and French, inserted before the title of the show to read, "Pasión: Mexican Modern Art, 1900–1950." The full version of the ad graced the cover of the visitors' guide, as well as some print advertisements (Figure 3).

In the painting, Kahlo faces the viewer, as a small monkey looks over her right shoulder. In the ad, the edges of the image are framed in vivid scarlet, and "pasión" is written across the top in the same colour, covering

Kahlo's hair. This painterly stroke, sympathetic to the aesthetic of her work, looks as if it were part of the original. Other promotional materials reduced Kahlo's image further, focusing on her lips. For instance, the exhibition invitation showed only her mouth and part of her cheek, beside which "pasión" was written in the signature red brushstroke (Figure 4).

Similarly, the MMFA collaborated with the dairy Liberté to place its ads on the lids of the company's yogourt containers. They too featured Kahlo's mouth and the word "pasión" (Figure 5).

Newspaper ads reduced the design even further, displaying the word "pasión" written in white on a large red brushstroke. The focus on passion was especially prominent in the use of Kahlo's lips, an aspect of her body

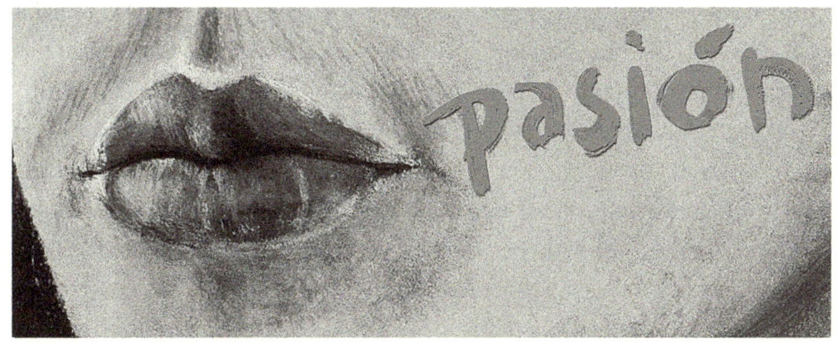

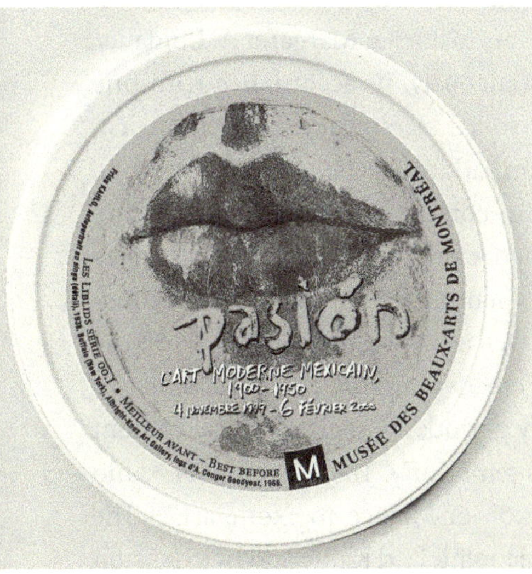

FIGURE 4 MMFA exhibition invitation for *Mexican Modern Art,* detail from Frida Kahlo, *Self-Portrait with Monkey,* 1938 (Collection Buffalo AKG Art Museum) © Banco de Mexico Diego Rivera Frida Kahlo Museum Trust, Mexico, D.F./Artists RightsSociety (ARS) New York/CARCC Ottawa 2024. Image courtesy of MMFA.

FIGURE 5 MMFA yogourt lid advertisement for *Mexican Modern Art,* detail from Frida Kahlo, *Self-Portrait with Monkey,* 1938 (Collection Buffalo AKG Art Museum) © Banco de Mexico Diego Rivera Frida Kahlo Museum Trust, Mexico, D.F./Artists Rights Society (ARS) New York/CARCC Ottawa 2024. Image courtesy of MMFA.

related to her sexualized mythology. This advertising presented Mexico as something to be consumed. Artist Guillermo Gómez-Peña explains the tendency to mythologize Latin America as exotic: "Our art is being described as 'colourful,' 'passionate,' 'mysterious,' 'exuberant,' 'baroque' etc. – all euphemistic terms for irrationalism and primitivism. These mythical views can only help to perpetuate the colonizing notions of the South as a wild and exotic preindustrial universe ever waiting to be discovered, enjoyed and purchased by the entrepreneurial eye of the North."[74]

The promotional campaign also echoed in the gallery space. Upon stepping into the Montreal galleries, viewers saw "the word Pasion [sic] splashed on a wall at the entrance to the show," one reviewer noted.[75] The MMFA even offered a "Pasión Contest," giving visitors the chance to win a four-day trip for four to Mexico City sponsored by the Mexico Secretariat of Tourism.[76] The NGC offered a similar contest with the same prize but under a different name.[77] Exoticism was also emphasized in the exhibition catalogue, where the MMFA and NGC directors described *Mexican Modern Art* as "an expression of ... attraction [to Mexico] and of our interest in discovering the art of a near neighbour."[78] How exhibitions are promoted to the public can be equally as important as their content. Here, Mexico was offered as a site for Western consumption.

The choice of Kahlo for the promotional materials added to this theme. Art historians have often conflated her life with her work. "Kahlo's character development and life story," art historian Margaret A. Lindauer argues, "have been produced simultaneously, in accordance with one another, in such a way that various social classifications – nationalist, invalid, rebel, hypochondriac, lesbian, adoring wife, childless mother, sexually desired object, antibourgeois, communist – are seen as being illustrated in her paintings."[79] Lindauer refers to this mythologization as "Fridamania" – a focus on Kahlo as a feminine icon that omits the historical details of her life and work as well as the realities in Mexico at the time.[80] She adds, "Although Kahlo's creative production is classified in relation to Mexico's postrevolutionary period, the social political content of her work is diluted by the focus on femininity. The reduction of Kahlo to woman resonates with the reduction of Mexico to exotic art."[81] The MMFA's promotional campaign thus depoliticized Kahlo and by extension

Mexico itself. As art historian Shifra Goldman suggests, "20th century Marxists like Kahlo and Diego Rivera ... [are] packaged into a handsome continuum of genius, detached from their historical context."[82] Shorn of her contradictions and voice, Kahlo became "simply a sanitized icon of the exotic, deprived of her politics."[83] By depicting her as a body part, the MMFA represented her as a myth.

Although the NGC had its own advertising campaign for *Mexican Modern Art,* it too relied on Kahlo's artwork, this time her 1940 *Self-Portrait with Thorn Necklace and Hummingbird.* Whereas the MMFA used "pasión," the NGC employed the tagline "Sol y Vida." Nevertheless, Mexico was again portrayed as an exotic place, full of "sun and life." In the Foreword to the exhibition catalogue, Pierre Théberge and Guy Cogeval described Mexico as "a country very different from our own – warm, colourful, legendary."[84] A promotional television commercial featured a montage of close-up shots of Kahlo's self-portrait, unrecognizable as a whole until the camera zoomed out and the entire painting became visible. A voiceover sketched the experience that awaited visitors to the show: "At the turn of the 20th century, a movement began that lasted fifty years. It captured the colour ... the passion ... and the soul of a beautiful country. Now at the beginning of the 21st century, we've captured it for you. Sol y Vida! Don't miss *Mexican Modern Art* at the National Gallery of Canada."[85] This approach to Mexico continued the long history of displaying so-called primitive cultures, often from colonies, at world fairs for consumption by Western tourists.[86] The promotion of Mexico in both the NGC and MMFA ad campaigns can be read as a gesture toward tourism, whether recreational or cultural. And, the exhibition itself was a form of cultural tourism. Latin American studies scholar George Yúdice explains, "Such exhibitions appeal to the metropolitan desire to indulge in a 'comfortable exoticism.'"[87] This was evident even in the details of the opening ceremony in Ottawa, where beer was provided by Corona.[88]

In the context of NAFTA, *Mexican Modern Art* became a vehicle of cultural diplomacy, an avenue through which political overtures were made. In particular, for the politicians and corporate sponsors who had a vested interest in tightening the ties between Canada and Mexico, it provided a way to publicly align themselves with narratives of the new

North America envisioned by NAFTA. Political and business support for the exhibition came from diverse Mexican and Canadian sponsors: Corona Extra, CBC/Radio Canada, Mexicana Airlines, the Mexican Tourism Office, and Magna International, which were augmented by regional supporters in Ottawa and Montreal.[89] This use of *Mexican Modern Art* as a platform for Canada-Mexico relations was encouraged by the NGC and MMFA. Their directors, Théberge and Cogeval, made this obvious by stating that the show "marks an important moment in the cultural relations between Canada and Mexico, two countries that share a hemisphere and that can reach a greater understanding of each other's heritage through works of art."[90] Robert Hain, president and CEO of AIM Funds Management, the primary corporate sponsor of the exhibition, echoed this message: "Art speaks an international language and is one of the most effective cultural ambassadors in the world today."[91] Hain's comment mirrors the 1943 rhetoric from *Mexican Art Today,* when much was made of the ability of artworks to "speak for themselves" across borders. Hain also invoked the notion of Mexico as a constructed space, which was repeated by Cogeval and Stéphane Aquin, MMFA curator of contemporary art: "Modern Mexican art occupies an inviolable place in our cultural imaginary. Rivera, Siqueiros, Orozco, Kahlo, Álvarez-Bravo – these names and many others bring to mind powerful images and a certain concept of Mexico."[92] However, this image of Mexico is always changing, as it is socially constructed; its use in relation to exhibitions in Canada reveals more about Canadian understandings of Mexico than it does of Mexico itself.

The cultural diplomacy purpose of *Mexican Modern Art* was most evident at its opening in Ottawa on 24 February 2000. Internal NGC correspondence states that the opening was intended as a celebration of "the cooperation between the two countries as much as the exhibition."[93] At the vernissage in the NGC's Great Hall, the Canadian and Mexican flags hung side by side.[94] Opening day also coincided with Mexican Flag Day, further foregrounding ties between the show and Mexican national identity. The opening was thus a staging ground for political gestures and a platform for politicians and corporate sponsors to increase their links to Mexico. Business added a new layer to exhibition exchanges at the turn of the millennium, which was absent in the mid-twentieth century.

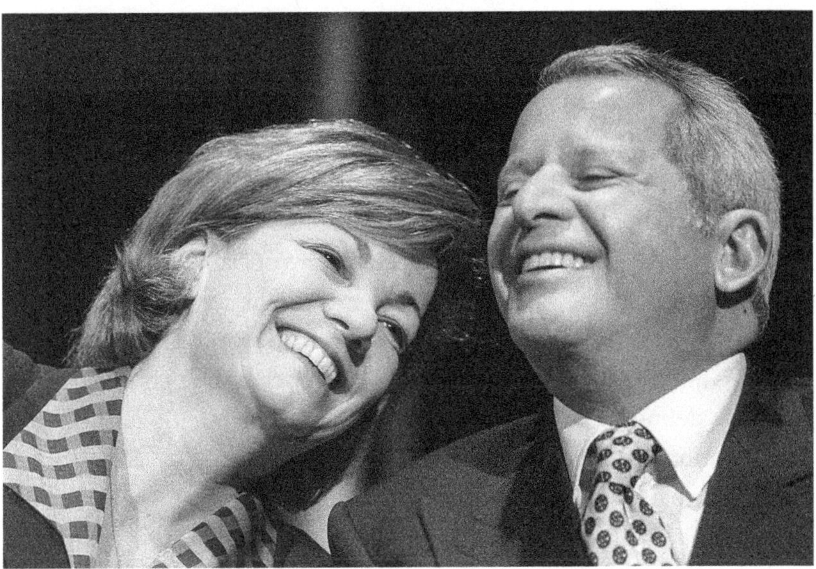

FIGURE 6 Sheila Copps and Ezequiel Padilla at the Ottawa opening of *Mexican Modern Art*. Photography by John Major, "Quiet Diplomacy," *Ottawa Citizen*, 25 February 2000, A5. Material republished with the express permission of the *Ottawa Citizen*, a division of Postmedia Network Inc.

The event hosted eminent guests from political, corporate, and cultural spheres, including the Canadian heritage minister, Sheila Copps, Théberge, Cogeval, Gerardo Estrada, the director-general of Mexico's Instituto Nacional de Bellas Artes, Alberto Fierro, the Mexican cultural attaché, Ezequiel Padilla, the Mexican ambassador, and Hain, representing the main corporate sponsor. A photograph of Sheila Copps and Ambassador Padilla sharing a convivial moment ran in the *Ottawa Citizen* the following day, captioned "Quiet Diplomacy" (Figure 6). The irony, of course, is that there was nothing quiet or subtle about the diplomacy of the event, which was imbued with overt political meaning.

Terre Commerciale

The use of art to negotiate a new relationship between Canada and Mexico was also apparent in the linkage between *Mexican Modern Art* and *Terre Sauvage: Canadian Landscape Painting and the Group of Seven*. A reciprocal exhibition of Canadian art, *Terre Sauvage* was curated by Charles Hill and organized by the NGC. Comprising seventy-six paintings by the Group of Seven and Tom Thomson, dating from 1912 to 1934, it ran in 1999 at the Museo de Arte Moderno in Mexico City, as part of a longer international tour.[95] The press release noted that it included "major" and "important" works, as well as the fact that the Group of Seven was vital to establishing Canadian identity and was a national school of modern art.[96] The deployment of the Group as representative of Canada is not surprising, given that their work has long been used in the service of nationalist projects.[97] Art historian Lynda Jessup, who has examined the history of the NGC and the Group, writes that the gallery championed "the Group's narrowly defined, exclusive Canadian nationalism, a nationalism based on the notion that there is an essential Canadian identity."[98] Such criticism is still advanced by contemporary artists such as Deanna Bowen, who has pointed to anti-Black racism and, more broadly, the exclusionary nature of the Canadian national narrative, with specific reference to cultural institutions and artists, including the NGC and the Group of Seven.[99]

Terre Sauvage was initiated by diplomats. It was requested by the Canadian embassy in Mexico as part of the end-of-the-century celebration *Canada-Mexico: A Salute to the Millennium.*[100] The show was coordinated in part by Mary Culham, wife of Allan Culham, a Canadian diplomat who had worked at the embassy in Mexico City.[101] The importance of *Mexican Modern Art* as a cultural broker is supported by *Terre Sauvage.* In Canada, the press discussed the two shows in tandem, their association aptly expressed by arts reporter Paul Gessell: "These are the patrimonial works that define the essence of Canada and Mexico."[102] Artists who were seen as national icons, such as the Group of Seven, Frida Kahlo, and Diego Rivera, thus became envoys, symbolically representing their nations.

Together, the two shows sent the message that Canada and Mexico were culturally equal (invoking the narrative of cultural parity that was promoted in twentieth-century exhibitions). The NGC press release for *Terre Sauvage* outlined the similarities, stating that the Group of Seven

> was part of a larger international movement in which nations sought, through their art, to define their unique identities. Artists in Sweden, Canada, Mexico, and other countries set out to define and valorize what

> was unique in their own environment. Borrowing from modern art movements in France and elsewhere those elements appropriate to the expression of their indigenous culture, they set out to realize art that was truly expressive of their own land and people. In the older cultures of Sweden and Mexico, history and tradition were essential components of this new expression. In the relatively young Canada, it was Canada's wilderness, its Terre Sauvage that determined a new identity for the nation as expressed in art.[103]

This passage references indigeneity in terms of the quest to identify national distinction, laying bare how settler claims to indigeneity buttress national narratives that displace Indigenous sovereignty. Additionally, the press release reveals the emphasis placed on cultural parity, with Canadian art read within a larger international movement. This attention to parity makes sense when exhibitions are seen as a means of supporting political and economic ties between nations. The exhibition's support for the bilateral relationship was not covert. In fact, the media coverage suggested that the advancement of bilateral trade was all too apparent. Writing about *Terre Sauvage,* Gessell remarked that it "could have been called *Terre commercial* [sic]."[104] In his view, corporate sponsors such as Bombardier, SNC Lavalin, Canadian Pacific, and Newbridge overshadowed the art on display in Mexico City.[105]

Gessell may have felt a distaste for mixing art with business, but *Terre Sauvage* offers important context for *Mexican Modern Art.* That the show was tied to reciprocal exchange is notable because it places *Mexican Modern Art* within a longer tradition of mobilizing national patrimony as an instrument of cultural diplomacy. This tradition is significant in size and scope – for but one example, *First Peoples of Canada* (discussed in Chapter 4) was associated with several reciprocal shows that were linked to Canadian state interests. Recall that *Terre Sauvage* was displayed in Mexico at the urging of a diplomat's wife and functioned as an envoy for specific government-endorsed messages about Canadian cultural parity expressed through canonical works of modernism. *Mexican Modern Art/Terre Sauvage,* however, stand out from the longer history of Mexico-Canada art exchanges for the prominent corporate presence in both, which was absent from the earlier exhibitions. The narratives around cultural exchange had evolved; art that had previously been mobilized to evidence unique state identities now spoke of integration and parity.

The trade context is therefore key to understanding *Mexican Modern Art,* specifically that it was displayed in Canada just as the Canadian government was attempting to strengthen the new economic integration of North America, including its links with Mexico. Although the show was initiated by the NGC and MMFA, it was activated in a manner that augmented trade goals. It conveyed differing and contradictory ways of understanding Mexico, but nevertheless curator Luis-Martín Lozano constructed the country by utilizing a conventional survey format that charted a traditional Western art-historical narrative. The promotional materials underlined the exoticism of Mexico, positioning it as a sunny, colourful, passionate tourist destination and further depoliticizing the art on display. This depoliticization allowed *Mexican Modern Art* to become a political vehicle of another kind, employed to promote trade and economic ties between Canada and Mexico in the era of NAFTA. Further, the show provided sponsorship opportunities, which highlighted corporate interest in trade between Canada and Mexico. Altogether, it supported and enhanced NAFTA trade connections.

The art may have been depoliticized, but the show itself was not. Governments have long politicized seemingly neutral sites of exhibition to advance their objectives. Earlier in the twentieth century, alignment between the government and its institutions was expected. Thus, the Canadian government's connection to *Mexican Art Today,* initiated at the behest of the WIB in 1943, is not surprising. With *Mexican Modern Art* and its reciprocal show *Terre Sauvage,* however, one might expect to find greater separation, given that the NGC had become a Crown corporation under the 1990 Museums Act, which established a distance between it and the government.[106] Nonetheless, we still see art mobilized in the service of the nation and the exhibition deployed as a locus for diplomatic activity, with openings in Montreal and Ottawa functioning as meeting grounds for government stakeholders and sponsors.

But in the twenty-first century, the message subtly shifted from diplomatic relationships driven by the government to trade ties. *Mexican*

Modern Art took place during what may have been the heyday of Canadian cultural diplomacy, shortly after the Liberal government of Jean Chrétien (1993–2003) enshrined culture as a third pillar of Canadian foreign policy (along with politics and the economy).[107] The subsequent Conservative government under Stephen Harper (2006–15), for whom culture was a low priority, would disengage from cultural diplomacy initiatives abroad. This demotion was most apparent in the 2008 elimination of the government programs Trade Routes, run by the Department of Canadian Heritage, and PromArt, a program of the Department of Foreign Affairs and International Trade. Both had provided an important means for the Canadian state to fund the circulation of Canadian culture abroad.

The history of displaying Mexican art in Canada during the twentieth century reveals the government as a driving force behind exhibitions. The specific rationale may have changed as the years went by, but the prevailing ethos was always to use art in the service of political ends. This began in the 1940s, with the goal of diplomatic relations and shared alliance in the Second World War, and continued in the 1960s, when exhibitions exchanged between Canada and Mexico underscored their status as sovereign nations possessed of a significant cultural patrimony. Following NAFTA, exhibitions were exchanged as a means of emphasizing new linkages through trade and more broadly as a means to foster commercial partnerships. These varying aims aside, Canada's positioning of Mexican art and Mexico itself as exotic was remarkably persistent. As was the case with *Terre Sauvage,* Canadian art shows in Mexico similarly essentialized their country of origin. The lens of trade diplomacy deployed here reveals similarities in the underlying rationales and organizational structures of exhibitions, particularly the reciprocal ones. Throughout the second half of the twentieth century, institutions in Canada and Mexico circulated works by artists of comparable national stature, such as the Group of Seven, Rivera, and Kahlo. These exhibitions were also often linked financially through payment agreements in which countries subsidized their own shows in recognition that they would receive a show in turn. This was as true of *Arte Canadiense* in 1960 as it was for *Terre Sauvage* in 1999.

Reciprocity also demonstrates how states mobilize their culture in similar ways, further legitimizing its instrumental use. Problematically, the machinations behind such exhibitions are often not apparent to the viewing public, and thus the issue is one of public understanding. And a more pointed critique can be made of the shows themselves. Art historian Francis Haskell criticizes the totalizing appearance of international loan exhibitions. As he points out, all such exhibitions are presented as fully formed rather than as shaped by numerous factors including curatorial aims and institutional abilities.[108] This was certainly true for *Mexican Modern Art.* Moreover, such shows speak to Wallis's argument that they are "a blatant, self-admitted form of propaganda" rather than an example of the disinterested scholarship that they attempt to project.[109] In histories of cultural exchange, multiple actors, institutions, and contextual factors played a significant role in the project of an integrated North America under NAFTA. At the Montreal opening of *Mexican Art Today* in 1943, H.L. Keenleyside, assistant deputy minister of external affairs (and later Canadian ambassador to Mexico), stated, "Today it is beginning to be realized that a nation is not adequately represented by its diplomats, its military power and its commercial activities alone."[110] Art and culture are needed too. An examination of the history of Mexican art in Canada demonstrates that this remained true at the beginning of the NAFTA era.

2

Canadian Art at 49th Parallel

Just as the relationship between Canada and Mexico can be traced through the exchange of art exhibitions, Canada's connections with the United States have also been shaped through formal strategies of cultural engagement featuring visual art.[1] These efforts, however, differ remarkably from those deployed in Mexico. Part of this difference is grounded in the "special relationship" between the two allies, as well as Canada's historical emphasis on engagement with the US economy.[2] A notable initiative emerged in the 1980s, when the Canadian government allocated substantial resources to a decade-long project (1981–92) whose purpose was to promote contemporary Canadian art in the United States, all in an effort to advance Canada's standing in the American economy. The history of this project, a gallery known as 49th Parallel: Centre for Contemporary Canadian Art, reveals a great deal about the Canada-US connection, as well as how the Canadian government invested significantly in exhibitions, hoping to leverage art to promote state relationships and trade (in the broad sense and in the art market specifically).

The gallery took its name from the line of latitude that marks the boundary between the two countries.[3] A key element of the gallery was its hidden agenda as a Canadian government cultural diplomacy effort. From the outset, 49th Parallel emphasized innovative and experimental art, including video, installation, and performance, in a bid to fit naturally into SoHo, a trendy Lower Manhattan neighbourhood. In the 1980s, SoHo was a key site of the international art scene, with numerous private galleries and artist-run spaces. The *Calgary Herald* identified the gallery's 420 West Broadway address as one of the "most heavily trafficked gallery buildings in the heart of New York's art world."[4] It shared this prestigious spot with several large galleries, including renowned tastemakers Sonnabend and Leo Castelli.[5]

The gallery opened on 20 March 1981, and the Canadian government representatives and New York politicians who attended the event suggest something unusual about it. Rubbing shoulders with prominent artists, curators, and dealers from Canada and the States, the guests included Mark MacGuigan, Canadian secretary of state for external affairs; Ken Taylor, Canadian consul general in New York; and Ed Koch, the mayor of New York.[6] In fact, though ostensibly just another commercial gallery, 49th Parallel was actually a special "pilot project" and an "experiment" conducted by the Department of External Affairs.[7]

The dignitaries were there to mark the inaugural exhibition, *Plus Tard and Other Works*, comprising sculpture and photography by internationally established Canadian artist Michael Snow. Among the most prominent works was *Plus Tard* (1977), twenty-five colour photographs shot in the National Gallery of Canada and featuring paintings by Tom Thomson and the Group of Seven – canonical wilderness images associated with Canadian nationalism (Figure 7).[8] Snow's photographs blur and distort the paintings, commenting on the passing of time, each a testament to the artist's movements through the gallery.[9]

In part, the aim of 49th Parallel was to teach Americans about Canada. It was the brainchild of Guy Plamondon, cultural affairs consul at the Canadian consulate general in New York, who argued for it as an educational tool and marker of cultural parity.[10] "Americans don't know us as well as we know them," he told the *Ottawa Citizen*. "It's important to show that we have people who compare easily with what we see here [in the United States]."[11] Yet, the Canadian officials who sought to seamlessly integrate the gallery into its surroundings also downplayed its national orientation – which was its defining feature. The gallery closed on 30 June 1992, but its decade of operations was characterized by a rich history of solo and group exhibitions. It was active during the time of CUSFTA, a significant period of change in terms of Canadian government efforts in

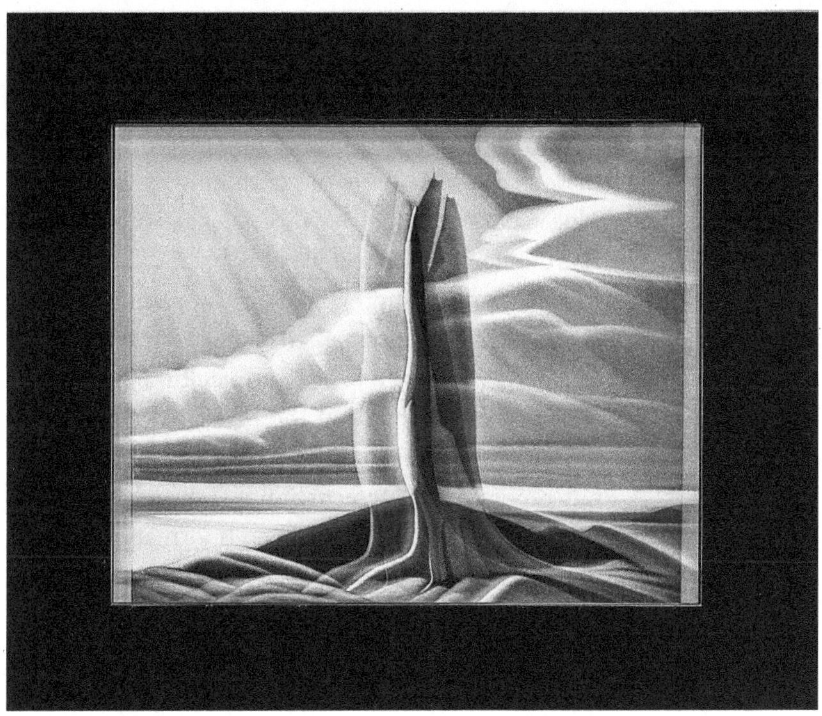

FIGURE 7 Michael Snow, *Plus Tard #15,* 1977, 1/25 framed dye coupler prints, 86.4 x 107.2 cm each. National Gallery of Canada, Ottawa. Photo NGC. Courtesy Estate of Michael Snow.

cultural diplomacy and policy that emphasized culture as a commodity. The gallery occupied an uneasy and sometimes controversial space in the political and arts spheres. In this chapter, I examine its trajectory, revealing the insights it offers into how Canada positioned itself vis-à-vis the United States during the free trade era and how it provided a new model of cultural exchange.

The history of 49th Parallel must be understood within the broader context of the cultural diplomacy efforts by the Department of External Affairs – key among them, its constellation of cultural centres.[12] Initially, the cultural centres existed only in Paris, London, and Brussels, where they were closely connected to Canadian diplomatic outposts.[13] As such, they were not integrated into local arts communities. They provided comprehensive arts programming in which visual art was one component. Their offerings in this field represented the broadest possible range of Canadian art through equal attention paid to various styles and geographic regions. Writing about the centres in 1981, Georges Bogardi characterized them as "very much aware of their official character."[14] For its part, the Canadian art community dismissed their visual arts programming as "pedestrian offerings."[15] This was due in part to the fact that professionals with expertise in the field did not coordinate the selections.

According to political scientist Andrew Fenton Cooper, the department's interest in cultural programming emerged in the 1960s, in response to initiatives by the Quebec government to engage in cultural promotion abroad, including its 1961 establishment of the Maison du Québec in Paris.[16] Such moves caused a great deal of unease among federal government officials. A draft report titled "International Cultural Relations" produced by External Affair's Cultural and Public Information Bureau makes this adversarial relationship clear: "The creation of our centre in Paris, for example, was motivated in part by the need to respond to the challenge posed by Quebec's efforts to promote its cultural presence in France. The Centre was intended as a deliberate assertion of the federal claim to represent the Canadian cultural fact abroad in its entirety, to speak on behalf of all Canada, including French Canada."[17] This explicit statement of antagonism and defensiveness reveals the stakes of federal and provincial cultural initiatives in the international sphere.

External Affairs officially took on the role of arts promoter in 1965, focusing on international tours of Canadian performing arts. By the 1980s, its public diplomacy activities were considerably more complex. Writing in 1985 about the promotion of Canadian visual art abroad, Joyce Wayne explained,

> Today, arts promotion is the title of one of seven divisions – including cultural policy, academic relations, external information, domestic information and the historical and international expositions divisions – that all come under the supervision of Richard Tait, director general of the Cultural and Public Information Bureau, one of three bureaus answering to the assistant deputy minister, Social Affairs and Programs Branch.[18]

Within these public diplomacy activities, 49th Parallel had something in common with the other cultural centres operated by External Affairs – a model that Canadian government representatives often employed to explain and contextualize it. In fact, however, 49th Parallel offered a different way for the department to promote Canada and its cultural accomplishments while connecting with an internationally recognized art scene. The gallery stands out – then and now – as a significant investment in contemporary art, a field rarely connected to national sentiment and state promotion projects. Its history demonstrates the gains it made in the New York arts community while also revealing the myriad challenges that beset External Affairs in supporting it.

A New Model to Showcase Canada (1981–84)

An employee of External Affairs from 1965, Guy Plamondon had a background in law, though he was greatly interested in contemporary art. Early in his career at External Affairs, he participated in a range of cultural programs, notably the creation of the cultural affairs division in 1966 and of Canada's cultural centre in Paris, which opened in 1970.[19] In a report produced for Canada's New York consulate in 1978, Plamondon presented a detailed proposal for an ambitious multipurpose arts space in New York to be run by External Affairs.[20] He suggested purchasing an entire building in SoHo, which would contain living quarters, studios, an auditorium, library, bookstore, professional art gallery, and potentially a second, smaller gallery space for young artists. He proposed a program for high-quality Canadian visual art, including residencies, contemporary art shows, and touring exhibitions from regional museums and private galleries in Canada. His report claimed that his scheme had been well received, noting "tremendous interest" from cultural communities and other stakeholders in Canada and New York.[21] Such a large project would be costly, but it was politically justified, Plamondon argued, because "Canada would have a very visible presence in this very powerful megalopolis" and be at "the centre of much of what is happening on the international scene in matters of business, finance, marketing, culture – in summary, in every conceivable field."[22] He identified Canadian art as the best means to connect with these disparate communities in New York while also raising Canada's profile abroad.

Of course, business and finance were of particular interest to the Canadian government, and Plamondon remarked that the United States had been a "priority target" since 1974.[23] He also mentioned that Canadians and Americans knew little about each other, citing the fact that Canadians and Canadian products were often mistaken as American and hinting that increased cultural distinction was important.[24] He emphasized the need for Canadian culture to access larger markets in the United States if it were to grow. His proposed Canadian Art Centre, which would ultimately inform the mandate of 49th Parallel, would help to educate Americans about Canadian art and, by proxy, Canada itself, thus presenting a solution to these various issues.

Plamondon championed his idea for several years before External Affairs approved a revised proposal in November 1980. In February 1981, Secretary of State for External Affairs Mark MacGuigan announced a pilot project under the name 49th Parallel: Centre for Contemporary Canadian Art/49e Parallèle: Centre d'art Canadien contemporain.[25] It would be a permanent outpost in the vibrant artistic neighbourhood of SoHo – an experimental, cutting-edge gallery devoted exclusively to contemporary Canadian art. Subsequent announcements by MacGuigan picked up on Plamondon's original proposal, noting that the gallery "reflected the Canadian government's view that New York is clearly the visual arts capital of the world, and is the place where the vitality, range, and proliferation of new and experimental Canadian artistic expression should be showcased."[26] Plamondon was appointed director of 49th Parallel, a duty he shouldered while fulfilling his other responsibilities at the consulate.

The gallery records from 1981 to 1992 reveal three distinct administrative periods, coinciding with the tenures of three directors: Plamondon (1981–84), France Morin (1984–89), and Glen Cumming (1989–92). During the first two periods, the leadership of Plamondon and Morin strongly shaped the direction of the gallery. The same cannot be said for the third period under Cumming, for structural reasons detailed below. In its first administrative phase, 49th Parallel was under direct administration by Pierre Trudeau's Liberal government. It was run by employees of the Canadian consulate general in New York and funded entirely by External Affairs. Robert Handforth, a cultural affairs officer who had been at the consulate general since 1980, assisted Plamondon, also continuing to work at the consulate. Handforth brought great expertise in Canadian art and theatre to the job. Prior to joining External Affairs, he had worked at the Canada Council and Stratford Festival. He also possessed significant knowledge of Canada's burgeoning art scene as a co-founder and publications manager at Art Metropole, a key Toronto institution established in 1974 by an art group named General Idea. Additionally, Handforth had been the director of A Space, a prominent artist-run centre in Toronto.[27]

Plans for 49th Parallel came together quickly, and by 6 February 1981, six weeks before the opening of *Plus Tard and Other Works,* the consulate had secured a lease on a gallery on the fourth floor of 420 West Broadway.[28] A *Calgary Herald* journalist described the location as a "competitive" and "critical art forum" that provided access to premier commercial galleries engaged in avant-garde art.[29] Handforth explained that in opting for the West Broadway address, "we have purchased a great deal of good will and visibility for our artists for a very reasonable amount of money."[30] Living up to its moniker as the "cultural capital of the USA," SoHo was home not only to the Leo Castelli and Sonnabend galleries, but also to André Emmerich, John Weber Galleries, Sperone Westwater Fisher, Nancy Hoffman Gallery, Paula Cooper Gallery, Sculpture Now, the Drawing Center, Max Hutchinson, O.K. Harris, Heiner-Friedrich, and Holly Solomon Gallery.[31]

Plamondon's interest in works that "reflect[ed] the newest, freshest and most contemporary Canadian art forms" was a perfect fit in SoHo.[32] The gallery's programming would include works in media such as installation, video, photography, and performance. A consulate statement reinforced this approach, indicating that 49th Parallel would present "contemporary and experimental visual arts and will include aspects of the literary and performing arts, as well as independent film and video, *in all of these stressing the new and experimental.*"[33] "We'll try to show the kind of art that New Yorkers naturally expect to see in Soho," Plamondon explained.[34] However, the commercial milieu of SoHo was somewhat incongruent because 49th Parallel was legally unable to sell the work it displayed.[35] Its lease had been secured by the consulate, which conferred tax-exempt status on the gallery. Sales of exhibited artworks were prohibited because doing so would jeopardize this arrangement.[36] The gallery may have looked like a commercial space, but any visitor who wished to acquire a work would be referred to the appropriate art dealer in Canada. If the sale went through, 49th Parallel suggested a 20 percent donation to the gallery in lieu of the 50 percent commission that was the norm.

The gallery's affiliation with the Canadian government was similarly complicated. Its purpose was to promote Canada, but as the *Globe and Mail* reported, the gallery "consciously tr[ied] to avoid any kind of 'institutionalized feeling,' both out of respect for their neighbours, and out of sensitivity for the kind of high quality Canadian work they want[ed] to introduce to the New York public."[37] Put another way, downplaying the gallery's Canadian government connections was necessary for 49th Parallel to fit in with the other galleries that surrounded it and a means to protect the reputation of the art it displayed (chosen because it had merit, not because bureaucrats thought it would sell). Media coverage makes clear the crux of 49th Parallel's model of cultural diplomacy in which nationalism was a covert but driving force. The art was intended to speak for itself as an exemplar of contemporary Canadian practice, holding its own in the international art sphere while concurrently promoting Canada itself. The masked role of the Canadian government is evident in debates over the gallery's name. In the end, 49th Parallel/49e Parallèle was selected because the reference to the international boundary did not overtly signal "Canada."[38] A 1981 memorandum recounts that the name boasted "low-key identification, memorability and suggestion of metaphor."[39] The gallery's ambiguous approach to national orientation would dog discussions about the efficacy of its promotion of Canada throughout its tenure.

Despite a proclaimed emphasis on new and experimental art, 49th Parallel's opening exhibition featured older work by an established figure. The gallery's entrance onto the New York scene came via Michael Snow, whose reputation was already very well established both within and outside of Canada. In fact, he was known in New York, having lived there during the 1960s when he produced some of his most iconic works, such as the experimental film *Wavelength* (1966–67). His reputation was cemented in key exhibitions during the 1970s, including when he showed at the

Venice Biennale as the first solo artist to represent Canada. In short, when 49th Parallel launched in 1981, Snow could hardly be considered an edgy choice. Before the show even opened, the director of the National Gallery of Canada (who loaned work to the exhibition) chided Plamondon: "While we are supportive of the principle of encouraging the exhibition of works by Canadian artists outside Canada, it has been our understanding that as a centre for contemporary art, the Consulate's Gallery would *primarily be exhibiting current work*. We are concerned that in the future the Gallery's collections not be viewed as a standard source for exhibitions."[40] Artist Leslie Reid voiced similar criticisms at a 1981 Federal Cultural Policy Review Committee meeting in Ottawa, where she decried 49th Parallel's programming just one month after the gallery opened as "history on display."[41] Thus, the Canadian arts community clearly felt that 49th Parallel was not honouring its mandate to showcase contemporary art.

Certainly, Snow's work did not entirely lend itself to Plamondon's rhetoric regarding the fresh and the new.[42] The most recent work in the exhibition was *Plus Tard*, which dated from 1977. Almost everything else had been produced during Snow's residence in New York, including the photograph *Atlantic* (1967) and sculptures *Scope* (1967) and *Blind* (1968). Given the accelerated timeline of the gallery's opening, the works had to be assembled quickly, based on their availability. However, given their display in a quasi-commercial gallery that emphasized new production, the fact that they had been exhibited before was significant. Moreover, none were for sale.[43] I hesitate to place too much emphasis on the first exhibition, but it was important because it garnered wide attention in Canada and in New York. Subsequent shows, such as that of art collective General Idea in 1981, came closer to fulfilling the profile that Plamondon espoused.

The gallery would come to draw on Canada's network of artist-run centres for its programming, connecting these relatively new alternative spaces with new audiences. The centres, which emerged across Canada during the late 1960s and the 1970s, were initially known as parallel galleries. In his seminal essay "The Humiliation of the Bureaucrat: Artist-Run Centres as Museums by Artists," artist AA Bronson describes their development:

> Suddenly there were galleries (and other hybrids) by artists popping up all over the country: Open Space in Victoria, Video Inn and the Western Front in Vancouver, the Parachute Centre for Cultural Affairs in Calgary, Plug-In in Winnipeg, Artspace in Peterborough, the Music Gallery, 15 Dance Lab and Art Metropole in Toronto, Vehicule in Montreal, Powerhouse in Montreal, the Centre for Art Tapes in Halifax, and many more ... Soon there were little artists' bureaucracies having exhibitions and promotions and educational programmes and video workshops and concert series and anything else you might care to think of in this parody of that museum world we all supposedly were trying to escape.[44]

Their presence on the cultural scene was such that by 1976, the Association of National Non-Profit Artist Centres was established.[45]

Parallel galleries differed from commercial galleries in that they were non-profit and were led by artist-administrators. They widened the possibilities for what a gallery could accomplish. Art historian Clive Robertson explains that they were "multiply-coded and constructed as intermedia spaces for production and display practices, as material sites, and as *loci* for cultural and community activities."[46] Their arrival provided new roles and responsibilities for artists, such as curator and critic, which enabled them to play a more active part in cultural policy formation.[47] Supported by the Canada Council, parallel galleries contributed significantly to the development of the Canadian art scene and provided crucial support for artists working in emerging media, including video, performance, and conceptual art. In New York, 49th Parallel was able to harvest from the parallel gallery system, and the works it showed during its early years reflected the production of these key nodes in the Canadian cultural landscape.[48]

Thus, 49th Parallel achieved a mixed success during its first few years. Initially, it caught the attention of US art magazines, including *Art in America* and *Artforum*. Much of the coverage concentrated on its opening, announcing its premiere location and innovative mandate, as well as the art on display. The response was largely positive, but it died down after the opening, reflecting 49th Parallel's weak ties to the New York art world. In addition, Canadian artists and gallerists criticized the gallery's lack of commercial viability despite its mandate to increase sales of Canadian art. Arts professionals in Canada did not hesitate to express their concerns. Canadian dealers saw the gallery as a disincentive to open their own branches in New York. Regina artist David Thauberger, whose work was shown at 49th Parallel during its first year, commented that it was "confused," acting simultaneously as "trade exhibit, museum, [and] commercial gallery."[49] Additionally, its ambiguous relationship with Ottawa ignited criticism. Some wondered if the government's use of artists were appropriate, and others, whether the Canadian origins of the gallery were too concealed. The gallery's nationalistic purpose, its desire to avoid overt branding, and its interest in being seen as a player in New York set up a conflicting mandate and a framework that made it difficult to advertise its Canadianness and that of the works it displayed.

Even as the gallery fielded some criticism from the Canadian arts community, its innovative approach also generated a great deal of interest from other constituencies, as confirmed by press coverage. Plamondon's – and by extension the Canadian government's – calculation that contemporary art could best represent Canada as an inventive nation and attract the attention that eluded the other Canadian cultural centres appeared to have paid off. A further defining element was the full commitment of External Affairs to the gallery, which would acquire other government and private partners as it developed. At the same time, this phase reveals that the gallery was always burdened with a complex mandate that required it to promote Canadian art (and by extension Canadian artists and Canada per se) but in a subtle manner that was not overly nationalistic. This mandate posed ongoing problems for its operations. After two years, Plamondon stepped down from the directorship to take on other duties at External Affairs, which used the opportunity to implement several key changes in the gallery's administration, demonstrating flexibility and responsiveness. First, it announced the creation of a seven-member advisory committee in March 1983.[50] The committee members, as reported in *artmagazine*, represented the regions of Canada.[51] Second, External Affairs recognized the difficulties inherent in having a director who simultaneously maintained a full role at the consulate. Plamondon's replacement would be devoted solely to the gallery.

Becoming Professional (1984–89)

When France Morin was appointed its director in 1984, 49th Parallel gained a new orientation and outlook. Morin's tenure was characterized by an increasing professionalism and a deepening of the gallery's ties to the SoHo art scene, as well as to arts communities in Canada. Her appointment marked a further separation of the gallery from the consulate, though External Affairs continued to oversee it and to provide substantial funding. Well versed in contemporary Canadian art, Morin was a curator from Quebec affiliated with Vehicule gallery, who, with Chantal Pontbriand, founded the esteemed arts periodical *Parachute*. Furthermore, her knowledge of French and of Quebec's contemporary art world allowed 49th Parallel to rebut criticism that it did not fully represent Canadian art.[52] The institution was a prominent international posting, and Morin's appointment could be considered an affirmation of the gallery's commitment to Quebec and francophone communities.

Morin brought a strong vision to 49th Parallel's programming. Her first exhibition featured photographer Robin Collyer (b. 1949). Another early show, *Canada/New York*, pointedly commented on Canada within a New York context by featuring Canadian artists who lived in the city.[53] Morin went on to undertake ambitious collaborative projects with other New York commercial galleries, such as *Icarus: The Vision of Angels*, a 1986 show that dealt with flight and was lauded in *Artforum*. Created with Ronald Feldman of Ronald Feldman Fine Arts, *Icarus* brought together Canadian and US artists with historical icons associated with flight, from Leonardo da Vinci to Alexander Graham Bell – a move away from the national focus that had underwritten programming during the gallery's first period. Canadian gallerist René Blouin underscored the shift at 49th Parallel, identifying Morin's expertise in contemporary art as essential to its success. "France Morin is not a bureaucrat," he explained; "she doesn't work from nine to five and attend cocktail parties. She takes risks and fights for the artists she exhibits."[54] Morin's appointment provided a clear indication that the mandate of the gallery was now to seriously engage within the sophisticated New York scene and execute innovative programming.[55]

Only one year into Morin's tenure, however, 49th Parallel experienced its most significant setback to date. In March 1985, a confidential report titled "Canadian Cultural Centres Abroad" was leaked to the press. Commissioned by External Affairs, it had been written by Woods Gordon, a Canadian consulting firm. Known as the Woods Gordon Report, it assessed Canadian cultural centres in Paris, London, Brussels, and New York. It drew 49th Parallel into the public eye in Canada and cast it in a negative light. Using strong language, it decried the gallery, noting its lack of impact and condemning its failure to overtly promote its identification with Canada. It advised that both the gallery and the cultural centre in Brussels be closed.[56] As debate over the gallery's future played out in the press, supporters countered that the report was superficial, relying on limited and inappropriate sources. No dealers, museum directors, art consultants, or critics had been interviewed, only bureaucrats and two Toronto-based artists. By this point, 49th Parallel had exhibited work by approximately two hundred artists, and under Morin it had secured corporate sponsorship from Air Canada and ongoing collaborations with other commercial galleries in New York. Supporters further mentioned that other countries, including Australia and New Zealand, were interested in 49th Parallel as a model for their own cultural diplomacy.

The debate reveals attitudes toward cultural diplomacy in the period, with key figures expressing their support for 49th Parallel alongside others in government who voiced lingering doubts. Several famed members of the New York art world backed the gallery, including American painter Leon Golub, New Museum founder and art historian Marcia Tucker, and art historian and critic Donald Kuspit. As Kuspit asserted, the gallery "is an important representative of Canada, diplomatically and intellectually as well as specifically artistically."[57] Tucker went farther in her praise, noting that the gallery "fosters a valuable exchange between American and Canadian artists, which results in increased dialogue, joint exhibition and publication projects, and mutual respect."[58] German artist and New Yorker Hans Haake made a clear case for the gallery's achievements: "Canadian art was practically unknown outside of Canada before the establishment of the 49th Parallel."[59] Support from such high-profile individuals provided a significant defence of the gallery and also spoke to the inroads that Morin had made in New York.

The negative response was considerable, however, and no consensus about the work of the gallery and its objectives could be reached in the public realm. In the aftermath of the Woods Gordon Report, it was obvious that 49th Parallel enjoyed strong support from arts communities on both sides of the border. However, whether that backing extended beyond artists, curators, dealers, and cultural critics was far less clear. The debate raised hard questions about Canadian cultural diplomacy: What was worthy of government spending? What could art do to promote the state? And, how exactly could Canadians know if such programs were working? The consulate in New York affirmed the gallery's purpose, stating, "any nation that wants to be taken seriously in financial and diplomatic circles must have a certified cultural presence."[60] In the lead-up to CUSFTA, trade provided the main reason for External Affairs to continue supporting 49th Parallel.[61] Broadly understood, the gallery's promotion of Canadian art was an attempt to bring Canada into a closer relationship with the United States, which, it was hoped, would increase trade between the two nations. The challenge for bureaucrats was how to substantiate the connection between the gallery and trade.[62]

The trade and diplomatic context of the gallery is essential to understanding the relationship between art and free trade in this period. The 1980s were a significant epoch in the development of Canada's "special relationship" with the United States. Under the leadership of Brian Mulroney, elected prime minister in September 1984, Ottawa pursued a free trade agreement that would increase the integration of the American and Canadian economies. A particularly famous moment in Canada-US relations was the Shamrock Summit of March 1985, when Mulroney met with President Ronald Reagan. It was characterized by a warm relationship between the two men, exemplified by their televised rendition – with their spouses – of the song "When Irish Eyes Are Smiling."[63] Increased economic integration with the United States, however, provoked fears among many Canadians about American imperialism, especially in the cultural sphere. These anxieties were conveyed in the work of Condé + Beveridge, as described in the Introduction, the video art discussed in Chapter 6, and the organizing work of the Independent Artists' Union, as examined in the Epilogue. Concerns regarding free trade were complicated by the economic recession of the early 1980s. In a political climate dominated by cost cutting, art was seen as a frill.[64]

The Woods Gordon Report threw 49th Parallel's future into uncertainty for many months and ultimately cast a large shadow over its remaining years. Almost immediately following the release of the report, the gallery needed to renew its lease, which prompted further discussion about ongoing support from External Affairs and the expense involved. In the months that followed, 49th Parallel was drastically restructured. It received recognition from the Canada Council and became a non-profit corporation with a board of directors in 1986.[65] But discussion of its direction persisted. By the end of this period, it had significantly diversified its funding structure. No longer subsidized solely by External Affairs, it drew programming support from the Canada Council and the federal communications department, while it also sought private backing.

A Private-Public Partnership (1989–92)

Morin continued to lead the gallery until 1989. When she left, Glen Cumming assumed the directorship (beginning in November).[66] Like Morin, Cumming was well versed in contemporary art, having served as director of the Art Gallery of Hamilton. The shift in leadership was marked by a full embrace of commercial aims, a step initiated in the mid-1980s under Morin's guidance. Cumming's tenure marks the third administrative phase of the gallery, which lasted until its closure in 1992 and witnessed the most radical changes to its mandate and administration. Compared to his predecessors, however, Cumming had the least impact on gallery programming, which was due to structural changes that increased the roles of others in deciding what exhibitions were staged. This development was brought about by a three-year partnership between External Affairs and the Professional Art Dealers Association of Canada (PADAC). Founded in 1989, PADAC stressed the commercial potential of the gallery, even though art could not be sold on the premises. PADAC assumed administrative control of 49th Parallel, with the result that the gallery rededicated itself to promoting commercially viable contemporary Canadian art in

New York's competitive market. Nevertheless, most of its funding still came from External Affairs, which provided $400,000 of its $600,000 annual budget. The new administration sought to secure the remaining $200,000 from corporate funders.

The gallery, in effect, had become a public-private partnership, spearheaded to a large degree by Olga Korper, a Toronto gallery owner who was PADAC president during the 1980s. The new assertive approach of 49th Parallel was labelled a "major assault" on the New York market by journalist Isabel Vincent and, by implication, something that had been missing since its inception.[67] The gallery now concentrated on placing Canadian art in US exhibitions and collections.[68] Accordingly, Korper noted that it would not borrow works, choosing instead to focus on art that was for sale or available for exhibition at other galleries. In a bid to signal this change to visitors, "gallery" replaced "centre" in 49th Parallel's name in November 1989.[69] Addressing the arts community directly, Korper expanded on the new approach in a 1990 letter to *C Magazine*. In it, she clarified the unique partnership between External Affairs and PADAC and explained that dealers could apply for shows and benefit from cost sharing, while public galleries (including parallel galleries) could also provide works for display. Pushing back against criticism that a commercial focus would lead to poor-quality exhibitions, she stated,

> The intent of the new priorities of the 49th Parallel is not to become a purely commercial venture which would compromise the quality of the exhibits, but to focus on placing the work in Public Galleries, private galleries, group exhibitions beyond our borders, collections of some significance, and lastly, to make the work overtly available to the general viewing public.[70]

This mandate, according to Korper, did not constitute an extreme departure from 49th Parallel's previous activities. However, the input of PADAC did have a marked impact on its work, namely in reducing the autonomy and vision exerted by its director.

Despite the new administration and mandate, the fact that the gallery was not financially viable became obvious within about eighteen months.

The poor economic climate that weakened the sales market did not help. The gallery also had difficulty building profiles for the artists it exhibited, who were largely unknown to American audiences. In part, this was because it deviated from the commercial gallery practice of programming a select roster of artists through repeat showings, opting instead to program new artists in each exhibition. In 1991, Korper and Cumming publicly acknowledged that 49th Parallel would never be financially self-sustaining and cited difficulties in obtaining corporate support.[71] At this point, the gallery was besieged by rumours of its own demise, which were relayed by a Canadian press that was eager to rehash the debates of the Woods Gordon Report. Aware of the gallery's precarious situation, Cumming told the *Globe and Mail* in April 1991 that he had heard the talk of its closure and expected, at the least, a major restructuring.

In the end, 49th Parallel did not respond to these challenges, as it had in the past through creative changes to its structure and administration. Instead, it shut up shop on 30 June 1992 when its lease at 420 Broadway expired.[72] For over a decade, it had successfully faced competing pressures to provide a new model for promoting Canada abroad. Its hybrid character – part cultural centre, part commercial gallery, part envoy for the Canadian government – rendered it unable to fully satisfy the various communities that it served, thus drawing criticism from all sides.[73] Its most successful period came in the mid-1980s under the direction of France Morin, when it made significant strides toward connecting with arts communities in Canada and New York through quality programming. This goodwill was later eroded by a shift toward the commercial value of art. Once that occurred, the gallery's failure to sell the works it displayed was tied to its perceived inability to sell Canada's image abroad. This failure was compounded by structural factors, including the gallery's organization and the prohibition on direct sales, as well as market factors that made it difficult for the gallery to demonstrate fulfillment of its new aims.

Whereas 49th Parallel is often cast as a failure, the fact that this experiment in cultural diplomacy operated for over a decade is proof of its success and of the potential of its hybrid structure. Its history and programming stand as evidence of the government's strong investment in visual arts as a form of cultural diplomacy. The significant resources lavished on the gallery stand in contrast to the lack of US efforts to advance similar endeavours in Canada. I argue that 49th Parallel should be recognized for what it did, rather than for what it did not do. That is, it ought to be upheld as confirmation that cultural diplomacy projects can productively mobilize a diverse range of actors. Moreover, 49th Parallel's work in New York reveals the possibilities for engagement when dominant modes of representation – in this case, of historical Canadian landscape art – are challenged. The gallery's changing mandate demonstrates its response to criticism, and its flexibility also allowed it to explore differing approaches to cultural diplomacy. It was a space of possibility, one that benefited from a high public profile and a desirable location.

In a wider sense, the gallery's trajectory tracks the ongoing privatization of culture that occurred during the late twentieth century, as well as the advent of free trade and continental integration and changes to cultural centres more broadly.[74] Learning from criticism, the institution showed flexibility and creativity in continually restructuring in an attempt to succeed. These changes, however, indicate that it was perhaps not given adequate time to find its footing and that the demand to turn a profit was always unrealistic. The record shows that 49th Parallel was burdened by expectations, many of which could not be easily assessed and some that did not directly link to the work undertaken by gallery staff.[75] Here, Cynthia P. Schneider's comments regarding the efficacy of cultural diplomacy are relevant: "Cultural diplomacy cannot be effectively measured; it makes a qualitative, not quantitative, difference in relations between nations and peoples."[76] The issue of identifying appropriate metrics for success continues to plague many discussions of cultural diplomacy for practitioners and scholars.[77]

The history of 49th Parallel demonstrates that new and creative approaches to cultural diplomacy could pique the public's interest, for better or worse. Despite the gallery's ultimate closure, it garnered attention in New York's competitive art market and, later, that of commercial dealers in Canada, who saw it as a foothold in the US market. The gallery bridged the divide between diplomats and professional art communities in Canada, and its sensitive approach to cultural diplomacy established a new means of connecting to foreign audiences who were outside the traditional purview of Canada's cultural centres.

49th Parallel and the North American Imaginary

In 2017, the Standing Senate Committee on Foreign Affairs and International Trade opened a study into how culture was deployed in the service of Canada's foreign affairs.[78] Among testimony from scholars, former diplomats, representatives of arts organizations and arts councils, and Canadian government stakeholders, the Senate notably allowed for the voices of cultural producers – who are rarely brought into discussions of international affairs.[79] Conceptual artist Jana Sterbak, who exhibited her work at 49th Parallel in 1986, spoke to the difficulty of employing contemporary art in the pursuit of foreign policy aims, emphasizing the innovative nature of professional art production – precisely what 49th Parallel was created to foreground. She argued that the excellence of Canadian art provided its currency abroad. "If you ask any seasoned art professional," she stated, "they will confirm that the *experimental nature* of Canadian art is precisely what makes it attractive in international circles." Notably, such art is not always palatable to the masses. Sterbak underscored this point, counselling the senators, "Please remember that we are not obliged ... to like it, but you are obliged to afford the kind of respect to contemporary artists that you would accord to any other specialized professional in their field."[80] Here, Sterbak's testimony made clear that the challenges of employing art for national promotion had not faded away after 49th Parallel closed down in 1992, pointing to the complexities of how culture is deployed in cultural diplomacy projects.

In terms of free trade histories, 49th Parallel spoke to government efforts to employ culture in encouraging trade during the lead-up to increased economic integration under CUSFTA and NAFTA. The gallery promoted Canadian art as a cultural commodity, whose sale was understood to correlate to the political and economic power of Canada in the United States. The debates surrounding 49th Parallel in the 1980s reveal a pervasive understanding of US cultural dominance over Canadian culture. This far-reaching dynamic endured through CUSFTA and NAFTA, with the trade deals providing another moment where anxieties were articulated over the status of Canadian culture and its ability to withstand competition from its powerful neighbour.

For more than a decade, 49th Parallel demonstrated Ottawa's commitment to employing culture to change attitudes south of the border. The gallery encouraged trade, preparing the ground for both increased bilateral cooperation and a market-based approach to fine art. In minimizing differences between Canada and the United States, and by making the point that Canadian artists were already engaged in transnational art practice, 49th Parallel's programming exemplified the potential of cultural diplomacy to establish mutuality – in this case, within a targeted community of artists.

PART 2

Picturing North America

3

Exhibiting the Continent

The implementation of CUSFTA and NAFTA changed dominant understandings of North America. This process was complex, involving a perceived expansion of the scope of the continent. With CUSFTA, Stephen Clarkson explains, "the notion of the old North America was extended far into the Pacific Ocean, since the state of Hawaii was constitutionally part of the United States, and deep into the Caribbean, owing to the agreement's provisions applying to the US territory of Puerto Rico."[1] NAFTA furthered this enlargement with the addition of Mexico. Thus, it led to what Clarkson and other scholars identify as the creation of a "new North America."[2]

This so-called new continent should be seen as a conception, a hegemonic narrative that must be contextualized in the longer history of North America if its significance is to be understood. It is worth emphasizing that perceptions of North America have often been in flux. The new version under NAFTA was predicated on complex international relationships, of which the connection between Mexico and Canada was particularly ambiguous. In part, this was due to the dominance of the United States, which greatly occupied the focus of its northern and southern neighbours. Economist and political scientist María Teresa Gutiérrez Haces asserts that the "clear predominance" of the United States "has strongly influenced the nature of the relations between Mexico, the United States, and Canada."[3] Characterizing these connections as "dual bilateralism," Pablo Heidrich and Laura Macdonald regard Canada's relationship with Mexico as indifferent: "Canada's ties with Mexico have often remained half-hearted and conditioned by each country's relationship with the United States."[4] Quoting Jack Ogelsby, historian Asa McKercher attests to a persistent sentiment held by Canadians in the twentieth century that "'even appeared to deny Mexico its place in North America,' preferring instead to limit the continent to Canada and the United States."[5] The revised understanding of North America necessitated cultural programming that recognized Mexico's new relationship to the continent under increased economic integration.

Changes in regional understandings are not new. As international relations scholars Luis Ochoa Bilbao and Jorge A. Schiavon suggest, Mexico's place in the western hemisphere has long been debated and has shifted over time.[6] For instance, William A. Orme Jr. argues that "in the 19th century Mexico was in the West. Now it is in the South."[7] Mexico is also distinct in its relationship to North America due to its simultaneous ties to South America, adding to its ambiguous place in the continent.[8] In 1994, NAFTA integrated Mexico economically into North America, but the country retained its cultural associations with Latin America. Mexicans continued to use the term *norteamericano* (North American) to refer to a "culturally and geographically demarcated reality distinct from themselves," namely citizens of the United States.[9] Although the topic of identity is "deeply complex and polarizing," Ochoa Bilbao and Schiavon draw on data from 2004–14 to show that Mexican public opinion in the twenty-first century continues to demonstrate multiple ties of belonging.[10] They characterize this "dual [Mexican] identity" as simultaneously North American and Latin American, suggesting that Mexico "is physically in North America (and appreciates more what this region offers in economic terms), but it is Latin American in terms of history, identity, and culture."[11] Understanding these tensions, as well as historically shifting conceptions of North America, can help us to see why government actors in Canada, Mexico, and the United States concluded that cultural diplomacy initiatives asserting a new North American identity were needed and worthwhile. This also underscores the fragility of the continent's alliance under free trade. The new North America came about because of specific developments at a certain moment, so it is not surprising that continental integration has not endured (as discussed in the Epilogue).

The new perception of the continent as a unified entity was rooted in economics rather than culture. Political scientist Guy Poitras even asserted in 2001 that the concept was largely a corporate one: "There is no such thing as a North American per se." He explains, "Individuals are not North American, but companies and firms are more frequently than ever becoming North American. Regionalism or regionalization has only just begun to affect loyalties or identities for most people."[12] The new perception of North America needed to be created to reinforce and naturalize economic linkages. One way of doing so was through cultural initiatives that both explicitly and implicitly reaffirmed the parameters established by free trade. This chapter focuses on three art exhibitions staged between 2001 and 2005 that reflected the new mapping of North America, mirroring NAFTA's supposed erasure of its borders.[13]

On the one hand, the fact that the three shows did not appear until several years after the 1994 implementation of NAFTA simply reflects the reality that preparing a museum exhibition typically takes a long time, especially at larger institutions. On the other hand, and as I argue in this chapter, the exhibitions reveal a government interest in promoting a certain concept of North America, as well as civil society's response to the links made in economic agreements. Although their cultural impact was not immediate, the trade deals provided an important rationale for the three shows discussed in this chapter. Further, their timing may have related to negotiations regarding the development of an expanded Free Trade Area of the Americas (FTAA). Although the talks started in 1994 at the Summit of the Americas in Miami, key meetings in the process included the Third Summit of the Americas held in 2001 in Quebec City, which was accompanied by major protests.[14] Proponents of the FTAA hoped to produce a deal by 2005, well within the period of the exhibitions discussed in this chapter, but the negotiations collapsed.[15] Nonetheless, the goal of achieving a hemispheric trading bloc provided important context for ongoing conversations at the time.[16]

Panoramas: The North American Landscape in Art

The online exhibition *Panoramas,* endorsed by the Governments of Canada, Mexico, and the United States, was promoted as a "one-of-a-kind project" and widely lauded as the first trilaterally supported online art show.[17] Its origins in this unprecedented partnership are notable. It employed landscape art as a means to project a message of unity among the three nations. When it opened in 2001, it was celebrated with events in each country, linked by a three-way digital video conference.[18] In Canada, the launch was held at the Canadian Museum of Civilization (CMC, now the Canadian Museum of History), in Gatineau, Quebec. Among the attendees was Heritage Minister Sheila Copps, who stated, "The art in this exhibit reflects not only our natural environments, but also our histories, our industries, our cultures and our belief systems."[19] Thus, Copps stressed the shared cultural heritage of North America, but exhibition records reveal an emphasis on free trade as well. The intended audience for the video conference consisted of "guests from the media, the museums and arts community; cultural and educational organizations, and *foreign-policy organizations with an interest in NAFTA affairs.*"[20] In Mexico City, the launch was at the Museo Nacional de Arte (MUNAL) and was attended by a mix of leaders in arts and foreign affairs, including Ignacio Toscano, director-general of the Instituto Nacional de Bellas Artes; Gerardo Estrada, director-general for international education and cultural cooperation for the Ministry of Foreign Affairs; Jeffrey Davidow, the US ambassador; and Keith H. Christie, the Canadian ambassador.[21]

State and institutional support for *Panoramas,* as demonstrated at the CMC and MUNAL openers, was enduring, and the exhibition remained online and accessible for over a decade.[22] In fact, it was closed only in 2013 when the website no longer met current accessibility requirements.[23] Beyond its extremely visible government support, *Panoramas* is distinguished for being one of the first projects hosted by the newly created Virtual Museum of Canada (VMC).[24] Announced in the 1999 Speech from the Throne, the VMC was a component of the Canadian Heritage Information Network (CHIN), a division of the federal Department of Canadian Heritage.[25] Coordinated by CHIN, *Panoramas* united four North American partners: the Winnipeg Art Gallery (WAG), the CMC, the Smithsonian

American Art Museum (SAAM), and MUNAL.[26] Several other cultural organizations contributed to the show.[27]

The theme of the exhibition was the North American landscape, which necessarily encompassed a diverse range of topographical and conceptual landscapes. Within this broad theme, *Panoramas* was structured around four modules: the Evolving Landscape, the Social Landscape, the Mythic Landscape, and the Personal Landscape. According to the agreement between the four partners, "these themes provide the potential to explore areas of comparison, contrast and similarities among value systems and perspectives as expressed in the chosen works of art."[28] The exhibition was available in English, French, and Spanish to maximize accessibility across the continent.[29] This was an inherent aspect of the online platform, which allowed free access at any time of day. It featured over three hundred pieces by artists from all three countries, approximately a hundred of which were Canadian, drawn from the permanent collections of the CMC and the WAG. The exhibition also represented an extensive temporal range, with works spanning two hundred years. Clearly, *Panoramas* boasted considerable size and scope.

The show was aimed at a broad North American audience, as evidenced by its trilingual presentation and reinforced by its focus on the landscape genre.[30] Landscape is perhaps a surprising choice for an exhibition with a continental focus, given the genre's long association with national narratives. As W.J.T. Mitchell explains, landscape is a powerful social medium that is essential in constructing the nation.[31] He writes that it "is central to the national imaginary, a part of daily life that imprints public, collective fantasies on places and scenes."[32] The landscape theme appeared in *Panoramas* planning documents as early as February 2000, just a month following the birth of the exhibition, suggesting that it was chosen by the high-level Canadian and American politicians who first conceived of the show.[33] Exhibition records indicate that the theme was set well before a Mexican partner was identified, implying that Mexico tacitly agreed to it.[34] The four partners who were tasked with bringing the project to fruition probably had no say in the selection of its theme.[35] This unusual level of political involvement in an art show demonstrates the significance of *Panoramas* to the governments concerned as a means of cultural diplomacy.

The use of culture to convey values, beliefs, and ideologies on behalf of individuals and communities is not new, and visual art has often been employed to negotiate a variety of relationships. It is well suited to such a role, given the Western perception of culture as a universal conduit that transcends differences of language, religion, and ethnicity. Thus, control of cultural goods and their circulation, which often lies in the hands of the state, can provide a very important means of building connections between communities.[36] "If the artworks are of universal significance, speaking across cultural boundaries," Judith Huggins Balfe argues, "so is their discerning patron or owner."[37] This relationship is grounded in mutually reinforcing assumptions of value – the value of the objects, which are accorded cultural and national importance, and the prestige and power of the institutions and communities that are associated with them.[38]

Thus, the long-standing value accorded to the works featured in *Panoramas* allowed it to serve as a form of public diplomacy – a means to manage and influence the international sphere – relaying a message of unity to North Americans. Historian Nicholas J. Cull identifies cultural diplomacy as a subset of public diplomacy, defining it as "an actor's attempt to manage the international environment through facilitating the export of an element of that actor's life, belief or art."[39] Therefore, cultural diplomacy encompasses state-to-state relations (wherein a government employs culture to advance its foreign policy objectives), as well as state(s)-to-people and people-to-people relations (when states or groups use cultural goods to send a message to a population). This expanded understanding of cultural diplomacy is in keeping with the new public diplomacy, which acknowledges a shift from the "club" diplomacy of the twentieth century to the "networked" environment of the present day.[40] As such, state-to-state, state-to-people, and people-to-people relationships are all part of the single mechanism of public diplomacy. *Panoramas* evidences state-to-state and state-to-public relationships as the three governments attempted to redefine how Canadians, Americans, and Mexicans saw themselves and their continent.[41]

Cultural envoys, such as the paintings featured in *Panoramas,* provide new narratives and images that change perceptions and convey information. As political scientist Patricia M. Goff explains,

> Cultural diplomacy can tell another story about a country (or province or state or regional grouping). This may be a story that differs from what official policy would imply. It may be a story that counters what opponents are recounting. In doing so, cultural diplomacy can offset negative, stereotypical or overly simplistic impressions arising from policy choices or hostile portrayals. It may also fill a void where no stories of any kind exist.[42]

Panoramas presented a new story about the continent of North America, one in which Canada, Mexico, and the United States were an integrated unit.

SAAM documentation characterizes the exhibition as "being sponsored by and organized at the urging of the Canadian government."[43] In fact, the Canadian Department of Heritage supplied the bulk of the funding, contributing C$228,000, whereas SAAM added US$100,000 (Mexico was not a formal partner at the time).[44] The proportion of funding provided by Heritage attests to the significant value that Ottawa placed on cultural diplomacy initiatives at the time.[45] Its investment also speaks to a larger trend in several of the case studies discussed in this book, where the Canadian government funded exhibitions to a greater extent than its American and Mexican partners.[46]

In January 2000, Canadian deputy minister of heritage Alexander Himelfarb met with Evelyn Lieberman, the US undersecretary of state for public diplomacy and public affairs, to initiate *Panoramas*.[47] Shortly afterward, the scope of the project was expanded to include Mexico in light of the NAFTA alliance. Exhibition records attest to Lieberman's interest in bringing in Mexico to give the show a North American focus.[48] This development probably also reflected Canadian and US interest in further economic integration of the Americas through the FTAA. Correspondence between Canadian Heritage employees shows that the project was initially perceived as a cooperative endeavour between Canada and the United States in the "non-irritant" sphere of heritage.[49] This comment demonstrates that Ottawa viewed cultural initiatives as an important tool in attaining economic and political goals and that they were seen as a non-antagonistic means of strengthening relations – ironic, given Canada's insistence on a cultural industries exemption during negotiations for CUSFTA and

NAFTA.[50] Documentation also underscores linkages across the Americas as a broader aim for the exhibition, which at one point was slated to unfold in increments. Under this plan, it would have expanded to Mexican, and then to Latin American and Caribbean partners, and would have launched at the 2001 Summit of the Americas in Quebec City. This scheme confirms that the political context of trade negotiations was integral to the planning and development of the show.[51]

Ultimately, *Panoramas* was shaped by the interests of the US and Canadian governments. Early in the development process, the US Department of State informed SAAM that the show needed to encourage North American cultural understanding. Summary notes from a meeting record the department's request that the "overriding objective ... be that the exhibit promotes the understanding and appreciation of one another's countries." The department added that it "would like to see this statement reflected in the proposal [for the exhibition]."[52] Satisfying these criteria was necessary to secure funding.[53] The staff at SAAM were also made aware that US State Department funding was contingent on the project being trilateral and addressing a general audience.[54] However, SAAM correspondence reveals that its interests were slightly at odds with those of CHIN, given the "aesthetic goals" of the Canadian partners and their wish that the exhibition should target children.[55] Eventually, a compromise was found: the project would be pitched to two audiences, youth (ten to fourteen years old) and the general public, thus satisfying everyone.[56] Education programs provided a key means of compromise, allowing for a focus on youth. As detailed in the exhibition agreement, the contract outlined the agreed-upon plans for the show: "The target audience of the exhibit will be the general public although educational components targeting youth will also be included."[57] This resolution demonstrates how the partners negotiated their interests, with the final result leading to a broader audience for the show.

In the United States, Helena Kane Finn, acting assistant secretary for educational and cultural affairs, identified *Panoramas* as a form of diplomacy: "The website gives testimony to the powerful role of art and interactive education in promoting mutual understanding of the similarities and differences among these nations' citizens. This is modern public diplomacy at its pinnacle."[58] Her comment is in line with public diplomacy's emphasis on relationship building. Cull explains that recent public diplomacy initiatives – the so-called new public diplomacy – may not focus exclusively on foreign audiences. Instead, he suggests that "the relationships ... could usefully be between two audiences, foreign to each other, whose communication the actor [instigating the public diplomacy initiative] wishes to facilitate."[59] In the case of *Panoramas*, the three governments not only wanted to influence foreign publics but also sought to inform domestic audiences about their new relationships to the other North American countries. Potential educational ideas revolved around topics such as "Globalism," which included "NAFTA and free trade," and "possible educational telecomputing activities," such as "email exchanges exploring perceptions about free trade." These were not realized, but organizers were clearly thinking about how the show could teach the public about new connections between the countries and free trade.[60]

Interestingly, in the face of overt political proclamations such as Finn's, one *Panoramas* partner, the WAG, attempted to downplay the connection with free trade. The gallery's head of communications, Marilyn Williams, distanced the show from geopolitical developments, insisting that it "has nothing to do with free trade. It has everything to [do with] being neighbours on the continent."[61] Why the WAG took this stance is unclear, but it probably wanted to concentrate on the artwork rather than trade alliances, affirming an institutional view that separated art from politics. Perhaps it felt that the exhibition would seem too nakedly ideological. Nonetheless, Williams's comment about being neighbours was very much in line with the goals of NAFTA. That she felt the need to make this statement also suggests that *Panoramas* was being read publicly in relation to NAFTA.

Throughout the creation of the exhibition, there was an uneasy mix of advancing alignment between the three governments while simultaneously downplaying their political support. In designing the website, the team weighed how to emphasize the US State Department and the Mexican government on the splash page. To this end, they considered linking *Panoramas* to the North American Partnership website run by the State Department.[62] At the same time, the curators wanted the splash page to foreground the museum logos to avoid giving the impression that the show was a government project. As SAAM's virtual exhibitions specialist Jeana Foley reported, "All of the curators felt very strongly that the museum logos should not be removed completely from the splash, so I hope that does not happen. We feel it is important to have that immediate identification of the cultural organizations involved so that it doesn't only look like a government website."[63] An early version of the promotional brochure for the exhibition referred to "cultural diplomacy," but this was later removed, and the emphasis was placed on art and history instead.[64] The opinion of the partners seems to have been that fostering cultural cooperation and exchange was acceptable, whereas an overt promotion of trade ties was less desirable.

A reading of the exhibition as a foray in public diplomacy is furthered by the way in which senior politicians mobilized it at the third annual Trilateral Ministerial Meeting, which was held in Santa Fe, New Mexico, on 11 and 12 August 2000. Together, the Canadian foreign affairs minister Lloyd Axworthy, the American secretary of state Madeleine K. Albright, and the Mexican foreign secretary Rosario Green announced the project under the title *Pan-American Perspectives: The Land in Art*. The exhibition was introduced amongst larger conversations about building North American connections. Specifically, at the Santa Fe meeting the ministers discussed the "ways in which the people of Canada, the United Sates, and Mexico can deepen and widen their relationship," and identified "civil society" as a site from which to promote "the growing synergies of North American interconnectedness."[65] Thus, even before *Panoramas* was completed, it was already being conceptualized as evidence of North American unity. These discussions spoke to a recognition of public diplomacy as a means of changing understandings of the region.

The larger significance of *Panoramas* was not lost on the institutional partners. WAG chief curator Donna McAlear stated, "Culture and education play an important role in generating greater understanding of the cultural histories and outlook of the three countries. Here the virtual exhibition being produced by the WAG and its partners has a major role to play."[66] The Mexican curator, Esther Acevedo, argued that the contrast between the deep economic connections of the three countries and the relative lack of cultural connections justified the creation of *Panoramas*. "We trade in millions of dollars each year," she pointed out, "but we recognized that we were doing almost nothing as far as cultural cooperation at the official level."[67] In the United States, R. Susan Wood, deputy assistant secretary for western hemisphere affairs at the Department of State, contended that the North American countries had an inherent connection, which was in the land:

> Canada, Mexico and the United States are united first of all by our geography. This unique virtual exhibit enables anyone with access to the Internet to view that geography through dramatic works of art depicting North American landscapes, and – very appropriately on the eve of the Summit of the Americas – it exemplifies the cooperative spirit of our North American Partnership. This wonderful exhibit is a splendid example of modern technology at the service of cultural diplomacy and mutual understanding.[68]

Here, Woods refers to the Third Summit of the Americas held from 20 to 22 April 2001 in Quebec City, where the proposed FTAA was under negotiation. At the MUNAL opening, Canada's ambassador to Mexico, Keith Christie, also mentioned the summit, stating of *Panoramas*, "La computación borra el tiempo y el espacio, y las sociedades dialogarán entre sí, apreciarán la cultura del vecindario continental y se fortalecerán relaciones extraordinarias, en el marco de la Cumbre de las Américas que iniciará los próximos días."[69] (Computing erases time and space. Societies will dialogue with each other, appreciate the culture of the continental neighbourhood, and strengthen extraordinary relationships in the framework of the Summit of the Americas that will begin in the coming days.) That *Panoramas* generated political associations shows that its aims went beyond those typically given to exhibitions. This was probably the result of high-level political involvement.

To achieve these associations, *Panoramas* slotted national landscapes into a North American framework, severing the traditional connection between landscape and nation. By taking this approach, the organizing governments demonstrated their careful management of nationalist narratives.

The featured works included many iconic pieces, which retained a semblance of their past meaning, but they were displayed in a manner that emphasized continental associations. Canadian artists included Tom Thomson, Edwin Holgate, and Alex Colville; Mexican artists included Frida Kahlo, David Alfaro Siqueiros, and Diego Rivera; and American artists included Winslow Homer and Georgia O'Keeffe. A small flag indicated the national origin of every work, but each one also included a hyperlink that, when activated, opened a map of North America. This map allowed viewers to locate the region or city that corresponded to the artwork. In this way, national associations were maintained, but continental perspectives were emphasized in line with the stress on the promotion of North American unity.

The message of cultural parity mirrored the creation of a North America that was united by free trade. This concept of parity is significant because the economic relationships of the trade partners were not equal. Even so, articulating cultural similarities was central to this and other exhibitions that appeared at the time. A key component of the new continental narrative was the similarity between the states rather than their differences. This change was necessary because economic integration challenged conventional understandings. *Panoramas,* therefore, upheld and constructed a North American landscape that was in accordance with NAFTA requirements.

Throughout its development, the educational potential of *Panoramas* remained a priority. At the launch, Lawrence M. Small, the Smithsonian's secretary, stated, "We have much to learn from each other," implying that *Panoramas* would prove useful as a teaching tool.[70] On the *Panoramas* website, an educational section encouraged students to contemplate various issues, from the influence of landforms on human occupancy to the diversity of North American cultures. The website suggested activities and provided lists of additional textual resources. Rheingold Associates – a consulting firm helmed by Howard Rheingold, a leading proponent of virtual community – was hired by the US Department of State to make this component of the project highly visible.[71] The consultants worked with teachers and students in Edmonton and Winnipeg to show them how to maximize the potential of the exhibition as an educational resource.[72]

This included on-site visits, "training on use of virtual community software, ... inform[ing] participants of expected performance as part of the educational activity, ... coach[ing] students and teachers, and otherwise facilitat[ing] participation in activity."[73] In these ways, the pedagogical capacity of the exhibition was fully activated.

The VMC also created supplementary educational material, which was separate from the exhibition website and located on the online VMC Teachers' Centre. When the *Panoramas* site closed in 2013, these resources remained accessible for several more years, until September 2021.[74] Among them, "Virtual Tours and Media Exhibition" and "The Artist's Perspective" drew on the content of the online exhibition and provided material specifically aimed at educators of senior secondary students and undergraduates (fourteen to twenty-one years of age). "Virtual Tours and Media Exhibition" presented "tours" of *Panoramas* that took a certain work or theme as a guiding point, such as "Female Imagery and Landscape."[75] Some tours confined themselves to a single piece from the exhibition, whereas others covered several. One featured historic and contemporary videos of North America, whose footage included Niagara Falls, Yellowstone Park, and the Mexican countryside during the revolution (1910–21). "The Artist's Perspective" was organized through a series of images devoted to five themes: the environment, transportation, waterways, horses, and artists' worldviews.[76] A final tour offered activities for students to explore the artwork in *Panoramas* in conjunction with a range of learning objectives, including gaining an appreciation of art as a form of communication.[77] The content in these supplementary collections thus offered further insight into the art and the concept of the North American landscape through text and media. That these materials were publicly accessible for over two decades was evidence of ongoing state support for the messages delivered by *Panoramas*.[78]

SAAM developed its own supplementary pedagogical program, called the "Panoramas Education Project," which consisted of "a series of online education activities structured as a global classroom within a virtual community."[79] In early 2001, hoping to strengthen institutional linkages across North America, the WAG sent Marnie Butvin, one of its curatorial interns who had helped to develop *Panoramas*, to Washington DC to work on the educational component of the project.[80] In her view, it "fosters exchange and understanding between students throughout North America"; and it "involves teachers and students from all three participating countries. They will engage in a series of activities that happen both in actual classrooms and in an on-line global classroom."[81] This aspect of the exhibition bolstered the public diplomacy of the project by initiating people-to-people connections.

Panoramas was augmented by a small in-house exhibition at the WAG. Titled *Selections from Panoramas: The North American Landscape in Art,* it demonstrated the gallery's ongoing investment in the digital show. In fact, the WAG devoted considerable resources to *Selections,* including eight employees who began work on it in August 2000.[82] Curated by Tricia Wasney, it was on display from 8 to 29 April 2001 and so coincided with the Third Summit of the Americas in Quebec City. It was intended to provide a glimpse into the online show and to highlight the gallery's involvement in the trilateral collaboration.[83] According to chief curator McAlear, *Selections* gave the gallery "the chance to publicize this international website exhibition collaboration with our local audience, and to showcase the diversity of the WAG collections."[84] It featured thirty-one of WAG's seventy-six works in the online exhibition, all from its permanent collection.[85] They dated from 1799 to 1994, but most were from the twentieth century.[86] Artists included Molly Lamb Bobak, Emily Carr, Alex Colville, Greg Curnoe, David Brown Milne, Tom Thomson, Janet Kigusiuq, and William Kurelek.[87] The wall text, which also mentioned the online show, made clear the theme of North American unity: "The works of each country are presented alongside each other on the web, highlighting both the commonality of human experience and the diversity of geography, history, culture, and climate."[88] Everything on display in *Selections* was Canadian, but references to the larger North American framework of the online show linked to the concept of cultural parity – that a common core united the three North American countries. This theme was significant, given widespread Canadian fears about the dominance of US cultural products under free trade. North American unity was also reinforced in text noting the institutional alliances and continental cooperation developed through *Panoramas.*[89]

Panoramas was designed as a multifaceted platform to educate the public about North American integration, deemed necessary because of the economic integration of the new North America under NAFTA. Its political origins reveal the interest of the three governments in teaching their citizens about the connections between their countries.[90] This objective was accomplished through art, leveraging cultural patrimony as a non-aggressive means of transmitting the message. *Panoramas,* as McAlear explained, "is aimed at increasing cultural understanding and appreciation among the peoples of North America. It will also provide people around the world with access to the collections of museums in three countries."[91] By carefully selecting works from a genre that is traditionally associated with nationalist projects, the exhibition negotiated a place for Canada, Mexico, and the United States within a larger continental framework. Its emphasis on encouraging integration was amplified by its prominent educational component and adjunct elements that were aimed at youth. *Panoramas* also served as a Canadian-initiated public diplomacy project – a substantial means of state-to-people engagement and cooperation that involved civil society partners. Additionally, it was a traditional diplomatic project – a means of state-to-state engagement between the Canadian, Mexican, and American governments – employing art to communicate messages about unity and parity. Throughout, Ottawa took the lead, provided significant funding, and interacted with numerous partners, revealing its full-fledged support for this type of public diplomacy.

Carr, O'Keeffe, Kahlo: Places of Their Own

Featuring works by Emily Carr, Georgia O'Keeffe, and Frida Kahlo, the exhibition *Places of Their Own* was promoted as the first time that all three artists had appeared together.[92] It toured four venues in Canada and the United States between 2001 and 2002. Opening at the McMichael Canadian Art Collection (MCAC) in Kleinburg, Ontario, it then travelled to the Santa Fe Museum of Fine Arts, the National Museum of Women in Art in Washington DC, and concluded at the Vancouver Art Gallery.[93] The iconic statures of the three painters was evident during the development of the exhibition, whose working title was simply *E, F and G,* indicating that the organizers deemed the first letter of each woman's first name to be adequate.[94] Clearly, they were widely recognized as the "outstanding twentieth-century women painters of their respective countries." In fact, their nations of origin were frequently mentioned in association with the show; one reviewer, Layne Christensen, categorized the artists as "national treasures."[95] Scholar Kirsty Robertson notes that popular interest in all three peaked amid pop star Madonna's refusal to loan paintings to the show and in advance of the movie biopic *Frida* (2002), which starred Salma Hayek.[96]

Although the three artists were roughly contemporaries, born in 1871 (Carr), 1887 (O'Keeffe), and 1907 (Kahlo), they had little interaction with each other. Since their deaths, their art has been examined in relation to their homelands and their contributions to national narratives. According to the curator of *Places of Their Own,* Sharyn Rohlfsen Udall,

> They observed their surroundings and then reinvented the image in paint. As a result, the United States, Mexico, and Canada we know from their paintings are, in substantial part, the terrain they imagined; we can scarcely envision what their places were like beforehand. As advocates of their native lands, these painters' inscriptions of self upon those places became their ultimate subject and most radiant achievement.[97]

This sentiment was echoed by the MCAC, which stated that each artist was "considered to be her nation's outstanding female painter of the twentieth century ... [They] were, and remain, legendary in their respective countries."[98] The thrust of the exhibition was to align these three icons.

The continental focus of *Places of Their Own* was in line with the economic integration of North America that was under way at the time, mirroring the new trade alliance between Canada, Mexico, and the United States. Paul Gessell, an Ottawa-based critic, associated the three artists with NAFTA, characterizing them as "the best-known women artists this century from the three NAFTA countries."[99] Others mentioned NAFTA in passing as a descriptor for the artists, including Hadani Ditmars, who referred to them as the "Nafta Feminist 3."[100] NAFTA is central to understanding the framing of and support for the exhibition, despite the fact that it did not explore geopolitical developments in detail. The curatorial approach demonstrated an acceptance of NAFTA's economic integration, and the exhibition naturalized the new understanding of North America by affirming the cultural associations of the continent.

Udall originated the concept for *Places of Their Own* and published a book of the same title in 2000. Divided into three sections, the volume considers landscape and identity, as well as the private selves and public careers of the artists. It includes a detailed chronology of their lives, presented in tandem so that milestones in their biographies can be compared and contrasted. It maintains that Carr, O'Keeffe, and Kahlo's perspectives as female artists are a key commonality, as all three broke through gender norms during an era dominated by men. All were linked to prominent male artists – Carr to Lawren Harris, O'Keeffe to Alfred Stieglitz, and Kahlo to Diego Rivera – relationships that Udall underscores as another similarity among them.[101] She argues for a comparative consideration, despite a lack of contact between the three, suggesting that they shared fundamental similarities, from their connections to their countries to their interest in Indigenous cultures and nature.[102] She also points to the fact that they resisted, at one time or another, family, religion, and artistic expectations.[103]

Udall's curatorial approach repeated that of her book, exploring the identities of the artists and examining the similarities and differences in their lives, as well as their achievements and difficulties. Work began on the exhibition in 1998. Udall selected approximately sixty paintings, with roughly equal representation for each painter.[104] They were augmented by archival materials, including correspondence, journals, and statements from all three artists.[105] Udall structured the show around three themes: nature, culture, and the public self.[106] The paintings of each artist were grouped thematically. This allowed for juxtapositions in the gallery space. For instance, Carr's 1931 oil painting *Big Raven* could be viewed in proximity to Kahlo's 1937 *Self-Portrait Dedicated to Leon Trotsky* (Figure 8). Similarly, O'Keeffe's large-scale *Cross with Red Heart* (1932) took centre stage elsewhere, visible in proximity to Kahlo's *Itzcuintli Dog with Me* (1938), as well as other works.

These juxtapositions spoke to the settler perspectives of Kahlo and Carr, revealing their colonial appropriations. Kahlo's works and dress

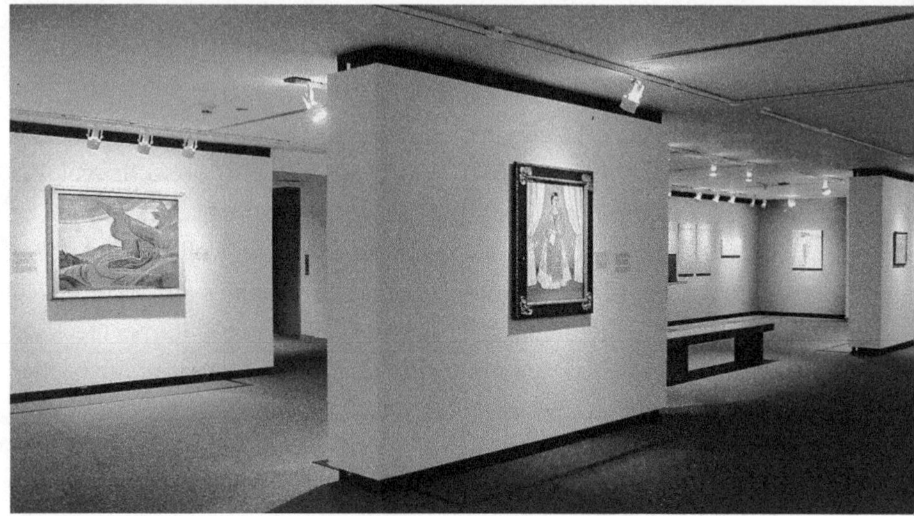

FIGURE 8 *Carr, O'Keeffe, Kahlo: Places of Their Own,* installation of Emily Carr and Frida Kahlo in Gallery 12. Exhibition at the McMichael Canadian Art Collection, 2001. McMichael Canadian Art Collection Archives. Visible (left to right): Emily Carr, *Big Raven,* 1931, oil on canvas, 87.0 x 114.0 cm, Collection of the Vancouver Art Gallery, Emily Carr Trust; and Frida Kahlo's *Self-Portrait Dedicated to Leon Trotsky,* 1937, oil on masonite, 30 x 24 inches, Collection of the National Museum of Women in the Arts © Banco de Mexico Diego Rivera Frida Kahlo Museum Trust, Mexico, D.F./Artists Rights Society (ARS) New York/CARCC Ottawa 2024.

reflect the *indigenismo* movement, a "fraught conflation of racial, gender, and class politics playing out in post-revolutionary Mexico," which scholar Camila Sutherland describes as a "conceptualization and deployment of indigeneity [characterized by] ... the weaving of living indigenous peoples and traditions into a larger discourse of populist nationalism."[107] Kahlo was known for favouring Tehuana attire, as captured in photographs of her and in her self-portraits.[108] Carr similarly drew on Northwest Coast Indigenous culture in her art and writings, including her memoir *Klee Wyck.*[109] Her interest was rooted in primitivism, and her approach reinforced the salvage paradigm.[110] According to writer Marcia Crosby, Carr's work evidences "a deep bond with an imaginary, homogenous heritage," an inclusion that is "parasitic" and contingent on othering Indigenous culture.[111] Such appropriation "denies the existence of systems of signs encoded in visual images, dress, language, ritual, that have specific socio-political and religious meanings for specific nations of people."[112] Critically examining Kahlo and Carr's engagement with Indigenous culture uncovers a naturalization of a settler-colonial framework, which was also embedded in the exhibition.

Throughout the show, Udall strongly emphasized the biographies of the artists and their similar narrative arc. This was underlined by the photographs that hung alongside the paintings, including striking portraits of the artists (Figure 9).

The Toronto advertising campaign to promote *Places of Their Own* at the MCAC also concentrated on biography. One ad reproduced Kahlo's famous *Self-Portrait with Monkey* (1938), adding a headline in block letters: "The Drama. The Passion. The Estrogen."[113] This essentializing and exoticizing tagline reduced the artist's oeuvre to her biography and a reference to gender. Interestingly, much the same approach had featured in the promotional materials for *Mexican Modern Art,* as discussed in Chapter 1. The Kahlo ad was one of a three-part series. Carr's tagline read "Scandal. Rejection. Separation," whereas O'Keeffe's was "Passion. Sexuality. Angst."[114]

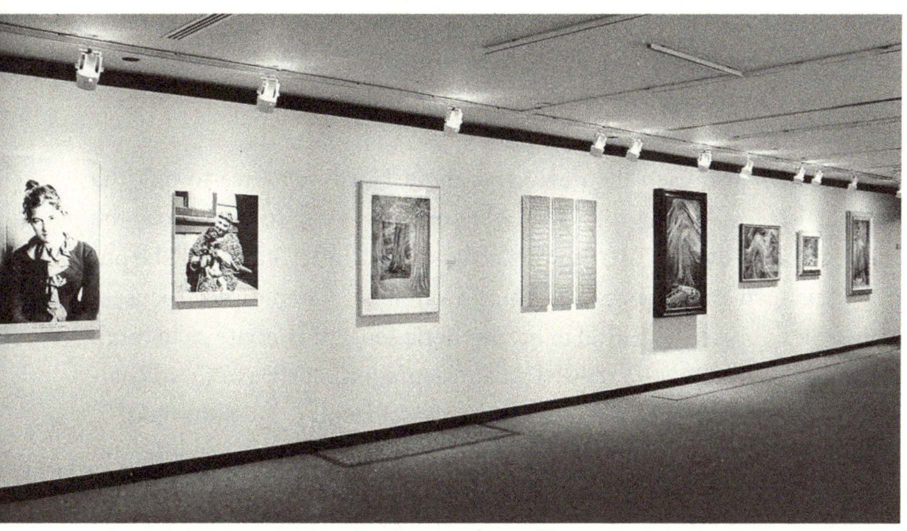

FIGURE 9 *Carr, O'Keefe, Kahlo: Places of Their Own,* installation of Emily Carr biography section in Gallery 12. The section features photographs of Carr (dating to ca. 1891 and 1943), along with five Carr paintings and didactic text. Exhibition at the McMichael Canadian Art Collection, 2001. McMichael Canadian Art Collection Archives.

Udall also emphasized the national associations of the artists, noting that "each was fiercely devoted to her own country," grappling with "the challenge of defining what it might mean to be a Canadian, American or Mexican painter in her day."[115] Critic Michael O'Sullivan picked up on this argument:

> Isn't it true that there is something quintessentially American about O'Keeffe and her affection for the Southwest? Something intrinsically Canadian about Carr's obsession with the totem poles and primeval woodlands of her homeland's aboriginal culture? And something ever so Mexican about Kahlo's conflicted sense of her mestizo heritage (her mother had Spanish and Indian blood; her father was of Austro-Hungarian descent)?[116]

Nations are often expressed through female associations; for example, allegorical references construct the land as a contained female body.[117] Such personifications are paradoxical because though women have been "given a special symbolic status in relation to the nation," they have experienced inequality throughout history and have been disenfranchised and "distanced from active membership of the polity."[118] *Places of Their Own* continued this narrative by highlighting the national origins of Carr, O'Keeffe, and Kahlo.

But Udall also used the new ideas about North America to link the three artists, explaining that their work asked viewers to reconsider the connections between Canada, Mexico, and the United States. As she put it, "Their own movements and their awareness – sometimes focused, sometimes diffuse – of a kind of hemispheric sensibility invite us to think about the possibility of a revised axial orientation, north-south, to challenge the entrenched east-west cultural consciousness they inherited."[119] These associations also appeared in media discussions of the exhibition. Critic Sarah Milroy regarded it as being about continental ties: "Udall has provoked a rethinking of our traditional notions of East-West cultural axis along North-South lines."[120] Here and elsewhere, the rhetoric about North America, arising from the economic integration brought about by free trade, provided context for reinterpreting the relationship between the three artists.

Places of Their Own thus supported the construction of the new North America by naturalizing continental associations. The similarities in the artists' biographies contributed to the idea of cultural parity, and like *Panoramas,* the show emphasized a cultural unity among Canada, Mexico, and the United States. Referring to the three painters, the MCAC accentuated the continental bonds: "Collectively, *their work gives form to a mythos of North America,* linking region and nationality to larger forces at work in Western consciousness."[121] In art-historical terms, the show demonstrated a new approach, drawing on transnational regionalism as the logic for examining the work of artists who were traditionally tied to their national canons.

Nonetheless, *Places of Their Own* differed significantly from *Panoramas* in that it was not conceived as a political project. There was no direct state sponsorship, even if the Canadian Department of Foreign Affairs and International Trade (DFAIT) was involved peripherally by helping to secure loans of paintings from Mexico.[122] During a conference call regarding further collaborations, the *Panoramas* partners discussed *Places of Their Own,* which is listed on the agenda for the meeting alongside a possible exhibition on scientific inventions in Mexico, Canada, and the United States. Although not politically motivated, *Places of Their Own* fit the narrative the partners wished to promote.[123]

Governments also voiced support for *Places of Their Own.* In a review, Gessell noted that "the show is being encouraged at the highest levels in Mexico and Canada, where the two national governments are trying to capitalize on the North American free trade agreement with increased cultural links."[124] State support also figured in an online exhibition inspired by the show: *Perspectives: Women Artists from North America,* created by the Virtual Museum of Canada (VMC) in 2002.[125] Encompassing numerous women artists from across the continent, *Perspectives* celebrated female art production and advanced a message of North American cultural unity, indicating the extent to which messages of integration gained traction in art shows that resonated with the trade alliance. *Places of Their Own* demonstrates how national narratives could also resonate from within larger transnational agglomerations. Beyond state diplomacy, it articulated new art-historical methods of understanding art in a manner that corresponded to geopolitical developments.

Baja to Vancouver: The West Coast and Contemporary Art

Novel ideas for exhibiting the continent were also evident in *Baja to Vancouver,* a 2004–05 touring show of contemporary West Coast art. It was the first museum show to address the West Coast from a transnational perspective.[126] As art critic Robert L. Pincus wrote, "The West Coast is growing in the post-NAFTA era – at least when it comes to the art world."[127] *Baja to Vancouver* presented a more conceptual than literal understanding of the West Coast, stretching from southern British Columbia to Baja California in northern Mexico. This limited definition of the region as a transnational space exemplifies Stephen Clarkson's claim that global regional structures "are notoriously unstable in their geographic definition."[128]

Branded "B2V," *Baja to Vancouver* featured over fifty works by thirty-three West Coast artists, including Brian Jungen, Marcos Ramírez ERRE, and Kota Ezawa. All dated from 1998 to 2003. The intent of the show was to highlight contemporary art on the transnational Pacific coast, to work against traditional regional categorizations that were limited to sub-state areas, and to refute conventional organization by nation.[129] The West Coast was described as a "distinctive cultural terrain" and "North America's most vital region of contemporary art making," in the face of the northeast orientation of the art world, dominated by New York.[130] Like *Panoramas, Baja to Vancouver* was the product of North American institutional collaboration, though no Mexican partners were involved. The reasons for the lack of a Mexican partner are unclear; it is notable given the show's emphasis on art produced in Tijuana. (In contrast, Mexican institutions were involved in the binational art festival inSite, discussed in Chapter 5.) At *Baja to Vancouver,* Mexican participation came in the form of the artists displayed, and the exhibition catalogue received significant support from the Jumex Collection in Mexico. The four participating institutions were all in the United States and Canada: the Seattle Art Museum, the Museum of Contemporary Art San Diego, the Vancouver Art Gallery, and the CCA Wattis Institute for Contemporary Arts in San Francisco.

These partners began organizing the show in 2000.[131] The process affirmed relationships across national boundaries, even as the exhibition itself transgressed the boundaries through its curatorial premise. It opened in Seattle on 9 October 2003, where it remained until 4 January 2004, after which it ran in San Diego from 23 January to 16 May 2004 and then appeared in Vancouver from 5 June to 6 September 2004. The final stop on the tour was the CCA Wattis Institute, from 6 October 2004 to 10 January 2005. *Baja to Vancouver* also received some support from DFAIT, which partially funded the tour, probably because Ottawa wanted to create new cultural connections with Mexico following the implementation of NAFTA. The curatorial team was composed of five members, with representation from all four institutions: Lisa Corrin in Seattle, Toby Kamps in San Diego, Daina Augaitis in Vancouver, and Matthew Higgs and Ralph Rugoff in San Francisco.[132] Missing from this list is any representation from Los Angeles, a significant centre of art production on the West Coast.[133] Although some reviews criticized this absence, the potential creation of new transnational networks was suggested by the institutions that did participate. Christopher Knight of the *Los Angeles Times* noted, "The show's institutional consortium draws the fragile outlines of an independent network that, with some effort, could operate with considerable freedom from the limited mandate represented in New York."[134] Knight's comment speaks to the network of regional alliances and the possibility that new alliances and approaches could open up novel partnerships in the art world.

The *Baja to Vancouver* curatorial team grouped the works into categories that pushed certain juxtapositions: Pop Media Culture, Edge City Culture, Culture of Individuals, and Communal Culture.[135] Abstract art was excluded, and all the art was required to deal with the West Coast and its social landscape.[136] The attention paid to the social aspects of landscape echoes the approach of *Panoramas* and *Places of Their Own.* In all three exhibitions, the works on display went beyond topography to address shared culture, values, and relationships in North America. However, *Baja to Vancouver* diverged significantly from *Panoramas* and *Places of Their Own* in marking out the Coast as a new framework within a unified continent.

The curators sought to present "the shared social, historical, and topographical conditions that set this area apart from the rest of North America."[137] This emphasis indicates a mild resistance to continental integration as a totalizing force. *Baja to Vancouver* advanced cultural connections as the basis for a regional identity. It saw the West Coast as a culturally cohesive entity, thus breaking free from the economic unity reinforced by the continental focus of *Panoramas* and *Places of Their Own.*

Asserting that there was a "need to redefine regionalism in art centers," the curators attempted to free the concept of region from its traditional national constraints.[138] The exhibition catalogue argued that the assessment of unity among geographical areas should go beyond the idea that a region was inevitably the subset of a nation. "By offering evidence of creative cross-talk and shared aesthetic concerns among artists living and working on North America's West Coast," the curators stated, "this exhibition reveals the need to redefine our notions of 'regional' art centers, expanding them beyond considerations of national identity."[139] During an interview, *Baja to Vancouver* co-curator Toby Kamps explained that intranational regionalism no longer applied to contemporary art in a globalized world. The curators, he said, "think 'regionalism' doesn't hold anymore. Everyone is hyper-connected these days, electronically and physically. But there are themes in common. So we tried to focus on this basic idea of 'social landscapes' – that's sort of the world and its people. It's kinda broad."[140] For Ralph Rugoff, this transnational approach was a means of going "beyond the limiting dichotomy of international and local ... a more expansive way of demarcating zones of cultural production."[141] Ultimately, it pushed back on national and continental framings, providing another way to understand region within North America.

It is paradoxical that the *Baja to Vancouver* curatorial team would argue against intranational regionalism, given their dedication to the idea of regionalism, albeit a transnational one. Their approach to region accords with the rethinking of national boundaries undertaken at roughly the same time by scholars such as urban studies theorist Richard Florida, who wrote that "mega-regions have replaced the nation-state as the economic drivers of the global economy."[142] Florida coined the name "Tor-Buff-Chester" to define "the economic powerhouse region stretching from

[Florida's then] new hometown [Toronto] to Buffalo and Rochester."[143] Such mega-regions were one result of free trade agreements that facilitated economic exchanges across borders. Discussing the changes to the Mexico-US landscape due to free trade, Orme argues that NAFTA was instrumental in creating four new regions: Las Californias, the Rocky Madres, the Monterrey Metroplex, and the Gulf Coast.[144] The West Coast region defined by *Baja to Vancouver* may not be an economic powerhouse in the same sense, but the exhibition revealed that the cultural sphere was also tackling the issue of defining place in a globalizing world. At the same time, it expressed a slight pushback to the kind of continental integration advanced by *Panoramas* and *Places of Their Own*. This resistance indicates the uneven nature of economic and cultural integration in North America during the period.

Baja to Vancouver encouraged new readings of the landscape. The region it carved out dispensed with conventional associations of culture as nationally bounded. This shift was as much economic as cultural, according to Orme; North American trade routes would be reconfigured along north-south pathways under NAFTA, connecting Canada and Mexico through the United States.[145] Focusing his analysis on Canada, economist Thomas J. Courchene argues that CUSFTA and NAFTA "transformed Canadian geo-economic space from the traditional east-west trading axis to a north-south trading axis."[146] *Baja to Vancouver* redefined regional culture in the same way that free trade redefined economics (by foregrounding north-south associations as opposed to nationally bounded east-west ones). Thus, its emphasis on region unsettled the nation as a dominant framework. It also demonstrated that new art-historical narratives might result from the transnational connections formed by processes of neoliberal globalization. The curatorial intent to establish such links allowed for larger social and cultural associations to emerge among the artworks, which supported cross-border ties.

The exhibition's focus on the distinct nature of the West Coast, however, resulted in a lack of aesthetic consistency and thematic unity. The art on display did not emphasize a specific style or theme; rather, it promoted new ideas about a region.[147] Consequently, it tended to examine conceptual understandings of the area, such as the notion of periphery or utopian site. Stan Douglas's *Every Building on 100 West Hastings* (2001), for example, depicts Vancouver's Downtown East Side, a low-income neighbourhood frequently represented in media coverage for its significant social challenges. As art historian Gabrielle Moser explains, its "poverty, homelessness, drug use, and sex work have increased as the divide between the rich and poor deepens," making it "a point of contrast for the rest of the city."[148] Douglas's work is a twelve-foot-long, digitally manipulated panoramic photograph that documents a strip of predominantly vacant buildings.[149] It foregrounds the contested nature of the neighbourhood and raises questions about the power dynamics between its residents and other groups, including the media and police, as well as the photographer and urban subjects.[150]

Despite the connections between free trade and the novel understandings of North America, press reviews of *Baja to Vancouver* rarely touched on NAFTA or economic unity. Many did mention globalization, in reference to the transnational focus of the exhibition, speaking of the need to understand the art world as an international entity that transcended national borders.[151] Only in passing did journalists note the geopolitical relationships that were reshaping the continent. One anonymous review defined the West Coast as "linked geographically, economically and culturally." Art critic Robert Pincus concluded that NAFTA necessitated new regions and that "this show ends up touting regionalism for the post-NAFTA era."[152] Pincus did not pursue this point in any detail – perhaps an indication of the extent to which the revised North American landscape had already been naturalized by 2004–05.

Certainly, some of the works included in *Baja to Vancouver* invited discussion of the material conditions of existence. These were linked to employment, a hot topic under free trade, so it is surprising that NAFTA was not cited more often in media coverage. For example, *Urban Survival Unit,* a 2002 work by Torolab (an art group founded by Raúl Cárdenas Osuna and Marcela Guadiana de Cárdenas), consisted of a backpack that contained a portable shelter – a camouflaged tent for use in spaces between and behind billboards. The tent was intended for Tijuana residents who lacked safe housing, as billboards are ubiquitous in the city's landscape.[153] The pointed commentary and site-specific focus of *Urban Survival Unit* are similar to those espoused by many artworks featured at inSite, discussed in Chapter 5.

At least one of the curators, Ralph Rugoff, hoped that *Baja to Vancouver* would help viewers understand the North American landscape in a new way. He described the show as an educational road trip that "transforms the manner in which we see the places and cultures around us."[154] It thus continued the pedagogical function of *Panoramas* and *Places of Their Own*. For Rugoff, "This show astutely recognizes that, in a globalizing world, regional identity changes. It codifies the shift."[155] *Baja to Vancouver* exemplified how changing regional identification under globalization "means continually redrawing borders, not erasing them altogether."[156] It reinforced a different North American orientation and also rejected the pan-continentalism of NAFTA, deploying art to make sense of the constantly shifting borders and alliances. This function of art informs the idea of cultural diplomacy that undergirds much of the discussion in this book.

Visualizing Change

The nation has long been a dominant structure in the study of art history.[157] With the rise of neoliberalism in the late twentieth century – a political formation that supports the demise of national barriers to trade – and globalization, which increases connectivity and mobility, the role of the nation is being questioned in this and other disciplines.[158] David Palumbo-Liu suggests that the ascendancy of national frameworks for reading and understanding art becomes less certain when global connectivity weakens national distinctiveness.[159] He explains, "The way we 'locate' art may be altered by the fact that traditional historical points of reference and framing now seem outmoded, inadequate to the task of locating as precisely as they may have done before."[160] Artists, however, have long questioned such categories, particularly nationalism. In fact, Palumbo-Liu insists that "art today, at and across the borders of nations, calls for a questioning of those categories – do they make sense any more, or do they refer to a constellation of facts no longer as immediately and self-assuredly relevant as before?"[161] Néstor García Canclini argues that the national terms used to categorize art movements contrast with the reality of "the transnational conditions in which art is produced, circulated and received at the end of our [twentieth] century."[162] García Canclini identifies free trade and regional economic integration as challenges to national terms. "What do national identities mean in a time of transnationalization and interculturalism, of multinational co-productions and 'Paris-Berlin' or 'Paris-New York' exhibitions, of free trade agreements and regional economic integration," he asks, "where art works, artists and capital constantly cross borders?"[163] As the exhibitions examined in this chapter indicate, these developments have necessitated changes in art-historical narratives. Whereas the nation remained a key denominator, it was reconfigured in these shows in acknowledgment of transnational flows and reformulated in a manner sympathetic to broader transnational connections. In North America, new ideas for exhibiting the nation began to highlight north-south associations that crossed borders. Moreover, I suggest, these exhibitions even helped to create (not simply reflect) these ongoing changes by naturalizing transnational narratives.

In presenting the new frameworks for understanding North America, these exhibitions demonstrated the central role of art shows in reformulating narratives about the continent, visualizing it for the education of its inhabitants. All three shows displayed art in a manner that promoted the land as a key determiner of identity but refrained from bounding the land by national definitions, as past display strategies had done. *Panoramas* was a state-sponsored initiative directly resulting from geopolitical developments and concerns. *Places of Their Own* and *Baja to Vancouver* were only implicitly related to political agendas but nevertheless reflected changes in civil society's understandings of North America. Even as the economic alliance structured by NAFTA reshaped trading patterns, the three exhibitions did their part in helping to redefine North America. They affirm Poitras's assertion that the continent needed to be united by more than economic ties: "North America is a regional experiment in commerce and investment. Inventing North America may go well beyond the world of business."[164] According to the exhibitions discussed in this chapter, the revisioned landscape included Canada, Mexico, and the United States, and it encompassed the land between the Pacific and the Atlantic Oceans. These shows informed North Americans that they were connected – broadly through trade (under NAFTA) and in transnational regions such as the West Coast (depicted in *Baja to Vancouver*).

The use of art to naturalize these connections should be understood as an attempt to invent tradition. Historian Eric Hobsbawm argues that this occurs when a change is deliberately rooted in a fictionalized past to make it palatable in the present. In his words, "'Invented tradition' is taken to mean a set of practices, normally governed by overtly or tacitly accepted rules and of a ritual or symbolic nature, which seek to inculcate certain values and norms of behaviour by repetition, which automatically implies continuity with the past." He adds, "All invented traditions, so far as possible, use history as a legitimator of action and cement of group cohesion."[165] The three exhibitions discussed in this chapter can be read as part of this legitimating process, buttressing the naturalization of both North American unity and the free trade agreements that produced it. The art on display, understood to represent national histories, was redeployed to promote the revised image of the continent.

It was intended to knit together disparate national narratives and to project parity. Despite variation across Canada, Mexico, and the United States, the three exhibitions and their related educational materials emphasized cohesion among the countries, instructing the public in a new "imagined community." But, by frequently drawing on land and landscape art to normalize this unity, they also reasserted the denial of Indigenous sovereignty. As Eve Tuck (Unangax̂) and K. Wayne Yang explain, land is essential to the system of settler colonialism: "Settlers make Indigenous land their new home and source of capital, and ... the disruption of Indigenous relationships to land represents a profound epistemic, ontological, cosmological violence."[166] Thus, the invention and reinvention of settler traditions have stark and punitive repercussions for Indigenous-settler relations; they perpetuate colonial relationships to and possession of the land.

The need to make claims for unity becomes clear when we consider that in Chiapas, Mexico, the Zapatista uprising against NAFTA, which began in 1994, was still ongoing in the 2000s (the Spanish name of the group is Ejército Zapatista de Liberación Nacional). At the same time, a global justice movement was focused on protesting globalization (including free trade), with major demonstrations in Quebec City and Seattle.[167] Against this backdrop, government interest in supporting the kinds of exhibitions examined in this chapter, either directly or implicitly, reinforced their assumed ability to mediate geopolitical transitions. The three shows all received some measure of state support, ranging from full and active planning and participation for *Panoramas* to partial support for *Baja to Vancouver* and tangential support for *Places of Their Own.* This interest was tied to their perceived pedagogical value, which was especially prominent in the educational programming associated with *Panoramas.* Beyond government support, the exhibitions also reveal new transnational institutional connections, unique partnerships forged between North American institutions in the wake of CUSFTA and NAFTA. All three involved large-scale collaborations: *Panoramas* and *Baja to Vancouver* resulted from trilateral and bi-national partnerships, respectively, whereas *Places of Their Own,* organized by the MCAC, led to a larger collaboration via its educational component *Perspectives.* These alliances reflect the ongoing naturalization of North American integration, in which cultural initiatives mirrored economic partnerships.

4

Settler State Claims to Indigeneity

Whereas *Panoramas, Places of Their Own,* and *Baja to Vancouver* naturalized new visions of North America, none validated the original inhabitants and ongoing claimants of the land. *Rethinking Anthem* (2008), a three-minute video by Nadia Myre (Kitigan Zibi Anishinabeg), exemplifies the contradictions inherent in myths of the Canadian settler state. The video plays with a phrase from the Canadian anthem – "home and native land" – which asserts settler ownership of the land and erases Indigenous histories.[1] Consisting of a short performance, the video shows a tightly cropped aerial view of a white piece of paper with two lines of capitalized text: "HOME AND" and "NATIVE LAND." As it opens, "HOME AND" stands out against the paper, whereas "NATIVE LAND" is barely visible. Two sets of hands appear in the frame, each holding a kneadable art eraser (Figure 10). In a trick of editing, one pair of hands rubs the eraser across the words "NATIVE LAND" until they are boldly inscribed. At the same time, the other hands slowly erase "HOME AND," which is ultimately reduced to a faint trace.

Through these acts of inscribing and removing, *Rethinking Anthem* points to the erasure and appropriation of Indigenous histories in the construction of Canada. The video troubles settler claims to the land, undermining the nation-state's legitimacy. Mohawk scholar and curator Ryan Rice suggests that it also "inserts and establishes a Native presence in the anthem." In this way, it offers a challenge to national narratives. As Rice puts it, the video "metaphorically reveals traditional territories, land

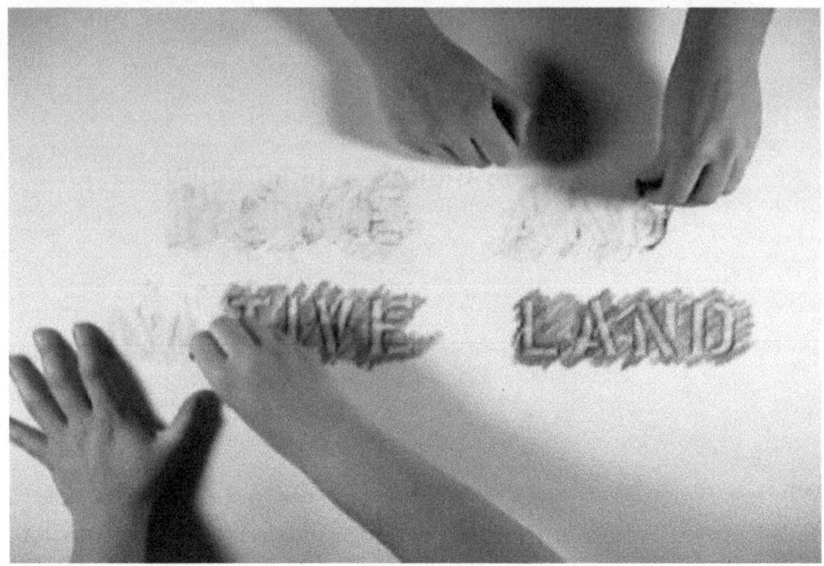

FIGURE 10 Nadia Myre, *Rethinking Anthem,* 2008, video still © Nadia Myre/CARCC Ottawa 2024.

claims, and forms of displacement as part of the living collective memory that should exist in the national conscience."[2] *Rethinking Anthem* lays bare the manipulations that subsume Indigenous cultures and communities into the settler state apparatus.

Given Canada's long-standing use of Indigenous (First Nations, Inuit, and Métis) visual and material culture to construct and promote itself domestically and internationally, it is necessary to consider how this unfolded under NAFTA. These dynamics are complex. Although NAFTA worked to erase some aspects of the settler state, such as international borders, much of the rhetoric around integration was just that, with the state apparatus revealed as enduring under neoliberal globalization. Moreover, this supposed obliteration of borders did not address either Indigenous sovereignty or the violence with which colonial boundaries were imposed, tied to ongoing settler claims to the land.[3] The boundaries also divided Indigenous communities between settler states, as was true for the Akwesasne Mohawk territories that predate and straddle the Canada-US border.[4] Addressing Indigenous sovereignty in the face of competing claims to territory, *Rethinking Anthem* wipes out "HOME AND" – but not completely. The words leave an impression on the paper that speaks to the persistence of settler colonialism despite assertions of "NATIVE LAND," such as the Indigenous-led Land Back movement.[5] Thus, the video addresses the complicated terrain on which settler states foreground Indigenous culture to further their own interests.

The ongoing mobilization of Indigenous culture seems incongruous, given the long histories of violence enacted against Indigenous populations and because the nation-state accords very little to Indigenous peoples in constructing itself. Even as it upholds Indigenous culture as a means of distinguishing itself internationally, it also seeks to conceal the realities of its violence, a process that is premised on forgetting, or selective remembrance. This paradox, according to scholar of settler colonialism Lorenzo Veracini, is typical of settler states. In fact, Veracini identifies a "narrative deficit" in such countries, which springs from the need to elide the violence.[6] Writer and historian Patrick Wolfe labels this phenomenon as a "native counter-claim" (the settler state claims itself as indigenous to the territory). He sees it as part of the "process of replacement" that is inherent in settler colonialism, which normalizes settler privilege while enacting long-term structural genocide against Indigenous populations.[7]

Other scholars have identified settler colonialism as a form of white possession. Writing about Australia, Aileen Moreton-Robinson, a Goenpul woman of the Quandamooka people (Moreton Bay), explains that its social, legal, and cultural practices function to rupture Indigenous ontological relationships to the land. She writes, "Indigenous people's position within the nation-state is not one where colonizing power relations have been discontinued. Instead these power relations are at the very heart of the white national imaginary and belonging; they are postcolonizing."[8] To put it another way, the settler state works to normalize narratives that its claim to the land is legitimate, despite being based on disavowing the violence needed to create itself (through displacement of Indigenous peoples).[9] Even when settlers acknowledge colonialism, they tend to do so at a superficial level rather than in a way that calls for change. As scholars Eve Tuck (Unangax̂) and K. Wayne Yang characterize it, this acknowledgment can be understood as a settler move to innocence – an attempt to assuage responsibility rather than to espouse decolonization (discussed further in Chapter 6).[10] Ultimately, settler colonialism seeks to sustain the settler state, thwarting Indigenous sovereignty and nation-to-nation relations between settler and Indigenous communities.

Despite disavowing Indigenous sovereignty, national settler-colonial narratives also mobilize Indigenous culture to override Indigenous presence and claims to the land, and to speak to peaceable relationships with Indigenous communities.[11] A 2008–11 exhibition titled *First Peoples of Canada: Masterworks from the Canadian Museum of Civilization* is an example of this disingenuous use of Indigenous culture to promote Canada abroad. Another show, *Remix: New Modernities in a Post-Indian World* (2007–09), probed contradictions of identity for Indigenous artists from an Indigenous perspective. Touring multiple venues, both featured Indigenous visual and material culture; *First Peoples of Canada* concentrated on historical objects and *Remix* on contemporary art.

Although this book deals with the government mobilization of exhibitions to disseminate narratives, it must be reiterated that its role is often nuanced and is sometimes difficult to parse. *First Peoples of Canada* was created by a Canadian national museum – the Museum of Civilization (now the Canadian Museum of History).[12] *Remix* was produced by two curators for display at private institutions, even less subject to government control; though one institution, the Art Gallery of Ontario, is funded in part by the Ontario government. Thus, we cannot read these institutions as direct instruments of the Canadian government, as we could in the presentation of *Panoramas* by Heritage Canada (in the previous chapter). Nevertheless, in what follows I aim to demonstrate how narratives – particularly those from the CMC – reinforced Canadian nationalism overseas.

Tensions between Ancient and Contemporary: Planning the Exhibition

The CMC designed *First Peoples of Canada* to be all-encompassing; as it explained, the show "reveals Aboriginal peoples' diversity and ancient relationships to the land, now known as Canada."[13] Produced "in house" by CMC curators Nicholette Prince and Jean-Luc Pilon, it was billed as the "finest collection of Canadian Aboriginal artifacts ever to tour internationally."[14] It premiered at the Art Museum of the Imperial City in Beijing, where it ran from 1 August to 15 October 2008.[15] Developed in conjunction with the National Museum of China (NMC),[16] the Beijing version of the show coincided with the 2008 Summer Olympic and Paralympic Games. In 2009, the CMC sent *First Peoples of Canada* on a three-continent tour, opening on 24 April at the Niedersächsischen Landesmuseum (Lower Saxony State Museum) in Hanover.[17] In September, it appeared at the National Museum of Ethnology (Minpaku) in Osaka. The final stop was the Museo Nacional de las Culturas (MNC) in Mexico City, where it remained from 6 October 2010 to 23 January 2011.[18] This coincided with Mexico's bicentennial and the centennial of its revolution, as well as the reopening of the MNC.[19]

The Beijing iteration drew a great deal of attention as the premiere of the show and due to the Olympics. It therefore provides an opportunity to discuss the key messages disseminated by the exhibition, to highlight changes in the Mexico City version, and to examine the larger circuits within which these blockbuster shows typically travel. The Beijing display of *First Peoples of Canada* speaks to the substantial global networks that underpin museums' roles as cultural diplomacy actors. The exhibition emerged from a 2005 partnership agreement between the NMC and the CMC that laid out terms for an exchange of shows and specified that the CMC would submit one during the Beijing Olympics.[20] According to art historian Ruth B. Phillips, "Moments when museums organize comprehensive and *definitive* exhibitions in connection with a major event in the life of the community" can be defined as "show times." In these moments, "relationships of dependence" between museums, business, and political organizations become more readily apparent, making them important sites for understanding exhibition meanings.[21] There is increased publicity on these occasions, and shows are often supported by unique funding arrangements from both political and business sources.[22]

In both Beijing and Mexico, *First Peoples of Canada* was a public demonstration of a bilateral relationship that also imparted knowledge of Canada. Thus, it can be understood as an aspect of Canada's international relations strategy. For example, the Government of Canada website mentioned the Beijing display as evidence of Canada's strong bilateral relationship with China in the areas of culture and sport.[23] The show was staged at a key moment for relationship building, when Canada was hoping to strengthen its ties with China.[24] Whereas the previous Liberal government had seen China as a site of "strategic partnership," the Conservative government of Stephen Harper criticized Beijing's human rights record while simultaneously attempting to increase trade with China (an approach summed up as "cool politics, warm economics").[25] When this strategy was not successful, the government pivoted. Thus, *First Peoples of Canada* launched in Beijing during an ambiguous moment in relations with China. In times where bilateral ties are weak, strained, or in need of development, cultural events such as exhibitions can provide a conduit through which to build trust and advance political agendas. Such was the case for the Beijing version of *First Peoples of Canada.* In Mexico, the messaging around the exhibition was different. There, as we will see, it was linked to the goal of promoting continental integration within the framework of NAFTA.

In both China and Mexico, the exhibition strengthened international relationships through reciprocal shows in Canada. Honouring its agreement, the Beijing government sent *Treasures from China,* which ran at the CMC between 11 May and 28 October 2007.[26] It consisted of 120 objects, most of which were fine artworks noted for their "national and cultural significance."[27] As the titles of the shows reveal, the Canadian and Chinese governments were interested in sharing specific types of objects, namely "treasures" and "masterworks" – a conventional blockbuster strategy that draws attention to the uniqueness of items and frames them as the products of the nation. Somewhat paradoxically, many of the objects included in *First Peoples of Canada* predated the 1867 creation of Canada (and the People's Republic of China did not exist when the objects in its exhibition were made). Historicization is necessary to uphold the nation's primacy, to produce it as a natural political formation that "loom[s] out of an immemorial past," according to scholar of nationalism Benedict Anderson, and that, "still more important, glide[s] into a limitless future."[28] In this way, cultural displays play an important role in facilitating international relationships and in producing specific narratives about nations.

The Mexico City version of *First Peoples of Canada* was followed by a reciprocal exhibition titled *Maya: Secrets of Their Ancient World*. It was a collaboration between the CMC, the Royal Ontario Museum in Toronto, and Mexico's National Institute of Anthropology and History. *Maya* was displayed at the Royal Ontario Museum from 19 November 2011 to 9 April 2012 and at the CMC from 18 May to 28 October 2012. For the CMC, these reciprocal shows were extremely beneficial as a way to "share our expertise, foster partnerships with museums around the world, and bring home important foreign exhibitions."[29] This speaks to the other side of cultural exchange, the forging of relationships between cultural practitioners – beyond those in the government's diplomatic realm.[30]

The Canadian government and the CMC clearly identified *First Peoples of Canada* as an envoy that would help to affirm bilateral national relationships. In discussing the exchange of exhibitions between China and Canada, the museum referenced state support: "Both governments saw the exchange as a gesture of friendship between our two countries, and as a means of promoting mutual understanding."[31] According to the CMC newsletter, the show was a "rewarding way for the world to get to know our rich culture."[32] In both China and Mexico, events that coincided with the presentation of *First Peoples of Canada* contributed considerably to the CMC messaging.

The CMC's work on *First Peoples of Canada* began in 2005. The exhibition ultimately included 150 objects structured in five sections and augmented with visual and audio materials: Masterpieces from the CMC's Collection; Wealth of the Salmon People; Ancient Farming in the Lower Great Lakes; Living in the Harshest Environment; and Glory of Hunters and Warriors.[33] The items on display were diverse; most came from the CMC ethnographic collection and the remainder from its archaeology collection. The most recent was a fur dance-parka sewn in 2002–03, and the oldest was a stone projectile point produced ten to eleven thousand years ago. Ceramic pots, feathered headdresses, ivory snow-goggles, and a birchbark canoe were also included.[34] The exhibition was comprehensive, seeking to showcase both historic and contemporary aspects of Indigenous lives in Canada. According to the CMC, its main message was that "Canada's Aboriginal people have ancient roots in North America and their adaptation to all parts of this vast and varied country is reflected in multifarious objects created from the resources of a rich land."[35] This clearly subsumed Indigenous cultural production to the nation-state and revealed an approach to the land as a resource for the state.

The agreement between the NMC and the CMC records that the show was to have been titled *Ancient Peoples of Canada: Collections from the Canadian Museum of Civilization.*[36] The use of the word "ancient" emphasizes Indigenous people's historic relationship with the land. Even as it historicized the nation of Canada and indicated that the past was over or ancient, the CMC dealt with contemporary Indigenous peoples through a virtual exhibition, which was to have been titled *First Peoples of Canada.*[37] The formal agreement between the CMC and the NMC mentioned it as a companion to *Ancient Peoples of Canada,* as presented in Beijing.[38] This could account for the title change of the physical exhibition.[39]

The initial title for the exhibition is somewhat perplexing, given that museological approaches had been advancing Indigenous agency for more than a decade. Although this trend was not limited to the 1980s and 1990s, it continued apace during the period of increasing economic integration under free trade.[40] A milestone in this history is a 1988 show titled *The Spirit Sings: Artistic Traditions of Canada's First Peoples.* Protested by the Lubicon Cree Nation, it became a catalyst for significant debates over Indigenous claims to territory and representational agency. Subsequent exhibitions *INDIGENA: Perspectives of Indigenous Peoples on Five Hundred Years* and *Land, Spirit, Power: First Nations at the National Gallery of Canada* foregrounded Indigenous perspectives and "disrupted long-held institutional discourses and practices."[41] Two policy documents are also vital in charting these developments. The first is Lee-Ann Martin's *The Politics of Inclusion and Exclusion: Contemporary Native Art and Public Art Museums in Canada,* a 1991 report to the Canada Council. The second is *Turning the Page: Forging New Partnerships between Museums and First Peoples,* a 1992 report by the Task Force on Museums and First Peoples. Reflecting on these reports in an interview, curator Rachelle Dickenson describes them as "documents of larger movements in Indigenous art and history in Canada that contributed to – if not entirely resulted in – significant change in representation of Indigenous arts and museum engagement with Indigenous people and collections in Canada."[42] *Turning the Page* outlined new standards of practice for museums that included consultation and collaboration with Indigenous communities. It also stipulated that Indigenous people had a right to access museum-held objects that came from their communities and noted that many of these items were illegally possessed.[43] The legacy of these exhibitions, reports, and shifts in museological practice is the prioritization of Indigenous agency over representation and a broader (ongoing) reckoning with the colonial histories of museums.[44]

To return to *First Peoples of Canada,* it seems likely that the name change was also a result of work by museum staff to ensure an emphasis on contemporary Indigenous communities. As revealed by documents created during the development of the exhibition, the CMC was concerned that its historical aspects would overpower the contemporary message it wished to present. Notes from a 2005 executive committee meeting state, "The team needs to clearly identify how they will address the point that 'Aboriginal people ... represent a continuing and vibrant part of Canada's culture' since this does not come through clearly at this point."[45] Correspondence between the two curators mentions the difficulty of conveying the position of Indigenous peoples to Chinese audiences, who might misconstrue the objects in the show as "colourful artifacts of a folk group(s)."[46] The CMC is well known for generating permanent displays of Indigenous culture, such as First Peoples Hall, whose "multivocal" approach foregrounds differing voices and perspectives (in opposition to an authoritative single narrator).[47] However, the focus on masterworks and ancient bonds to the land proved difficult for the organizers of *First Peoples of Canada* to navigate. That the messaging at the Beijing launch also highlighted contemporary aspects of Indigenous communities speaks to the ongoing complexity of this issue. When the show opened, for instance, CMC president and CEO Victor Rabinovitch mitigated the impression of Indigenous peoples as ancient by describing the artifacts on display as "a vital part of Canada's *living* history."[48]

The vitality and continuity of Indigenous peoples were also addressed in adjunct programming. For example, in the Art Museum of the Imperial City, representatives from the Department of Canadian Heritage screened several short films featuring contemporary Indigenous perspectives.[49] The films included *I'm Not the Indian You Had in Mind*, directed and narrated in 2007 by Thomas King, and *Nikamowin (Song)*, a 2007 experimental reflection on the Cree language by Kevin Lee Burton. This programming helped to avoid the "standard settler narrative of Canadian history," in which, notes Ruth Phillips, "Indigenous peoples are subsumed as *contributors* to a linear and progressivist historical trajectory of the nation."[50] The Canadian government's role in shaping the narrative is notable, as it underscores its interest in mobilizing culture in its service. Beyond revealing the parameters of the show and the efforts of the museum to emphasize the contemporaneity of Indigenous peoples, the exhibition's development points to broader tensions that arise in the use of Indigenous culture in national narratives.

From Beijing to Mexico

Even before it opened in Beijing, *First Peoples of Canada* was publicized as representative of Canada. This message was apparent at a 13 March 2008 promotional event at the CMC in Gatineau, whose purpose was to introduce the exhibition to the media. Important individuals from the CMC and the NMC were in attendance. Special guests from China included Haisheng Zhao and Caiyun Li of the Chinese embassy in Canada, as well as Chen Chengjun, Huang Yucheng, Wang Lei, Hao Yinxiang, and Sun Jing of the NMC.[51] Planning documents for the event note that CMC president Rabinovitch intended to refer to the museum as "the guardian of Canada's collective memory."[52] This talking point makes clear the relationship between country and institution, as well as the role the museum had cast for itself. When the show officially opened in Beijing, numerous dignitaries attended the event, including Rabinovitch and Robert Wright, the Canadian ambassador to China.[53] In the press coverage, Chinese officials voiced their support for the exhibition, citing it as evidence of links between their country and Canada. Identifying the show as "an important result of long-term friendly exchange and cooperation between the People's Republic of China and Canada," NMC director Lu Zhangshen also stated that it marked the beginning of a new relationship between the NMC and the CMC.[54]

Furthermore, the exhibition's power as representative of Canada was enhanced by the Olympics, which always arouse high national fervour. Lu claimed that *First Peoples of Canada* would "add luster to the 'One World, One Dream' Olympic stage of Beijing with its special charm."[55] The Canadian press drew analogies between the exhibition and the athletes who were competing for Canada: "While Canadian athletes strive to bring home gold," reporter Tim Wieclawski wrote, "150 Canadian cultural treasures will be winning people over."[56] The show also benefited from the unusually diverse audience of international visitors who had come to China for the Olympics, as well as an audience of Chinese residents. As CMC exhibitions planner Nicolas Gauvin wrote during the development phase, "This exhibition is a unique opportunity ... during one of the most important international events – the summer Olympic Games. The Museum will gain exposure to hundreds of thousands of people."[57] The significant international audience was a key part of what prompted the CMC to participate in the endeavour. Its use of Indigenous material to promote the nation was part of a "long-standing historical pattern by which Canada appropriates the First Nations to its national identity before an international audience."[58] This is achieved via processes of forgetting – eliding charged histories of violence toward Indigenous communities.[59] Only by omitting the realities of colonialism could *First Peoples of Canada* depict the settler state in a positive light.

Two years later, *First Peoples of Canada* arrived in Mexico City as "a gift from Canadians to the people of Mexico in celebration of the bicentennial of Mexico's independence and the centennial of its revolution."[60] This framing emphasized the exhibition as a state envoy. In Mexico, the Canadian embassy supplied help in various ways, including by obtaining support and sponsors. The launch on 6 October 2010 marked the reopening of the Museo Nacional de las Culturas after four years of renovations, with the exhibition constituting a collaboration between the CMC, Mexico's National Institute of Anthropology and History, and the Canadian embassy in Mexico.[61] It had the same general organization as in Beijing, with only slight changes in the titles of the five categories: Masterworks; The Glory of the Warriors and Hunters of the Bison; Ancient Agriculture in the Lower Great Lakes; The Arctic: A Severe Environment; and The

People of Salmon and Their Patrimony.[62] A promotional brochure described it as "an opportunity to demonstrate the great store of artistic, cultural treasures of the ethnic groups who first populated Canada."[63] Tellingly, this wording shifted the emphasis from presenting "Canadian" treasures to recognizing them as belonging to Indigenous peoples. The exhibition also referred to cultural treasures, rather than the "resources of a rich land." In other ways, however, it was still framed in terms of the Canadian nation.

In addition to embassy support, political backing was evident at the opening events, which were attended by Guillermo Rishchynski, the Canadian ambassador to Mexico, as well as CMC director Rabinovitch.[64] On the Mexican side, Alfonso de Maria y Campos, director general of the National Institute of Anthropology and History, was joined by Mexican president Felipe Calderón, which made support from the Mexican government equally apparent. Calderón took a prominent role, presiding over the launch and the museum's reopening.[65]

In Mexico, the context for *First Peoples of Canada* differed from that of China, as the relationship between the two countries was already well established rather than nascent. The Beijing show emphasized Canadian resources, whereas cultural discourse dominated in Mexico City. The messaging for the latter was perhaps more subtle, presuming a familiarity with both Canada and the importance of its links to Mexico. At the time, the Harper government was intent on building hemispheric ties.[66] It announced its Americas Strategy in 2007, following up in 2008 by appointing a dedicated minister of state for the Americas.[67] The emphasis on connections with Mexico was affirmed in rhetoric surrounding the exhibition. In Beijing, *First Peoples of Canada* was framed as a way for visitors to learn about Canada and the differences between it and China, but the Mexican version was about the similarities and close connections between the two countries.

Indigenous cultures were presented as a key element of both Mexico and Canada. According to Ambassador Rishchynski, the exhibition "highlights that common heritage at a significant moment in Mexico's history." He stated, "From ancient times to the present day, both Canada and Mexico have been greatly enriched by their Aboriginal cultures."[68] This was formally acknowledged in a 2005 letter that pledged to promote cooperation on Indigenous issues between the two governments, represented in Mexico by the National Commission for the Development of Indigenous Peoples (CDI) and in Canada by the Department of Indian and Northern Affairs (which is now two departments, Crown-Indigenous Relations and Northern Affairs Canada, and Indigenous Services Canada).

A panel discussion held in conjunction with the exhibition further highlighted the importance of Indigenous peoples as a commonality between Canada and Mexico. Titled "Canada-Mexico First Peoples Dialogue: Identities, Art and Culture," it was held at the MNC on 21 and 22 October 2010, and was organized by the Canadian embassy in Mexico, along with the CDI, the Technological Autonomous Institute of Mexico, and the MNC. Four Indigenous speakers from Canada represented the Inuit, Cree, Métis, and Mi'kmaq peoples. From Mexico, nine speakers, all members of Indigenous groups in the north, represented the Kikapú, Wixárika (Huichol), Conca'ac (Seri), Kumiai, Cora (Náayari), Mayo, Yoemem (Yaqui), Tohono O'odham (Pápago), and Cucapá peoples. The United States was invoked as a present absence because the territories of most of these Indigenous communities straddled the Mexico-US border, specifically the Kikapú, Wixárika (Huichol), Conca'ac (Seri), Kumiai, Yoemem (Yaqui), Tohono O'odham (Pápago), and Cucapá. All have distinct histories of migration and/or claim territories in the United States. The Kikapú are a case in point. In the late seventeenth century, they were based in what is now south Wisconsin. By about 1750, there were three groups of Kikapú across the United States, which subsequently divided further. By the nineteenth century, some Kikapú aligned with the Mexican government and subsequently claimed territory there. Currently, there are federally recognized Tribes of Kikapoo in both the United States and Mexico. For another example, the traditional territory of the Tohono O'odham extends from northern Mexico into southcentral Arizona.[69] Although Mi'kmaq territory also stretches into eastern Maine, the Indigenous speakers from Canada did not represent border-crossing territories to such an extent as the Mexican nations listed above. Thus, the United States was largely omitted from the conversation despite its geographic, political, and economic centrality in North America. However, perhaps this omission was not entirely accidental, as paying attention to Indigenous nations whose territories crossed the Canada-US border could potentially have evoked the unwelcome truth that the two nation-states were founded on stolen land.

The panel discussion promoted cultural diversity in a bid to combat discrimination against and exclusion of Indigenous peoples. It was as notable for giving voice to Indigenous peoples as it was for the way in which the two governments used Indigenous issues to bring Mexico and Canada together. An important goal, according to the Government of Canada website, was "to strengthen cooperation between Canada and Mexico on indigenous issues."[70] Government support was prominent; both the opening and closing ceremonies were presided over by government officials, including Ginette Martin of the Canadian embassy in Mexico, Xavier Abreu, director general of CDI, Teofilo García, president of the Indigenous Affairs Committee of the Chamber of Deputies, Andres Galván, president of the Committee for Indigenous Affairs of the Senate of the Republic, Duncan Wood, professor and researcher at the Technological Autonomous Institute, and Ambassador Rishchynski. At the opening, Ginette Martin asserted that the exhibition was "proof of the growing strength of the links between Canada and Mexico, as well as of the diversity of issues that are encompassed by the bilateral relationship."[71] Like the exhibition it accompanied, the panel discussion positioned "the indigenous cultures of Mexico and Canada as an essential part of the identity of both nations."[72] Thus, even when Indigenous people were permitted to speak, their cultures had already been absorbed into the supposedly inevitable totalizing structure of the nation. This points to the ongoing work of the settler state to normalize its construction in the face of contradictions.

At the time, Canada was looking to the southern hemisphere for potential trading partners, which meant that shoring up its economic relationship with Mexico in the wake of the FTAA's failure was a sound strategic decision on a number of levels. In Mexico, *First Peoples of Canada* was repurposed to emphasize indigeneity as a point of commonality between the two countries. This enabled the Canadian government to claim that Canada's cultural history was equally as long and impressive as Mexico's, once again subsuming the heritage of Indigenous peoples to the settler state. Thus, the exhibition may be read as a kind of riposte to comments made by Jaime Serra Puche, who held that Mexico did not require a cultural exemption under NAFTA, given its cultural richness and established stature (as discussed in the Introduction).[73] Thus, the political work performed by the Mexican iteration of *First Peoples of Canada* differed from that in Beijing. Even so, narratives in both locations relied heavily on promotion, events, and programming that featured Indigenous peoples and cultures, in addition to the objects on display.

Remix: New Modernities in a Post-Indian World

Remix toured Canada and the United States during the same period as *First Peoples of Canada,* but its curators took a different approach to Indigenous identity. By featuring the multiple identities of the artists whom it included, *Remix* questioned the constraints placed upon them and stressed the fluid nature of identity. The introductory wall text informed viewers that the show "explore[d] complexities that shape our individual and cultural identities." Signifying a departure from the state-sponsored notion of Indigenous identity, as in *First Peoples of Canada, Remix* introduced the concept of the "post-Indian." This term acknowledges the flexibility of Indigenous identity in the contemporary era. "As 'post-Indian,'" art critic Eleanor Heartney writes, the artists in *Remix* "embrace a reality in which identity is constantly being reshaped by surrounding circumstances."[74] In foregrounding Indigenous sovereignty, the exhibition provides a point of contrast with *First Peoples of Canada.*

A collaboration between the Heard Museum in Phoenix, Arizona, and the Smithsonian National Museum of the American Indian (NMAI), *Remix* was curated by Gerald McMaster (Plains Cree and member of the Siksika Nation) and Joe Baker (Delaware).[75] McMaster was based at the NMAI and Baker was at the Heard Museum. The exhibition toured to three venues: the Heard Museum from 6 October 2007 to 27 April 2008; the George Gustav Heye Center, NMAI, in New York from 26 May to 30 September 2008; and finally, the Art Gallery of Ontario (AGO) in Toronto from 4 April to 23 August 2009. It included works by fifteen artists, all from Canada, Mexico, and the United States, such as Hector Ruiz, Kent Monkman, Nadia Myre, Barnard Williams, and Dustinn Craig. The works represented a wide variety of media, including painting, video, and installation, and all dated from the first decade of the twenty-first century.

The decolonial thrust of *Remix* was prominent. In the catalogue, Joe Baker wrote about the burden of colonial interpretations of Indigenous cultures, which continue to influence contemporary Indigenous artists, observing that "a colonial yoke of cultural interpretation forces artists into the position of 'cultural representatives.'"[76] For Baker, it was important that *Remix* be an open space for Indigenous artists to experiment and move beyond the limiting Western framework. He was interested "in constructing a new platform for Indigenous artists – a resistance model for how their art is presented, discussed, and contextualized."[77] Likewise, McMaster acknowledged that identity could be a limiting lens through which to understand Indigenous cultural production. "For many Native artists today," he stated, "cultural identity is not a concern. Nevertheless, we hope that the gathering of this group signifies a new articulation of the expanse and inclusiveness of contemporary Native art."[78] Here, McMaster resisted colonial readings of Indigenous art, while also pointing to the need for breadth and flexibility in understanding it.

The exhibition was shaped around the musical practice of remixing. W. Richard West, Jr., founding director of the NMAI, explained the title of the show:

> Baker and McMaster have appropriated a title, *Remix,* from global hip-hop culture. There, it refers to the practice of using altered, but recognizable, pieces of earlier works to create new music, a technique that takes advantage of the astonishing tools of our digital age. Here, the curators offer remixing as a metaphor for contemporary concepts of identity, reflected in these artists' painting, sculpture, photography, video, and installation art.[79]

In the catalogue, Baker and McMaster elaborated on the implied affinity between hip hop and Indigenous cultural production, a connection that has been widely noted. Many Indigenous communities have embraced hip hop because it is a "possible strategy for decolonization," explains music scholar Charity Marsh. It enables them to "convey the contradictions, struggles, resistances, and celebrations of their current lived experiences while simultaneously attempting to acknowledge and respect the (hi)stories of their ancestors." According to Marsh, hip hop culture permits a fluid approach to identity, allowing "for a confluence of a multitude of national, regional, and cultural sensibilities with its aesthetics, styles, and pleasures."[80] *Remix* made prominent the multiplicity of identities in North America. In the gallery, each artist's work was accompanied by their photograph, a quotation from the artist about the work, and a note regarding their national affiliations. Although exhibition labels commonly refer to an artist's nationality or place of birth, *Remix* departed from the norm by citing all the affiliations. These were often numerous, including transnational and diasporic identities. For example, Kent Monkman identified as Cree, English, and Irish; Hector Ruiz as Kickapoo, Mexican, and American; and Steven Yazzie as Navajo, Laguna, and Welsh.[81] What is interesting in this approach is that none prioritized one identity at the expense of another – contemporary North American countries alone could not adequately convey their identities.

Remix was also transnational, encompassing artists from Canada, Mexico, and the United States. By promoting Indigenous alliances that transcended borders, it challenged the traditional use of Indigenous culture in international exhibitions. John Haworth, director of the George Gustav Heye Center, suggested a broader continental reading of the show: its works "remind us to pay closer attention to the complicated history and 21st-century culture not only of the United States, but also of Canada and Mexico."[82] This multifaceted approach to indigeneity is exemplified in both *Remix* and *First Peoples of Canada*, but whereas all the works in the latter were unambiguously Indigenous and linked to a specific nation-state, *Remix* took a stand against such a categorization. West saw it as a statement against the appropriation and erasure of Indigenous cultures: "No longer will curators acquiesce to the perpetuation of national myths, or the objectification of other peoples through the self-congratulatory collecting and exhibition of their material culture!"[83] Although he was not referring to *First Peoples of Canada*, his words could certainly be applied to it.

Through a flexible approach to identity, the works in *Remix* dismantled conventional notions of indigeneity, promoting a more nuanced understanding of belonging in the modern world.[84] Whereas many of the artists in the show dealt with issues of cultural identity, the manner in which they did so worked against stereotypes. The art in *Remix,* according to Heartney, addressed identity "in a way that throws definitions of 'Indianness' into doubt." Breaking with convention was a central theme of the exhibition. Frank H. Goodyear, Jr., a Heard Museum director, identified this spirit of possibility as a key component of the "'post-Indian world' – without the limitations or expectations of earlier times."[85] Some of the *Remix* works directly addressed historical tropes of identity. For instance, in her 2004 video *Let's Dance,* Anna Tsouhlarakis (Navaho, Creek, and Greek) documents her attempts to learn thirty types of dance associated with various peoples, including the Harlem shake, the hora, and the Irish jig (Figure 11).[86] Her efforts give the work a humorous tone,[87] while also commenting on the tradition of performance in Indigenous cultures, often for non-Indigenous audiences. In the video, Tsouhlarakis is "no longer the ethnic 'other' re-enacting her native traditions for the entertainment of curious bystanders," explains Heartney; "instead she becomes a kind of tourist herself, in the process subtly pointing out that everyone is an 'other' to someone else."[88] Thus, the video lays bare the conventions and assumptions we hold when engaging with cultural forms that are not our own, while also pointing to the limitations of homogeneous notions of identity.

Remix drew attention to a general North American framework through the transnational connections and multiple identities claimed by its artists. Many of these identities crossed international boundaries, revealing the artificiality of the latter. In this way, the show exposed the colonial origins of North America, bringing to mind the violence inflicted on the land during colonization. In other ways, however, *Remix* fit nicely into the promotion of the new North America. Although it had no direct ties to NAFTA or state governments, its theme of indigeneity as a common factor on the continent echoed the message of state-supported exhibitions such as *Panoramas,* which attempted to erase state boundaries by using landscape art as a point of commonality between Canada, Mexico and the United States. *Remix* was no NAFTA show, however. Rather, it managed to undermine the new North American identity in much the same way

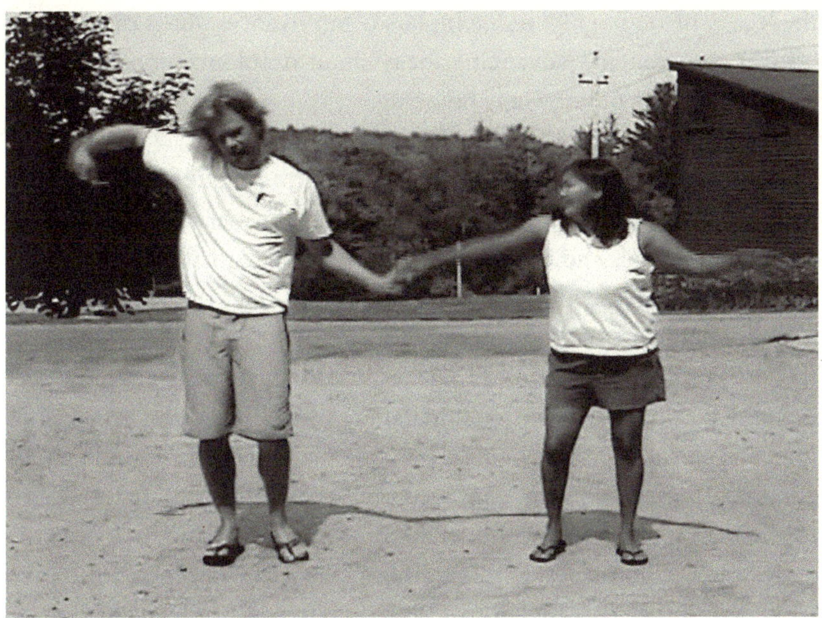

FIGURE 11 Anna Tsouhlarakis, *Let's Dance,* 2004, video still. Courtesy Anna Tsouhlarakis.

that it subverted older national identities by mining down into the granular identities of cultures and ethnicities rather than countries. *Remix* raised key issues about Indigenous identity within the North American framework. It encouraged viewers to think about how Indigenous artists negotiate national identities and suggested moving beyond conventional definitions of authenticity with regards to Indigenous cultures and nationalities. Thus, the exhibition stressed that Indigenous identification is only one factor influencing the creation of works, as opposed to the sole way of understanding or defining Indigenous artists.

Although I focus on the larger narratives around the exhibition, we cannot discount the individual agency of the artists involved and the works they created, which produce specific affective experiences for audience members. We can also understand the *Remix* works as espousing Indigenous American writer and scholar Gerald Vizenor's concept of "survivance" in their assertion of the complexity of Indigenous identity. "A condition contrary to dominance," Vizenor explains, "survivance creates a sense of presence and defines a resistance to sentiments of tragedy and the legacy of *victimry*."[89] As exemplars of survivance, works can provide critical commentary, advancing ideas about decolonization and other Indigenous ways of knowing and being.

Exhibiting Indigenous Culture in the New North America

In 2008, the Canadian government apologized to former students of Indian residential schools and launched the Truth and Reconciliation Commission, which concluded its work in 2015. After that, the contradictions inherent in the use of Indigenous culture in the service of the state and in the face of the lived reality of Indigenous peoples in Canada became particularly glaring.[90] Ottawa's reconciliation agenda has been criticized as imposed on Indigenous communities, one that homogenizes Indigenous peoples, denies their sovereignty, and relegates settler-colonial violence to the past, preventing an understanding of its ongoing and systemic nature, as well as its contemporary harms.[91] According to Yellowknives Dene political scientist Glen Coulthard, the terms of reconciliation are "still largely dictated by the colonial state."[92] In focusing on "Indigenous subjects," reconciliation does not address the colonial relationship; thus, as Coulthard argues, it "functions to assuage settler guilt ... and absolve the federal government's responsibility to transform the colonial relationship between Canada and Indigenous nations."[93] It also sets up a situation in which Indigenous peoples are subject to government, denying their sovereignty. Mohawk political anthropologist Audra Simpson sees reconciliation as one of the many "techniques that are used to manage 'the problem' of Indigenous people, rendered now as populations, to be administered to by the state. This moves Indigenous peoples and their polities in the settler imaginary from nations, to people, to populations ... categorical shifts [that] set Indigenous peoples up for governmental regulation."[94] Furthermore, according to Mushkegowuk (Cree) geographer Michelle Daigle, reconciliation is a form of spectacle.[95] Daigle characterizes the contemporary period as "marked by the spectacle of reconciliation – a public, large-scale and visually striking performance of Indigenous suffering and trauma alongside white settler mourning and recognition – which secures, legitimates, and effectively reproduces white supremacy and settler futurity in Canada."[96] Thus, though individuals who participate in reconciliation initiatives may be unaware of it, this state-driven project is fraught with tensions.

In the context of reconciliation, the mobilization of Indigenous culture in the service of the nation-state can be understood as a form of "hungry listening," a term coined by Stó:lō scholar Dylan Robinson to characterize relations between settlers and Indigenous peoples.[97] Robinson explains that this form of listening or witnessing "devours without consideration of those who have cultivated, harvested, and prepared the food of thought."[98] The kinds of relationships that appeared in *First Peoples of Canada* were not predicated on equal exchange. Instead, they revolved around the ownership and use of cultural forms, refusing to centre the voices and experiences of Indigenous people so as to foreground the settler nation and its concerns. Despite Indigenous-led resistance and resurgence, this continues to play out in state cultural diplomacy efforts abroad, which target international audiences. Such is the case at the Canadian Cultural Centre in Paris. Established in 1970 by External Affairs, the centre became part of the Canadian embassy in 2018, after which it made a concerted effort to present Indigenous culture. Its first exhibition, titled *Beauty and the Beasts,* featured Cree artist Kent Monkman, who is known for subverting the conventions of history painting to produce piercing critiques of settler colonialism.[99] A press release stated that its programming "highlights the importance the Canadian Cultural Centre wants to attach to the boldest and most remarkable voices from Canada's diverse Indigenous cultures."[100] Although the centre's approach is premised on inclusion, it is also a strategic co-optation. Discussing the contradictions of this programming, writer Julian Brave NoiseCat explains that Ottawa's use of Indigenous culture is a "product of a simple curatorial calculation: Indigenous arts and culture are the most unique and authentic thing Canada has to offer the world."[101] Here, NoiseCat points to the machinations of settler-colonial narratives, which seek to maintain the status quo and thwart decolonization.

The government use of exhibitions as a means of identity building is a theme that runs throughout this book. The advent of a reconfigured North America post-NAFTA disrupted the prevailing national narratives of Canada, Mexico, and the United States, requiring new formations that coincided with the economic integration of the continent. The ability of exhibitions to carry such messages is affirmed by curator Mari Carmen Ramírez, who refers to them as "privileged vehicles for the presentation of individual and collective identities, whether they consciously set out to be so or not."[102] Consequently, we can read both *First Peoples of Canada* and *Remix* as revealing changing perceptions of North America, even though neither exhibition explicitly set out to do so.

First Peoples of Canada and *Remix* demonstrate the various ways that art shows can affirm national relationships or deconstruct them, just like free trade narratives, which were simultaneously affirming of the state and destabilizing through their rhetoric of open borders. *First Peoples of Canada* presented Indigenous peoples within the framework of the Canadian state, which successfully deployed it to endorse bilateral relationships. When it was shown in China, it furthered a relationship that was premised on difference, whereas in Mexico it emphasized similarity. In both cases, it maintained a national framework, thus preventing a reading of Indigenous communities as nations and precluding discussion of both Indigenous sovereignty and the reality of Indigenous nations whose territories are bisected by settler state boundaries. The exhibition also perpetuated the appropriation of Indigenous culture, this time to advance the new North America. Political scientist Amelia Kalant explains that in the national myths of Canada, Indigenous culture is displaced through "a complex acrobatics that moves settler to native, siphons nativeness from 'the Indian,' and moves 'the Indian' out of the picture entirely."[103] One of the many problems with the appropriation of Indigenous culture to represent the Canadian nation, as seen in *First Peoples of Canada*, is that it "connotes an intertwining that then entitles Euro-Canadians to Native traditions and lands."[104] Such a venture can have a very real impact on the status of Indigenous communities.

In making clear the complexity of identities – Indigenous and settler – *Remix* provided another, more nuanced way to understand the continent. Emphasizing that identity is a hybrid and evolving concept, its approach disrupted the primacy of national associations. It made clear that North America, too, is a colonial project. The importance of such a reading is affirmed by artist and scholar Jolene Rickard (Tuscarora), who stresses the hegemonic nature of colonial narratives. "Every country has a national narrative, and Canada is better than most at attempting to integrate multiple stories into the larger framework," she states, "but the process is still a colonial project. The Americas need to be read as a colonial space with aboriginal or First Nations people as seeking decolonization."[105] The exhibitions examined in this chapter demonstrate how such colonial messages were constructed and circulated through displays of visual art, but they also point to how exhibitions served as conduits for counter-narratives.

PART 3

Creating Resistance

5

Reading inSite against the Cultural Exemption

The Mexico-US border was a site for numerous art interventions during the late twentieth and early twenty-first centuries, when it became a locus of what is often referred to as border art.[1] Some observers see this genre as specific to the Tijuana–San Diego region, one that addresses disparity, comments on marginalized aspects of the border zone, engages with local populations, and is cognizant of the historic struggles of the Chicano community.[2] Others note the genre's activist tendencies, with artist David Avalos defining it as a means of "encouraging participation in community and confronting governmental unaccountability and abuse of power."[3] The charged dynamics of this particular border made it a poignant and rich site for artistic engagement.

This becomes even more apparent when compared to the situation in Canada, where the international boundary did not inspire a similar development. As I have argued elsewhere, while the Canada-US border was actually quite porous and permeable (at least until 9/11), many Canadians saw it as a "site of cultural self-protection, a line of defence from US cultural imperialism."[4] Ideas about the need to protect Canadian culture circulated widely during the free trade era (as discussed in Chapter 6) and played into Canadian demands for a cultural exemption in free trade agreements. Unlike their counterparts at the Mexico-US border, Canadians did not employ border art to highlight the cultural issues evoked by free trade.

In recent years – following the period covered in this book – Canadian cultural engagement with the international boundary has expanded, with increasing numbers of art and cultural projects exploring the region. Geographer Anne-Laure Amihat-Szary traces this development to the 2010s, citing examples from Quebec–Vermont and British Columbia–Washington State.[5] In Windsor, Ontario (which borders Detroit), curator Srimoyee Mitra's *Border Cultures* project ran at the Art Gallery of Windsor from 2013 to 2015. This series of exhibitions explored contemporary border art.[6] Nonetheless, these instances pale in comparison with the sustained and multifaceted artistic attentions at the Mexico-US border.

I employ the term "border art" as a broad category, referring to a genre that is united in its examination of any aspect of a border but that, beyond this, is an inherently ambiguous category encompassing a variety of media. Thus, the term can apply to any international border, yet certain circumstances made Tijuana–San Diego a prominent site for artmaking in this mode. In this chapter, I focus on inSite, a binational art festival often referred to as the "border biennial."[7] Offered in five installments between 1992 and 2005, it was held in Tijuana and San Diego, cities that flank the Mexico-US border. The scope and range of media employed in inSite defy easy categorization, but many works engaged with the border, as well as with issues that were specific to communities in the Tijuana–San Diego region.

A hallmark of the projects was an interaction with the physicality of the border. For example, in 1994 artist Terry Allen created an interactive work titled *Cross the Razor/Cruzar la navaja,* which dealt with communication. It consisted of two vans, which were parked on either side of the fence that marked the border. One was placed in Border Field State Park, California, and the other in the Mexican suburb of Playas de Tijuana. Only a few metres of space – and the fence – separated the two vehicles. Both were topped with sturdy wooden platforms that held microphones and amplifiers. Participants were encouraged to climb onto the platforms and project music or speech, with the aid of a translator, across the border as they saw fit.[8] In 2005, artist Javier Téllez's performance and video work *One Flew over the Void (Bala perdida)* employed spectacle and humour to play with the physical space of the border. The artist collaborated with a group of psychiatric patients from Mexicali, organizing an event at Playas de Tijuana that culminated in the carnivalesque launch of renowned human cannonball David Smith, who was propelled over the border and into California.[9] The projects offered at inSite revealed the border as more than a simple delineation of boundaries: it was a complex signifier that encompassed multifaceted referents such as culture and memory, as well as wealth and inequality. For over a decade, inSite hosted numerous projects like those of Allen and Téllez, providing a platform for artworks that engaged with all aspects of this region, as well as its communities.

The Border as Resource

Geography was key to inSite's development. Numerous factors contributed to the Tijuana–San Diego region's uniqueness. The San Ysidro port of entry, which lies between Tijuana and San Diego, was the busiest border crossing in the world.[10] The twin cities were separated not only by an international border but also by great economic disparity.[11] Architect Teddy Cruz, an inSite_05 participant, called San Diego the "world's largest gated community" due to the rigidity of the border that divided it from Tijuana.[12] This border zone is both a real and a symbolic site for contentious issues, including immigration, crime, and labour – it is the home of the infamous maquiladoras, manufacturing factories that proliferated at the border under NAFTA, structured to take advantage of free trade regulations. Washington's ongoing militarization of the border generated further tensions. The 1980s are noted for the rise of "anti-Mexican sentiment" in the United States.[13] In 1992, the US military and US Border Patrol erected a steel fence that paralleled the border, running from the Pacific Ocean to thirteen miles inland.[14] In 1994, Washington launched Operation Gatekeeper to "restore the rule of law" to the boundary, drawing further attention to policing.[15] All these developments fostered a specific notoriety for the Tijuana–San Diego region.

In addition, the Chicano civil rights movement, founded in the United States during the 1960s and 1970s, affected the artistic development of the Tijuana–San Diego area in various ways.[16] Cultural projects emerged from the struggle for Chicano rights, including the 1973 Chicano Park Mural Project in Barrio Logan, San Diego.[17] Three years earlier, the Centro Cultural de la Raza, a Chicano cultural centre, had been founded.[18] Located in Balboa Park, San Diego, it has a long relationship with border art, and several artists and collectives related to the genre are connected to it, including Las Comadres, a group of artists that included David Avalos, Louis Hock, and Elizabeth Sisco, and the Border Arts Workshop/Taller de Arte Fronterizo (BAW/TAF).[19]

Cultural initiatives between Tijuana and San Diego during the 1980s and 1990s helped to facilitate the development of border art as a genre, paving the way for events such as inSite. These included the 1984 International Festival of La Raza (subsequently renamed the Border Festival), which scholar José Manuel Valenzuela Arce identifies as "one of the most important events for the creation of a transborder arts environment."[20] Another key project was *Dos Ciudades/Two Cities*, a multifaceted cultural program spearheaded by the Museum of Contemporary Art, San Diego (MCA).[21] Funded in 1989 by a grant from the National Endowment for the Arts, this three-year binational project involved lectures, film screenings, events, billboards, public arts projects, publications, and exhibitions.[22]

The inSite festival emerged from this context as a major initiative in the rich history of cultural engagement across the border. A large-scale festival of contemporary art, it was often categorized as a biennale in the press – though it did not occur every two years and did not take the same format each time. Throughout its five incarnations, in 1992, 1994, 1997, 2000, and 2005, inSite was characterized primarily by its binational nature.[23] As the festival took shape, its priority became collaboration between Mexico and the United States. The differing versions of inSite each took the form of a large multivenue event. In most cases, artworks were commissioned to intervene in public spaces and were exhibited alongside public programming and publications, all over the course of several months. The festival expedited unique partnerships, especially between previously disparate entities, ranging from community and non-profit groups to established public institutions. It was deeply committed to artist engagement with the complexities of the Tijuana–San Diego borderlands, from Téllez's *One Flew over the Void* to *MAMA*, a video by Mauricio Dias and Walter Riedweg, in which US Customs officers spoke about the dogs used for border security. Part of inSITE2000, the video was shown at the San Ysidro crossing.[24] Later versions of inSite created artist residencies in the region, allowing artists to learn about the area and to liaise with new partners. This was especially important, as each version of inSite involved artists from many nations who were not necessarily familiar with the region.

The festival drew regional arts audiences, members of the general public, and tourists who were interested in contemporary art. It required a great deal of commitment from its audiences. Viewing it was difficult; every version included numerous sites spread across a wide area, and many works were located off the beaten track. Its later versions were particularly unwieldy; inSite_05, for example, incorporated online projects, conferences, symposiums, and lectures. The evolution of programming over the years marked a change in focus "from showcasing finished works to process-oriented projects."[25] Audiences at any one festival could find it difficult to experience the show in its entirety due to its extended run times, the number of artists involved, and the geographic range of the event, which frequently crossed the border. As a result, inSite was largely geared toward a local audience, as art historian Jennie Klein observes: "The people who benefit most from the projects commissioned by inSITE are those groups at whom the art interventions are directed – local communities who live and work on the border."[26] Thus, though inSite drew the global art world to the region, it was organized to prioritize and foster deep local ties.

However, inSite had an ambiguous relationship with the border. George Yúdice, cultural theorist, writes that "the border can be said to be *inSITE*'s prime 'natural' resource."[27] Conversely, inSite's directors emphatically asserted that the festival was not about the border and that its projects were not border art.[28] According to attorney and art collector Michael Krichman, who was inSite executive director from 1995, it was "never really conceived as a border exhibition, or an exhibition about the border." He added, the border "wasn't the impulse behind inSite. It wasn't the incentive to do it."[29] Nevertheless, with their emphasis on residencies, in addition to community and site engagement, most works produced for inSite ended up relating to the physical border itself or to issues arising from the border dynamic. The growing significance and centrality of the border over inSite's run is therefore central to understanding how the festival evolved and how artists came to respond to the border through it. In short, the border was inescapable.

As a result, inSite inevitably raised questions about the border and about who had authority to speak about the region. Many artists who took the border as their subject matter, Yúdice says, were not members of the communities with which they collaborated, even if they did come from the Tijuana–San Diego area: "Neither the artists in BAW/TAF nor the directors, curators, and artists participating in *inSITE* are 'organic' to these communities."[30] The festival became a target for such reservations, especially after it achieved international recognition and generated a great deal of press in both newspapers and arts journals.[31]

The organizers' insistence that inSite was not directly focused on the border further complicated the issue. As Krichman admitted, even though "artists were not invited here to do work about the border," it nonetheless "became ... a central feature in a number of works that in turn became somehow well known." The idea that inSite was synonymous with the border, Krichman said, was an easy analogy – art made at the border is like art made about the border. Quoting curator Olivier Debroise, who was involved in inSITE94 and inSITE97, Krichman stated, "The border is there, like it or not," so of course it would inevitably figure into the festival. When Krichman himself discussed inSite, he emphasized the uniqueness of the region rather than the international boundary. As he put it, the festival was about "cities on the margins, cultural institutions that consider themselves on the margins within their own countries ... And particularly in Mexico the notion that things would be produced in Tijuana, as opposed to being produced in Mexico City and exported to Tijuana, was almost foreign." Furthermore, the dynamics of the region were extremely interesting; Krichman referred to the borderlands as a microcosm of both globalization and immigration policy.[32] Echoing this, inSITE2000 artist Jordan Crandall suggested that the binational nature of inSite was foregrounded rather than the border itself. In describing the relationship between inSite and the border, he explained the latter as "a metaphor and an emblem. So, it ... embodies some of the dynamics of the area, and so that casts out onto the region, rather than reinforces itself as an object."[33] For organizers and artists, then, the border was just one part of a complex region, rather than a discrete focus of the festival.

Despite inSite's uncertain relationship with the border – embraced by some artists, dismissed by organizers – the border was undoubtedly of great significance to the festival. This is especially obvious in the public sphere, where inSite became conflated with the border. As inSITE97 artist Louis Hock explained, "The idea of the border was crucial [to inSite] ... at least in terms of [its] international recognition."[34] The charged nature of the Tijuana–San Diego region, I argue, gave inSite a specificity and currency that allowed it to market itself internationally. Furthermore, the border was a resource for all inSite artists. In some cases, their engagement was superficial or tangential, whereas other artists undertook more substantial or sustained interventions addressing the hegemonic relationships shaping the border.

Acknowledged or not, the border gave the festival currency and a raison d'être, underpinning many of its projects. Some of these were located at or near the border and were created in response to specific border dynamics or oriented toward constituencies or communities in the area. As a result, inSite was largely read, understood, and valued in relation to the border. In a period of increased attention to globalization and a rhetoric of post-nationalism mixed with the retrenchment of the nation-state, the border was a physical divider and a metaphor for understanding new global realities. A close look at the five festivals reveals the way in which they leveraged the border.

IN/SITE92

The inSite festival came about as a project of Installation Gallery, an alternative non-profit venture that was established in San Diego in 1981.[35] When it encountered financial difficulties during the 1990s, board members Mark Quint and Ernest Silva came up with an idea for a project to unite the region's fragmented art scene.[36] Their goal was to "galvanize the energy of then-current artistic practice – installation, site-specific work."[37] Cultural institutions in the Tijuana–San Diego area eagerly embraced inSite, with some reconfiguring their schedules to participate. They appreciated the chance to collaborate, as Silva noted: "The strength of the idea is that it is a cooperative venture. Each institution is using its own resources. No one has anything to lose and they have everything to gain."[38] Essentially, inSite sought to highlight site-specific work, uniting the programming of a number of institutions in a new collaboration. It augmented the impact of each institution's programming and also drew attention to the region as a cultural centre.

IN/SITE92 was held in September and October 1992 at sites on both sides of the border.[39] A pilot project of sorts, it was much smaller than the later versions. There were no organized residencies for artists and no catalogue; Mexican involvement was less than in subsequent festivals. It encompassed twenty-two venues, including large museums, private galleries, college galleries, cultural centres, and bookstores.[40] These included the MCA, the Centro Cultural de la Raza, the Casa de la Cultura, the Centro Cultural Tijuana (CECUT), the Southwestern College Art Gallery, and Sushi Performance and Visual Art. A pamphlet describing the event and providing a map of the venues divided the festival into six key areas, revealing the focus on the American side of the border. Forty-seven artists showed their work.[41] Projects included an installation by Lewis deSoto and James Luna entitled *Kísh Tétayawet Wampkísh (Dreamhouse),* which explored representations of home and exposed the conflict between European and Indigenous belief systems.[42] At the Museum of Contemporary Art, La Jolla, internationally renowned British sculptor Antony Gormley showed *Field* (1990), an installation of thirty-five thousand small terracotta figures.[43]

The press celebrated the innovative nature of the festival. One critic, Robert L. Pincus, praised the concept and its structure far more than the artworks. Intrigued by the opportunity to see arts groups working together, he wrote that "the uneven quality of IN/SITE '92 doesn't detract from its overarching success as a project. It fostered a spirit of camaraderie among participating spaces. This welcome outcome, coupled with planning for the next series of shows, has had a positive impact on the recently faltering Installation [Gallery] as well."[44] The success of IN/SITE92 was also confirmed by the fact that organizers were already talking about a second iteration.[45]

Krichman, who was not involved with the festival in 1992, explained why IN/SITE92 attracted his attention as a viewer. "What interested me most about it," he recalled, "was that they had made some effort to do some things in Mexico." He emphasized the binational aspect of the festival as a reason for his involvement in subsequent editions: "I saw it as a really interesting opportunity ... to get across the border." He had noticed the separation of the Tijuana art scene from San Diego's:

> There had been very, very little [exchange across] the border. It had been much more about artists going down to Tijuana ... There had never been any exchange on any sort of formal level, and there had certainly never been any kind of ... effort to co-produce something with institutions or artists in Mexico ... [This] quickly became the thing that interested me the most.[46]

The festival's focus on cross-border collaboration challenged the siloed nature of the Tijuana and San Diego art worlds and in doing so substantially transformed them.

Notably, the success of IN/SITE92 was partly due to the abundant press coverage it received in San Diego, including in the *Union* and the *Los Angeles Times,* which published a San Diego edition. In fact, the city was so plentifully endowed with arts reporters that getting reviewed was easy. Krichman added, "San Diego might not have been a great centre of cultural activity, but it was, for some reason, a centre of lots of newspapers, with lots of arts writers, which we don't have any more ... So IN/SITE92 got this sort of strange amount of attention."[47] In other words, "the first inSite generated a disproportionate amount of ink."[48] It may have captured attention, but its programming made only a few fleeting references to the border.[49] Instead, it emphasized US institutions.

inSITE94

The second inSite festival, directed by Lynda Forsha, drew together thirty-eight non-profit institutions from the Tijuana–San Diego region and presented the work of over a hundred artists in seventy projects between 25 September and 30 October 1994. Adjunct programming included lectures by participants, such as Christo and Carlos Fuentes, as well as a critics' symposium. This adjunct programming began in October 1993—prior to the installation of artworks—and extended the duration of inSITE94 a full year.[50] Involvement from Mexico was greater than in 1992, with Installation Gallery joined by the Department of Culture of the City of Tijuana, the State of Baja California through the Instituto de Cultura, and the Consejo Nacional para la Cultura y las Artes through CECUT and the Instituto Nacional de Bellas Artes (INBA). These parties, in addition to the MCA, were responsible for coordinating the festival in conjunction with numerous participating institutions in three areas: downtown Tijuana, downtown San Diego, and Balboa Park, in north San Diego.[51] Like IN/SITE92, inSITE94 acted as an umbrella organization, bringing together sponsoring institutions, each of which exercised autonomy over its projects.[52] Artists, in turn, directed their own projects, which were commissioned specifically for inSITE94. Forsha, the director, writes that "all those involved took a leap of faith by committing to a risky artistic process in which the end result isn't known."[53] The only unifying elements were a focus on installation and site-specificity.[54]

Projects at inSITE94 tended to have a stronger political message than those of the 1992 festival, and many now focused on the border, with some actually taking place there.[55] This change was probably aided by residencies that enabled artists to spend time in the Tijuana–San Diego region. Artists completed two periods of residency: in 1993, they selected sites for their works and began to develop them; in the summer of 1994, prior to the festival opening, they created their works.[56] Marcos Ramírez ERRE, a Tijuana-based artist, created an installation called *Century 21,* which consisted of a shack made of foraged materials: metal, wood, and cardboard. Robert Pincus described it as "a deeply affecting, satirical installation."[57] Imitating the haphazard housing in Tijuana, this "model home" was placed just outside the CECUT building, whose modern design provided a remarkable juxtaposition that enhanced the artist's commentary on living conditions in certain city neighbourhoods.[58]

The political tone of inSITE94 corresponded with numerous regional and national developments in Mexico and the United States. Gallerist, cultural worker, and later inSite executive director Carmen Cuenca mentioned the significant impact of political and economic turmoil in Mexico in 1994. In March 1994, Luis Donaldo Colosio, a presidential candidate for the Partido Revolucionario Institucional, the ruling federal party in Mexico at the time, was assassinated while campaigning in Tijuana. Cuenca recalled that "the resulting spotlight on corruption, violence, drugs, etc., hardly helped the city's image."[59] Furthermore, inSITE94 was affected by a change in directors at CECUT and by Mexico's economic crisis. NAFTA had just been implemented in January of that year, simultaneously with the uprising of the Zapatista Army of National Liberation. "The 1994 NAFTA treaty," Cuenca said, "forced governments and economies to confront each other and the bigger process of globalization. The art of inSITE94 was overshadowed by these huge uncertainties, but much of the art also resonated with some of those issues."[60] At the same time, binational endeavours were gaining support, and as Krichman observed, inSite happened to coincide "with a number of different things that were going on at that time," including the US-Mexico Fund for Culture (which provided support for binational cooperation).[61]

Increasing the inclusion of Mexican institutions in inSITE94 required a great deal of work. Having become associated with the festival in 1993, Cuenca played a key role in these efforts.[62] Active in the Tijuana art scene in the early 1990s, she ran a commercial gallery and also worked for CECUT, later becoming its liaison with inSite.[63] The differences between American and Mexican cultural institutions, particularly in curatorial authority, were apparent to her. She stated, "We didn't have curators in Tijuana at that time, or directors of institutions, in the way they are understood in the US. Clarifying the differences was crucial because the basic model for inSITE'94 was an umbrella of participating institutions expected to select and also financially support their own artists. That model wouldn't translate easily for collaboration in Mexico."[64] The inclusion of Mexican institutions was additionally complicated by the fact that these partners were under the control of different government parties who held power municipally and at the state and federal levels.[65] Krichman explained,

> There was very little understanding across the border of how institutions operated. In San Diego, we barely comprehended the thorny power issues associated with culture in Mexico. Indeed, inside Mexico those fissures had only just erupted in partisan splits between INBA [Instituto Nacional de

> Bellas Artes], controlled by the PRI [Partido Revolucionario Institucional] at the federal government level (wielding more money and more expertise), and institutions that represented Tijuana and Baja, which were PAN [Partido Acción Nacional], the first opposition government in Mexico.[66] At every level, including of course publicity, there was considerable partisan maneuvering between these institutional sponsors. And, of course, there was lots of suspicion of anything from north of the border.[67]

Despite these differences, inSite organizers were committed to expanding their Mexican relationships. Krichman was a driving force in securing the city of Tijuana as an equal partner. To acquire support for the festival, he and two colleagues travelled to Mexico to meet with officials.[68] Support from Gerardo Estrada at INBA in Mexico City was crucial.[69]

Important border issues, including trade, migration, and security, were clearly at the fore for the inSITE94 organizers. The festival catalogue mentioned Mexico's economic crisis, as well as the recent vote in California passing Proposition 187, which targeted undocumented immigrants, prohibiting their access to non-emergency health services and public education, a development that especially affected Mexican migrants.[70] The inSITE94 organizers indicated a desire to affirm ties on both sides of the international boundary in the face of these developments. As they noted, "All of these circumstances serve to strain rather than to strengthen the relationships that are needed to create the infrastructure of a binational region."[71] They suggested that inSITE94 would provide a basis for subsequent alliances between Mexican and American institutions.[72] Thus, it was positioned to go beyond the arts to affect the region in many ways. This assessment was affirmed by Cuauhtémoc Medina, an art critic, curator, and historian who saw the festival as a link between areas: "inSITE94 was far more than an art festival, an expression of budding local pride, or a decorative footnote to the capitalist internationalization embroiled in NAFTA. This transformation of the border could be a critical beginning."[73] Medina identified the significance of inSITE94 in its move to bridge the international boundary and fully involve both Mexico and the United States. Thus, as the festival evolved through its second iteration, it and the presence of the border expanded considerably. Coinciding with the implementation of NAFTA, it envisaged substantial linkages between Mexico and the United States, though Canada did not figure in the conversation.

inSITE97

The next version of inSite occurred in 1997 and was co-directed by Krichman and Cuenca.[74] It placed a new emphasis on curatorial direction, employing a team of curators from the Americas: Jessica Bradley (Canada), Olivier Debroise (Mexico), Ivo Mesquita (Brazil), and Sally Yard (United States). In the past, each participating institution had selected its own artists, but now the curatorial team took on this task. Throughout, their goal was to look at public space as a "*subject* to be explored, not merely as a *site* for locating works." These changes marked a break from previous incarnations of the festival.[75] Nevertheless, curatorial direction was still relatively open; according to Jessica Bradley, "It was important that we decided not to name the exhibition with an imposing title or ask the artists to respond to the specific thematic of the border itself."[76] Thus, artists were granted a great deal of flexibility in engaging with sites, and the result encompassed a variety of projects.

Despite (once again) the organizers' stated disinterest in the border, many artists continued to comment on its complexities. For example, ERRE, who returned to inSite in 1997, fashioned a ten-metre-tall wooden sculpture called *Toy an-Horse*, a play on the mythic Trojan horse, except that it had two heads.[77] Mounted on wheels, it was parked at the San Ysidro border crossing, directly between lanes of cars waiting to traverse the international boundary, positioned so that one head faced toward the United States and the other toward Mexico. According to the presidents of Installation Gallery, Gerardo Estrada and Eloisa Haudenschild, the border remained relevant to inSite because processes of globalization had increased international attention to borders: "Today as never before all countries are experiencing the reality of life on the edge of a frontier – one result of the process of globalization."[78] Their statement makes clear the anxieties that characterized this period of globalization and the concurrent push for amplified economic integration.

Press coverage noted that inSITE97 had achieved a more equal balance between Mexico and the United States. Visual arts writer Leah Ollman commented, "Perhaps the biggest step in the maturation of inSITE92 and '94 into inSITE97 has been raising Mexico to the status of equal partner in planning and supporting the $1.5 million project."[79] Krichman and Cuenca referred to the relationship between Installation Gallery and INBA as a "true partnership" that had "evolved from a cooperative effort."[80] The 1997 festival was also distinct in that all the participating artists came from the Americas. This is especially interesting in light of increasing political-economic efforts to unite the Americas under the proposed FTAA.

The 1997 inSite festival involved twenty-seven institutions in the Tijuana–San Diego region and featured fifty-seven works, as opposed to the thirty-eight institutions and seventy projects (by over a hundred artists) of the 1994 show.[81] Comparing the two festivals, Ollman described the 1997 offering as "reined in a bit and refined."[82] Like its predecessors, however, it included numerous public programs, such as lectures, artist talks, and a conference. It was structured as two components, an exhibition of forty-two artworks and fifteen community engagement projects. The latter focused on education; artists worked for a sustained period with a local community and interacted with the region through a two-week-long residency in the summer of 1996, followed by more time in the community to implement their projects.[83]

The inSITE97 curatorial team believed that it was important for artists to spend sustained research time in the area. By the beginning of the festival, each artist had averaged a hundred days on-site.[84] The organizers exercised caution in this aspect of the festival. Krichman characterized their difficult choices as "trial and error, thinking about ... how to bring artists in ... [and] how many artists at a particular time because ... it [can] become this kind of weird tourism ... that we were trying not to do."[85] The organizers and curators believed that having artists spend time in the region was crucial to the generation of work that fully, rather than superficially, addressed its issues. In this way, inSITE97 fostered a climate of sustained creativity and cultural production, facilitating engagement with the border despite its disavowal of such a focus.

At inSITE97, Mexico City–based artist Francis Alÿs exhibited his documentation of a performance piece titled *The Loop*. Building upon his oeuvre of walking works, Alÿs travelled from Tijuana to San Diego – but not by crossing the Mexico-US border. Instead, he headed south, embarking on a thirty-five-day journey that looped through Mexico City, Panama City, Santiago, Tahiti, Auckland, Sydney, Singapore, Bangkok, Rangoon (Yangon), Hong Kong, Shanghai, Seoul, Anchorage, Vancouver, Los Angeles, and finally into San Diego.[86] Ephemera associated with his trip, including airplane boarding passes, hotel receipts, postcards, and emails, was displayed in a file box placed on an unobtrusive shelf at CECUT.[87] Olivier Debroise noted Alÿs's "political stake about his 'non-effort' to cross the border," in contrast to the border crossings typical of migrants, "jumping the fence, facing the Border Patrol and all that it implies."[88] Alÿs's project hinted at contemporary art as an economic commodity, as well as the international circuits of the art world, particularly in its biennales. *The Loop* drew attention to the power and privilege of artists to travel internationally and explored the Tijuana–San Diego border as a resource that they mined in creating their work – criticism levelled at inSite more broadly. Yúdice suggests that the 1997 festival could "be conceived of as an artistic maquiladora whose executives (the directors of the art event) contract with managers (the curators) to map out the agenda for flexible workers-for-hire (artists) who in turn produce or extract (cultural) capital by processing a range of materials."[89] This assessment makes a key connection between processes of labour under free trade (the maquiladora model) and contemporary art (the bienniale model, which foregrounds privilege and access in the global art world).

Other projects, however, sought to intercede directly in the border zone, increasing its visibility and in some cases, creating tangible change. In *International Waters/Aguas internacionales,* Louis Hock explored the confluence of the borderlands in the context of the unyielding boundary line. Hock saw people and water as "dynamic national forces," so he provided a "transnational drink to visitors" by installing an ad hoc water fountain on either side of the border fence, one in Border Field State Park and the other in the Sección Monumental, Playas de Tijuana (Figures 12 and 13).[90] The fountains were marked by plaques informing passersby that the water was potable, and the materials and patina of the work were carefully matched to the environment.[91] Hock says the project was critical of the border and sought to provide a possibility, explaining it was about

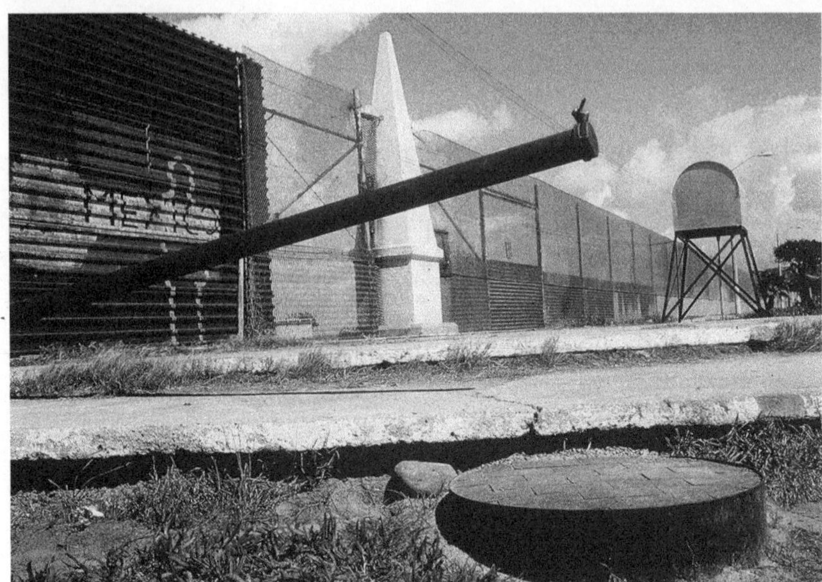

FIGURE 12 Louis Hock, *International Waters/Aguas internacionales,* 1997, installation, Border Field State Park and Playas de Tijuana. The round-headed tank in the distance contained the drinking water, which ran through the large pipe in the foreground of the photo. A push-button bubbler at its end could be manipulated to release the water. Courtesy Louis Hock.

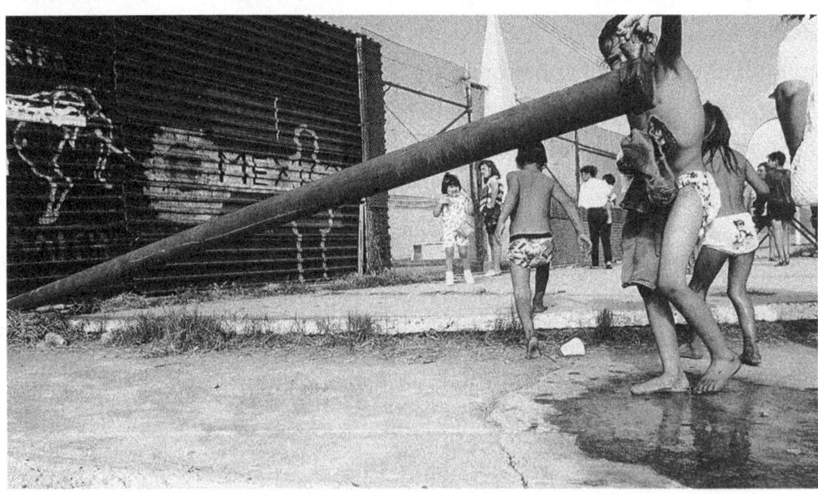

FIGURE 13 Louis Hock, *International Waters/Aguas internacionales,* 1997, installation, Border Field State Park and Playas de Tijuana. A child works the push-button bubbler at the end of the water pipe. Courtesy Louis Hock.

"creating ... a permeability ... creating a sharing ... and creating ... a human possibility for interaction."[92] Giving viewers a chance to experience the border in a new way, it also functioned conceptually to create a dialogue between the two nations, providing a "flow [of water] back and forth across the border" that "stitches together" Mexico and the United States.[93]

The location of the work drew attention to the artificial imposition of national borders on the landscape and to the rigid nature of the physical border, situated at the edge of the Pacific Ocean where the steel fence continued into the water. To enable interaction across the border, Hock had a window cut into the fence, so that participants could see each other as they drank from the water fountains. Although his project was relatively modest, consisting of a holding tank and some piping, he was required to obtain numerous permissions from various government agencies, one of which was to certify the safety of the water. Hock acknowledged that inSite's clout was essential in realizing the project: "I could never have done [it] individually. I was able to use the muscle of the Mexican–United States ... connections of inSite to be able to do the piece."[94] This was particularly true of the window that was cut in the fence, which made the US Border Patrol nervous. Officers were concerned "about people being able to see them, and they not being able to see who's looking at them, [so eventually] they welded up the hole."[95] Then Border Patrol replaced a portion of the steel fence with a chain-link fence, which created greater visibility across the divide. "They just opened the whole thing up," Hock said, "by putting a chain-link fence ... a hundred feet or so. So that they could see whoever was looking at them, rather than have to deal with a solid barrier." In this way, the work, intended as a commentary or "conceptual dialogue," physically changed the border itself. Hock recalled that "it ended up being actually ... a real physical change, a dialogue of a physical sort, rather than just a conceptual one."[96] His ability to engage the border in symbolic and unexpectedly physical ways speaks to the type of public projects that inSite was able to install in various locations across the region.

The 1997 version of inSite emphasized the Americas, bringing together a diverse curatorial team. The artworks engaged with the border in various ways, enabled in part by organizational strategies such as artists' residencies. Through some of the projects, relationships around the border changed – new infrastructure was created, new connections were forged, and new possibilities for embodied experiences were realized. In other ways, inSITE97 confirms that the border had increasingly become a resource for artists to exploit, seizing on its charged dynamics as fodder for their work. Thus, inSite's stature as a destination on the international art circuit exposed the cultural capital of those who presented it. Ironically, the festival seemed to mirror free trade's stress on movement, global connections, and capitalism, while underscoring the inequality and privilege at the heart of neoliberal globalization.

inSITE2000

The emphasis on curatorial vision expanded for inSITE2000. Four curators took charge of the festival, which ran from 13 October 2000 to 25 February 2001: Mesquita, Susan Buck-Morss, Osvaldo Sánchez, and Yard.[97] They began work in the fall of 1998, employing a model of the "city as a laboratory" and intending to "challenge concepts that have oriented previous versions of inSITE and similar international exhibitions: site specificity, community engagement, artistic practice, and public space."[98] The four continued inSITE97's focus on the Americas, inviting thirty-four artists from across the hemisphere to create new works under the sponsorship of twenty-seven non-profit arts institutions in the Tijuana–San Diego region.[99] Once again, the festival was a binational partnership organized by Installation Gallery and the Consejo Nacional para la Cultura y las Artes through INBA.[100] A full roster of public programming, including a series of forums called Conversations, accompanied the festival.[101]

The most striking development of inSITE2000 was that it did not prioritize the display of projects. As Krichman and Cuenca explained, the impetus for this transformation came from the curators, who did away with "any traditional notion of exhibition at all."[102] Krichman described the work of the curators as "privileging process over product ... privileging the residency and really not being concerned about whether there was something to see at the end."[103] The emphasis on process resulted in an extended public display of five months, though many works were visible only fleetingly as ephemeral events or were available only through documentation.[104] This approach "freed inSITE to look beyond traditional notions of site specificity, to look beyond traditional forums and forms of public art, and to think about the ways in which artistic practice might engage various sectors of our two communities."[105] Notably, the role of the public changed from passive to active, a shift that enabled the audience to become a "co-investigator."[106]

Nonetheless, a lengthy residency in the Tijuana–San Diego area remained an important component of inSite. In the summer of 1999, a group of artists participated in a combined residency that coincided with a symposium, which brought numerous critics, writers, and intellectuals to the region.[107] One of the artists, Jordan Crandall, recalled that the residency familiarized him with the area, contributing to his creative process:

> All the artists worked together and talked about what inSite was, and then we spent a lot of time going to Tijuana and various sites and learning about the area ... There were lots of people brought in from previous inSites ... to discuss inSite ... It familiarized us with the background of inSite, ... in addition ... to familiarizing us with the area.[108]

The artists later returned to the region for up to one month to develop their projects.[109] The inSite archive notes that organizers anticipated two further visits for all artists before the final residency and the opening of the projects in October 2000.[110]

This stress on residency and the curatorial attention to process rather than product resulted in a focus on community engagement, something that had begun at inSITE97. For example, Mônica Nador worked with ten families over two months in the impoverished Tijuana neighbourhood of Maclovio Rojas to develop *Project at Maclovio Rojas.* With the goal of increasing community pride, she facilitated the decoration of several homes with stencils representing the cultural traditions and regional heritage of their residents.[111] Another artist, Krzysztof Wodiczko, conducted a two-year project called *Proyección en Tijuana/Tijuana Projection,* in which he worked with two women's organizations in Tijuana, Factor X and Yeuani. The presentation phase of this work, which occurred over two evenings, 23 and 24 February 2001, consisted of a public performance conveyed through a large-scale video projection on the rounded facade of the Omnimax theatre at CECUT in Tijuana. Combined with pre-recorded footage, the live projection showed testimony from female employees in Tijuana's maquiladoras. Wodiczko referred to their testimony as a "public action," with the power to "intervene in real life." It revealed a range of contentious personal issues: "domestic and sexual abuse, exploitation in the workplace, police violence."[112] The project spoke directly to free trade by exploring the working conditions of the maquiladoras, demonstrating how cultural production could critically comment on the border, while also engaging community and other intersectional and local issues.

The festival also included work that concentrated on the border as a physical site. In his video *Heatseeking,* Jordan Crandall used military technology to explore policing the border.[113] The title of his film refers to the US military's use of heat-sensing technologies to track individuals attempting to enter the United States. Crandall used thermal imaging, surveillance cameras, a pinhole camera, and 16-millimetre black film. Shown on both sides of the border, his video comprised a series of segments on power, control, and surveillance, including erotic and violent imagery. In San Diego, it was shown on hand-held devices, whereas in Tijuana it was displayed on an electronic billboard.[114]

By the fourth incarnation of inSite, the focus on the border was readily apparent. The Tijuana–San Diego region, including the borderlands, occupied pride of place, and the festival encouraged deep engagement through residencies and an emphasis on process. In 2000, issues of free trade had come to the fore, which was also true of the 2005 festival. Discussions of free trade and the border were tied to contentious issues of migration, security, and labour, making them easy subjects for artists.

inSite_05

In 2005, inSite took its final bow, assuming its most extensive form yet. The public phase ran from 27 August to 13 November, but the actual project lasted much longer, from 2003 to 2005. It also had a more complex structure than previous versions. It was organized in four separate but interrelated components: Conversations, Interventions, Scenarios, and the exhibition *Farsites: Urban Crisis and Domestic Symptoms in Recent Contemporary Art.*[115] Its artistic director was Osvaldo Sánchez, who had been one of the curators of inSITE2000, and Krichman and Cuenca continued as executive directors. Several other curators were associated with specific projects within the four components. The Conversations component involved a series of sixteen public discussions held between November 2003 and November 2005. As Yard explains, they were "working sessions ... conceived to rethink issues of local import within a broader frame."[116] In the Interventions component, twenty-two projects by artists and artist groups "intervened" in the Tijuana–San Diego region. This component closely mirrored the main components of previous festivals. Three curators took the helm for Interventions: Sánchez, Tania Ragasol, and Donna Conwell.

The Scenarios component focused on new aspects of the public sphere – "the Internet, the spectacle, and the index" – those "less established practices that have nonetheless become key to the construction of the public sphere as a space of discourse."[117] The component consisted of three projects produced by teams of artists and curators. *Mobile_ Transborder Archive,* which was curated by Ute Meta Bauer, focused on border issues in the Tijuana–San Diego and Baja California–California regions. *Tijuana Calling,* an online show of commissioned web-based projects, was curated by Mark Tribe. And *Ellipsis,* a sound and visual event, was curated by Hans Fjellestad. The *Farsites* exhibition was curated by Adriano Pedrosa, consisted of works by fifty-two artists primarily from the Americas, and ran concurrently at the San Diego Museum of Art and CECUT.[118] According to Pedrosa, the works at *Farsites* addressed contemporary urban sites, specifically "moments or loci where the grid and the system fail or fall short."[119] As the first museum show jointly organized between Tijuana and San Diego, *Farsites* marked a significant moment of collaboration.[120]

Krichman notes that inSite_05 had to contend with a new political situation – the 2000 election of conservative political parties in Mexico and the United States.[121] This, combined with 9/11, produced a new climate at the border. Despite these developments and the radically expanded structure of the festival, it had much in common with previous versions. The emphasis on sustained engagement with the region continued, and artists who participated in Interventions undertook four residencies while developing their works.[122] The catalogue provided a timeline of significant moments for each project.[123]

The 2005 festival marked the first time the virtual sphere was a substantial site of engagement, in *Tijuana Calling,* an entirely web-based exhibition of five art projects focused on the border region. One of these was *Turista Fronterizo* by Ricardo Dominguez and Coco Fusco,[124] which playfully examined border tourism through an online game. Players could choose an avatar from among four people, two Mexican and two American, who crossed the border. They were El Junior, La Todóloga, El Gringo Poderoso, and Gringa Activista. Designed for individuals, *Turista Fronterizo* was loosely patterned after a conventional board game, and a roll of virtual dice determined a player's route from square to square on the board. The objective was to allow participants to easily engage with four distinct perspectives on the border.

In creating their work, Fusco and Dominguez drew on the history of game culture in avant-garde art from the Dada movement to the Situationists. They also conducted research on the Tijuana–San Diego area, depicting certain well-known sites, such as Fashion Valley Mall, Qualcomm Stadium, and various maquiladoras, on the game board. Explaining why they had chosen a game, Dominguez stated, "Coco and I felt that that kind of interface would allow a wider sector of the community [to engage with the work], with the expectations that it would be predominantly a Tijuana based ... community that would have the most [opportunity] to participate."[125] Keeping the game simple was essential:

> It had both instant availability of understanding, but also a distance from the normal logics of game culture ... but also a diagram of readability, of division, of control, of flows, and especially [as] one is thinking about NAFTA and the neoliberal entanglement and rearrangement that was going on. It was by keeping it flat, by keeping it ... a board-like game, by

constraining [the] narratives, that one could then accentuate what was readily apparent by moving in the flows between San Diego and Tijuana.

Dominguez tied *Turista Fronterizo* to inSite_05's aim of exploring new realms in the public sphere, observing that "games were obviously a model of thinking [about] online culture." He made an analogy between gaming as an economic industry and the many maquiladoras in the borderlands; the latter were "a different formation [from gaming], but perhaps playing with the same sort of economic games."[126] As a means to model these systems, norms, and actors, *Turista Fronterizo* drew attention to the larger dynamics of the border region.

Another, more controversial, project in the Interventions series also spoke directly to border flows. For *Brinco,* Judi Werthein designed shoes to help undocumented migrants cross into the United States – its title translates as "jump," a reference to jumping the fence.[127] Werthein's project revealed the contradictions of globalization, economics, immigration, and capitalism, and made a further pointed reference to global manufacturing circuits, by having the shoes produced in China. They were equipped with aids such as a map, compass, flashlight, and Tylenol. The project provoked debate about immigration and received a great deal of media attention. Like *Turista Fronterizo, Brinco* spotlighted the irony of "economic and political policies that promote the cross-border movement of foods, services, capital, and commodities, while simultaneously seeking to prevent the movement of labor."[128] The shoes were distributed free of charge in shelters in Tijuana, including Casa del Migrante, Casa de la Madre Asunta, and Casa YMCA de Menores Migrantes-Tijuana. In San Diego, they were sold at Blends, an upscale sneaker boutique.[129]

With its sprawling programming, the product of a firmly established organizational structure, and its fostering of long-term cultural engagement in the region, the 2005 inSite festival was clearly a success. Although organizers repeatedly downplayed the influence of the border, it was obviously a defining element of the area and one that artists engaged in fruitfully. Moreover, its enmeshment in flows of migration, as well as flows of trade and goods, came to the fore in many works.

inSite and NAFTA

As mentioned above, a key feature of NAFTA was its cultural exemption, which meant that cultural production was largely omitted from free trade. Despite this exclusion, art and culture provided the means through which many debates and ideas about free trade played out in public. Therefore, I propose that inSite needs to be read specifically in relation to its geopolitical context and against the NAFTA exemption.

NAFTA was instrumental in transforming the Mexico-US border. In 1993, one year before its implementation, curator Madeleine Grynsztejn summarized the changes, pointing out that the parties to the agreement were addressing the flow of "goods across their boundaries" while opting not to deal with formal and undocumented migration.[130] Historian Phoebe S. Kropp and urban geographer Michael Dear also comment on this paradox: "NAFTA is supposed to encourage a greater integration of the regional economy across the border, yet the border itself becomes more clearly and lethally defined."[131] This contradiction highlights what I see as a particular synergy between inSite and NAFTA. In attempting to open the border to transnational flows, albeit creative ones, the festival seems to mirror NAFTA, but it also reveals the strict controls and limits placed on the border with respect to goods and people. To put it another way, culture may have been exempted from the agreement, but ultimately NAFTA helped culture cross borders too.

Whereas scholars such as Néstor García Canclini maintain that linking inSite to the free trade agreement is a mistake,[132] I argue that the festival developed a specific relationship with NAFTA over time, at once reinforcing the transnational relationships of the NAFTA partners and opening up space for commentary on and questioning of these dynamics. Ricardo Dominguez regarded the festival as ambiguously related to neoliberal developments such as NAFTA, explaining that, though inSite did not have the political impact of the Zapatista emergence on 1 January 1994, it did have a "parallel evolution that on certain points is very involved ... either critiquing or [as] a product of and at other points is separated [from NAFTA]."[133] Dominguez made another connection between inSite, neoliberalism, and contemporary art circuits. "I'm not quite sure to what degree neoliberal policies are the core impulse of inSite," he stated. "We might say [its relation is through] globalization in a sense of the art market entering into this kind of frenzy of festivals and biennales, which one could say is part of the larger growth of the neoliberal agenda."[134] Thus, Dominguez acknowledged the ambiguous relationship between inSite and free trade, while also citing the festival's (and the art world's) larger imbrication in neoliberal globalization.

When asked specifically about how geopolitical developments such as NAFTA had an impact on inSite, Krichman demurred. However, he did mention the changes occurring in 1994 and afterward, conceding that they affected artistic responses to the region, especially at inSITE94.[135] As he explained, these political developments converged when Washington amplified its exclusionary measures at Playas de Tijuana:

> Almost to the day that they adopted NAFTA they finished the extension of the fence ... three hundred metres into the ocean at Playas Tijuana ... That was a, just a brutal ... signal for Mexico ... So the fence as a symbol of all of that became important; and there were certain works in '94 ... [that] took this fence, which was this recycled stuff from the Gulf War, as a starting point.[136]

Many artists homed in on the irony, Krichman explained, by "pointing out the absurdity ... of on the one hand adopting the North America Free Trade Agreement and on the other hand extending this ugly metal fence ... that started at a place that was called ... Friendship Park."[137] According to Dominguez, *Turista Fronterizo* was a commentary on NAFTA. As he put it, "NAFTA allowed commodity flows ... free and wild, unrestrained ... A Coca-Cola can had complete rights of flow, of protection, while those trying to work in maquiladoras or cross the border did not have any of those kind of basic rights."[138] Interested in the unequal distribution of freedoms under neoliberal globalization, he and Fusco saw the border as a device that limited some populations while enriching others.[139] Although inSite had no direct ties to NAFTA, unlike the state-sponsored exhibitions *Panoramas* and *Perspectives*, many works at the festival dealt with aspects of free trade and its impact. Furthermore, inSite benefited from funding programs aimed at North American integration, as well as government willingness on both sides of the border to assist the event, providing permissions and access for unique collaborative projects.

Several trends emerged from the five iterations of inSite, the foremost of which was the diverse ways that artists engaged with the border region and the border itself. This engagement was inherently conflicted and plagued by questions of authority: Who had the right to speak about the border? Many of the inSite artists were not from the Tijuana–San Diego area but were brought in to collaborate with local communities and organizations, a practice that raises the issue of disproportionate privilege and power. Yúdice flags the contradictions in the "almost ironic combination of artworks that raise political issues about immigration, race, and national and cultural identity, and that garnish ... a celebration of a dubious economic arrangement brought about by NAFTA."[140] The art at inSite commented on inequities in power but ultimately did not aid in redistributing power to marginalized communities. The artists employed the border as a resource but remained within the limits of the festival's artistic framing. That their works were praised for engaging with the dynamics of the border merely reaffirms the ineffectiveness or superficiality of their involvement. In short, the artists launched their critique from a position of privilege.

However, they were not blind to the limitations of the festival. Jordan Crandall recalled confronting the issue when Alfredo Jaar's *La nube/The Cloud* was presented at inSITE2000. This project involved the release of a thousand white helium-filled balloons that were intended as a memorial to the individuals who had perished while crossing the border during the previous decade.[141] Accompanied by live classical music, it was performed beside the border fence at Valle del Matador in Tijuana and Goat Canyon in San Diego on 14 October 2000. Six hundred people gathered to watch as the balloons dispersed across the sky. For Crandall, the juxtaposition of the ephemeral artwork with the potential agency of the crowd was jarring:

> We were at ... I think it was actually Alfredo Jaar's launch of the balloons ... [scholar] David Harvey was there ... The border fence was there and there was a crowd around it, and David Harvey said, "We should just charge that fence ... We should just charge it, you know. Burst through it, right?" And that "burst" was saying, why do we stand for this? We

> should just, you know, oppose it. We should just mobilize, you know ... But instead, of course, we're all gathering at [the border], all of us, to watch a gesture, which has no immediate political import ... So, the contrast was interesting.[142]

In Crandall's opinion, inSite's potential lay in its mobilization of audiences: "These artistic projects or interventions become catalysts for bringing together a whole host of people." Its success was also evident in its ability to attract participants from numerous fields, including urbanism, politics, sociology, philosophy, and critical studies to address the region from an interdisciplinary standpoint. Bringing together diverse groups was very productive, Crandall stated, because "the artistic projects become catalysts for assembly and reflection ... To get people who aren't necessarily in the same place, talking to one another, is something really of value in and of itself."[143] However, Crandall's anecdote about the balloon release encapsulates many of the contradictions of inSite's art projects, which claimed to critically engage with the border region but for the most part did not enact change, instead providing affective and aesthetic experiences.[144] The anecdote also exemplifies the problem of inaction by the people who attended inSite events and of the projects that addressed systemic issues of inequality at the border but did not result in political change. Many projects consisted of nothing more than a statement, belying the festival's rhetoric that presented them as actions. Thus, as Fusco argues, inSite "domesticated border art,"[145] taking it far from its origins in local Chicano community activism and turning it into yet another commodity that neoliberal westerners could enjoy.

More than in its art projects, inSite made its mark in numerous collaborations among individuals, organizations, and communities. In discussing the history of the festival, Krichman dwelt on the work that he and Cuenca did in negotiating relationships with institutions.[146] In 2001, Yúdice participated in an inSite event called *Conversation IV: Image Power: Cultural Interventions as Public Memory in Post-modern Spaces,* where he argued that attention should be paid to inSite as an organization – "its major achievement."[147] In a subsequent book, he suggested that "the *organizational work* done by inSITE directors and staff, deserves at least as much attention as the most successful art projects in the program."[148] Yúdice points to a tangible outcome of inSite – the networks and relationships forged between various individuals and institutions in Mexico, the United States, and farther afield.

Art about the Mexico-US border is characterized by a focus on the physicality of the boundary. This is due to the fact that it is heavily militarized, a process that developed at the end of the twentieth century and into the new millennium just as the continent was supposed to be drawing closer together. The attention to the physical nature of the border is also related to the strong sense of cultural othering of Mexico, the perception that the two states, and their respective citizens, are very different. This is tied to American fears about Mexican immigration. NAFTA may have stimulated commodity flows and opened the border to goods, but the movement of people was increasingly regulated.

The inSite festival lays bare the tangled mix of art, trade, and politics that aligned throughout North America's border regions in the period of free trade. It raises important questions about the ethics of engaging with the border, who was entitled to articulate border narratives, and the potential of art to challenge inequity and to effect change. Additionally, inSite demonstrates the development of binational collaborations between artists, communities, and a range of organizations. Thus, it allows us to parse North American borders during an era of increased economic integration, as well as changing understandings of the Mexico-US boundary and border region.

6

Changing Narratives of Free Trade in Video Art

Artistic responses to the announcement of NAFTA were swifter than those of galleries. For instance, Clive Robertson began production of his video work *Trade Winds (Canada) Ltd* on 13 August 1992, the day the trilateral agreement was proclaimed to great media fanfare.[1] Robertson's quick engagement demonstrates that artistic responses can be more agile and less beholden to government than the exhibitions discussed in previous chapters. Completed in just ten days, *Trade Winds* was a fourteen-minute snapshot of the Canadian and American media rhetoric surrounding NAFTA. It included footage of Robertson and artist Frances Leeming, interspersed with clips from television shows, newscasts, and documentary films, to create a multifaceted reflection on economic integration. *Trade Winds* reveals the artists' concerns with the implications of the agreement. In particular, it focuses on the claims of state representatives and commentators that NAFTA was a "prosperity deal" that would result in financial gain while simultaneously acting as a panacea for poverty in North America. The video contextualizes NAFTA within histories of free trade in Canada, making pointed connections to colonialism, power, and inequality.

Trade Winds offers a striking glimpse into how free trade was received by cultural producers and the public, as well as of its impact on popular culture. The video aired on Rogers Cable in Ottawa on 27 August 1992, as part of an artists' television show run by SAW Video. Robertson made the most of video's ease of circulation, which allowed him to share the work with audiences who might not necessarily attend conventional screenings or visit museum and gallery spaces. Television is deeply linked to news media and political discourse, so audiences were familiar with the format. Robertson's strategy of détournement – repurposing media clips to catch viewers off-guard – gave *Trade Winds* a particular significance. The broadcast intervened directly in the very political discourse the work sought to criticize.

Video is particularly well suited to responding to unfolding events in political ways. Thus, it is an important venue for tracing Canadian activist artists' responses to free trade and North American integration. The videos discussed in this chapter unsettle dominant understandings of the nation and the inevitability of continental economic integration. They exemplify "new documentary," a genre of video art that engages in social critique through political and narrative styles.[2] According to Sara Diamond and Gary Kibbins, new documentary works are heterogeneous, combining "the realism of documentary with narrative, experimental and appropriated elements."[3] The genre has no unifying aesthetic strategy but is identifiable by its ethical underpinnings, revealing a drive to "speak directly, to question the parameters of knowledge and to construct a network of communication which might assist in the construction of collective social identity."[4] These characteristics are obvious in *Trade Winds*, which questioned the status quo while speaking directly to viewers.

Trade Winds is just one of various videos that commented on free trade, a stream of production that is indicative of the rich cultural debates from the late 1980s through to the twenty-first century. That the responses to free trade so often came through art is notable, given the cultural exemption inscribed in CUSFTA and NAFTA, which prompted heated public discussions about national cultural distinction while enabling national cultural protections. Cultural production, of course, does not exist in a shining light of free and unfettered individual expression and socio-political critique. Canada has a long tradition of government funding for the arts, which dates to the 1949 Royal Commission on National Development in the Arts, Letters, and Sciences (known as the Massey Commission). Its 1951 report made the case for federal funding of arts and culture, and championed culture as a means to establish Canada internationally, inspiring a range of institutional and policy developments, including the creation of the Canada Council for the Arts in 1957.[5] Today, the production and exhibition of contemporary art are supported by municipal, provincial, and federal government funding bodies, in addition to private sources.[6] Thus, it is important to recognize that the artworks discussed in this chapter are not divorced from the economic and political context of their production.

Nonetheless, artists do have agency to advance messages and arguments that align (or not) in various ways with government. To put it more plainly, support for the arts does not result in an instrumental relationship between artist and the various levels of government that provide the funds. Peer assessment, which is employed by many government funders, allows for a level of independence for artists.[7] I argue for their abilities to speak back to government, while also acknowledging their location within funding and policy structures linked to government support. Recognizing their agency does not negate a concurrent recognition of a complex ecosystem of production, including the multiple sources of funding, administration, and policy structures in which artists work.

I discuss video because a focused body of work in the medium addresses free trade during the period covered by this book. Of course, work in other media also dealt with the subject, but by the time of CUSFTA and NAFTA, video was a well-established and easily disseminated medium with activist leanings.[8] Artist video emerged during the 1960s after Sony began to sell portable cameras. Curator Peggy Gale details why video was so alluring: "This new consumer item, with its grainy image that (unlike film) needed no development. Instant. And pretty cheap. Travelling light."[9] It was perfectly suited for quick responses to political developments and could be widely circulated.[10]

In general, I am critical of the category of Canadian art because its methodological nationalism leaves the state unquestioned. Moreover, the focus of the discipline of art history on white settler Canada, as art historian Erin Morton argues, is "settler-centric" to a significant end: it obscures the colonial violence at the heart of the national project, whereby "colonial-national texts" (often visual and material culture) bolster narratives that justify "genocidal moves in ongoing violence and dispossession."[11] Let me be clear: Canada's colonial origins and ongoing colonial relationships are evident in the history and present context of Canadian art. However, this chapter addresses art production in what is now known as Canada because the free trade debates were largely framed in nationalist terms due to the parameters of the trade deals themselves. Given this, any assessment of art that participated in these debates will necessarily follow nationalist lines. I have elected to focus on work produced in Canada because this book is concerned in part with filling a gap in scholarship – the response of the Canadian arts community to economic integration.[12] Additionally, scholarship in the field of contemporary art has determined that the path taken by art video in Canada differed from that in other locations, especially the United States. As Gale suggests, one notable variance is that the history of commercial and experimental film did not play into the development of artist video in Canada, whereas this was a significant factor in the United States.[13] For all these reasons, I pursue this examination of video work produced in Canada, albeit with reservations about the constructed boundaries of nation that are tied up in this topic. Thus, my approach is grounded in critiques of settler colonialism. This is not revisionism but a necessary framework that adds to our understanding. Canadian art is a colonial field of study because Canada was a British colony, a fact that shaped its domestic and international institutions, including museums and their collections. It is therefore important to conduct any study of Canadian art history within the scholarship on settler colonialism. This adds an essential dimension to my reading of artworks from the 1980s to the first decade of the twenty-first century. Finally, much of the art discussed in this chapter, and in this book more broadly, speaks to territory and sovereignty, concepts that are better understood when the longer colonial history of Canada is foregrounded.

My reading of free trade video suggests that its approach changed at about the turn of the millennium. During the 1980s and 1990s, it hearkened back to the cultural nationalism of the 1960s and also responded to specific debates in the negotiations, such as over split-run periodicals. (Split-run periodicals reprinted foreign editorial content with domestic advertisements, allowing publishers to circumvent tariffs. As such, they were the subject of a major dispute between Canada and the United States in the 1990s.)[14] Later video work discarded cultural nationalism, opting for other themes, notably gender, indigeneity, and transnationalism.

Cultural Nationalism in the Late Twentieth Century

In Canada during the late twentieth century, discussions of culture and trade commonly focused on cultural nationalism, which was evoked as a counter to US cultural imperialism. Fears of American dominance fuelled a pervasive belief that if Canadian culture did not receive policy protection, it would inevitably be swamped by content from south of the border.[15] This theme is evident in works such as Condé + Beveridge's *Free Expression*, as examined in the Introduction. Gillian Roberts identifies rhetoric about the hegemony of US cultural products as Canada's "nationalist sense of disempowerment vis-à-vis the United States."[16] It also prevailed in video production during the time that free trade was being implemented in North America. Here, I am interested in works by Lisa Steele and Kim Tomczak, Eva Manly, and Clive Robertson.

It is worth noting that far from originating in the free trade period, fears about the vulnerability of Canadian culture can be traced back at least to the Massey Commission of 1949. Artists had long expressed concern, wrapped up in apprehension regarding American imperialism. One prominent example is Joyce Wieland's 1968 film *Rat Life and Diet in North America*. This short 16mm colour film features rats (portrayed by pet gerbils) as American political prisoners who flee to Canada, which is portrayed as a utopia. Other Canadian artists, such as painter Greg Curnoe of London, Ontario, also espoused anti-Americanism. Curnoe's *Map of North America* (Figure 14) neatly excises the United States from the continent, stitching the borders of Canada and Mexico together.[17] Curnoe reworked the motif numerous times in various media, notably producing a colour lithograph version in 1989 – the year that CUSFTA was implemented.

In the period leading up to free trade, anti-US sentiment figured in public and political discussions of cultural policy. Susan Crean's 1976 book *Who's Afraid of Canadian Culture?* addressed the marginalization of Canadian content in Canada's English-language arts organizations. Crean argued that nationalism should be legitimized, calling for "anti-Americanism" in a bid to establish a Canadian cultural policy defined on Canadian terms.[18] Rather than recentre Canada as a new empire, Crean suggested that it should seize on its differences as assets and look for new ways of taking into account the existing "sensitivity to differences and

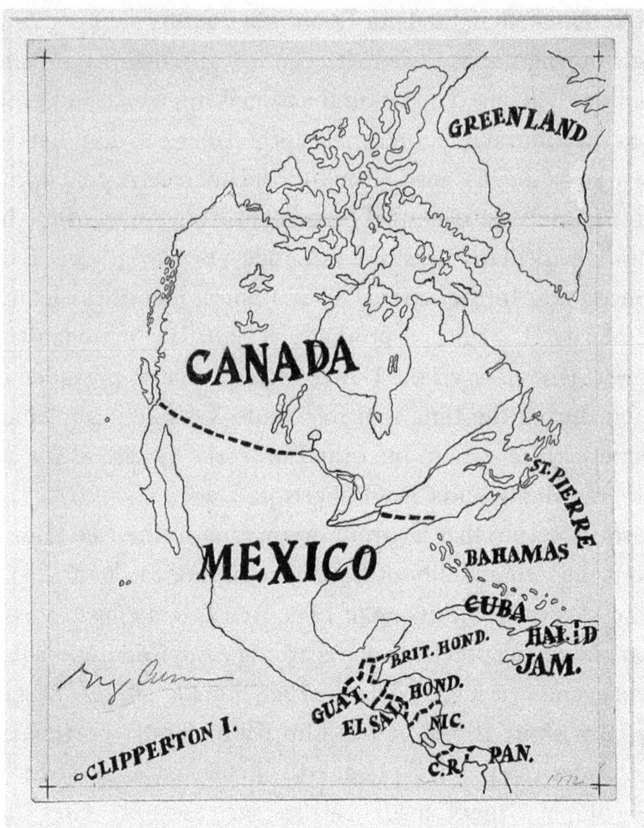

FIGURE 14 Greg Curnoe, *Map of North America,* 1972 © Greg Curnoe/ CARCC Ottawa 2024. Ink on paper, 29.5 x 22.2 cm, Dalhousie Art Gallery Collection, purchased from the Third Dalhousie Drawing Exhibition, 1978.

regions that few other societies have."[19] Many of her comments were echoed in artists' discussions of free trade during the 1980s and in the video works of the time.

White Dawn

The nine-minute video *White Dawn,* created in 1988 by Toronto-based artists Lisa Steele and Kim Tomczak, employs humour to comment on CUSFTA.[20] *White Dawn* engaged with the public debate over the CUSFTA negotiations, which often characterized the United States as holding the whip hand. People expressed fears that the final agreement would allow American culture to dominate in Canadian markets and negatively affect Canadian cultural products. In the video, Steele and Tomczak engage in an irony-laden presentation of the impact of free trade. They playfully invert typical concerns, drawing on the stylistic conventions of popular American television shows. The video tells the story of an American who awakens to find, to his confusion and horror, that he is surrounded by Canadian cultural products, which are submerging American culture.[21] In the artists' words, *White Dawn* portrays "an American who's losing it, who's insecure, doubtful of self but not quite sure why, who's grumpy but beginning to normalize the change."[22] They wanted to address the effect of "cultural imperialism" on Canadian society. "What happens," they ask, "to that most personal aspect of personality – the dream – when you lose your sense of yourself, when you are not reflected in the culture that surrounds you, when you're absent?"[23] Seriously engaging with the issue of cultural representation, the video inverts US cultural imperialism to humorous ends.

In a play on Canada's official bilingualism, *White Dawn* includes a voiceover that supplies the protagonist's thoughts. The protagonist, played by Kingston-based artist Gary Kibbins, awakens from a dream and notices a change in his environment (Figure 15): "Everything was so familiar. Just almost exactly right, just exactly almost right like it should be but not quite right. Not quite. Just off. And I couldn't think why. I didn't know exactly what was wrong."[24] Employing overly theatrical effects, including wolf howls, organ music, and thunderclaps, the artists convey the protagonist's dread upon realizing the pervasiveness and dominance of Canadian culture. Sitting in a car in an empty drive-in movie theatre, he sees posters for Canadian movies flash by, such as Denys Arcand's *The Decline of the American Empire* (1986). The voiceover reveals his surprise: "I couldn't get over it. Everywhere I looked it was just different ... I wanted to see, well, us. Us, you know, us, us, who we are." In the next scene, Kibbins, driving alone, turns on the radio to listen to music. As he adjusts the radio dial, images of album covers come out of the console, all by Canadian musicians, including Bruce Cockburn and Anne Murray. Here, Steele and Tomczak tackle the issue of Canadian music content regulation on the

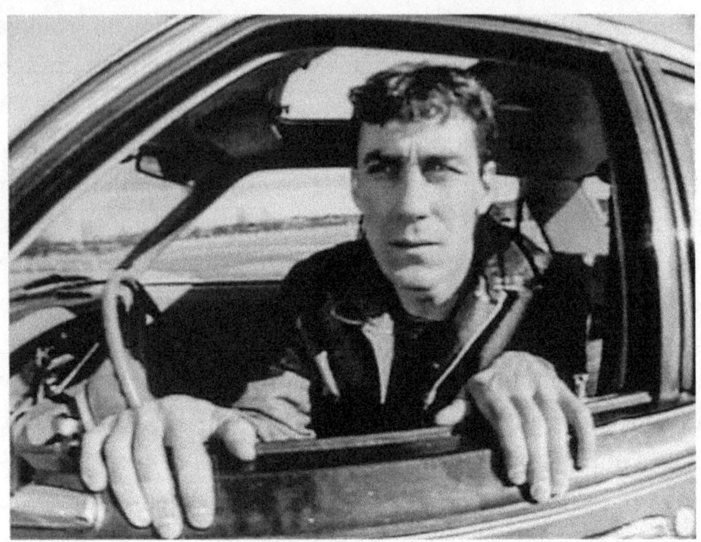

FIGURE 15 Lisa Steele and Kim Tomczak, *White Dawn,* 1988, video still. Courtesy of Lisa Steele and Kim Tomczak and Vtape.

radio. The voiceover articulates doubt about content regulations implemented to protect US music: "I didn't think we needed them. I thought we were beyond that. But I've heard that a lot of American bands are having trouble lately, getting gigs." Then the voiceover exclaims incredulously, "I've heard that [Bruce] Springsteen had to practically give away some of his last albums just to reach his audience." Underscoring the shocking nature of Springsteen's difficulties, the video comments on Canadian artists' prominent concerns over disseminating their work in a market that was advantageous to US cultural products.

Steele and Tomczak also address the importance of literature in creating a national cultural landscape, referring to novels used in the public education system. The voiceover explains, "When I was a kid ... they told us what books we had to read and they were, you know, normal books. Now a kid can't find any of those books." Images of book covers flash onto the screen, including Mark Twain's *The Adventures of Tom Sawyer,* Herman Melville's *Moby Dick,* William Faulkner's *Intruder in the Dust,* and Ernest Hemingway's *Men Without Women.* The voiceover refers to these so-called classic novels – "the ones we all had to read" – sadly noting their lack of circulation and explaining their shrinking relevance: "Well, they're gone. Not gone exactly, just diminished, not as important somehow." This discussion of literature plays with the US canon to set up an antagonistic relationship between American and Canadian cultural products.

In a scene set in a school library, the camera zooms in on a stack of geography texts, including the *National Geographic Atlas of the World*, the *National Atlas of Canada*, *Mon Atlas*, and the *Canadian Junior Atlas*. The voiceover expresses the personal dislocation that has resulted from the new political and economic integration of Canada and the United States. It hints at the reconceptualization of national boundaries due to globalization: "It's strange but even when we look at a map the colours seem all different. It's like we're looking at a picture of where we are that we never saw before. It's different. It's like a geography that we never lived in." Here, *White Dawn* accentuates how free trade influences US and Canadian narratives by disrupting the way in which each country is understood in relation to the rest of the world. It alludes to the constant restructuring of history and the process by which a dominant broker's recounting of events becomes the accepted version.

Near the end of the video, the issue of Canadian periodicals is addressed, pointing to the pervasive presence of US cultural products in Canada. Against a bright blue sky, American magazine covers flash by, including *Time*, *Esquire*, and *Vogue*. As each magazine disappears, it makes a loud popping sound, emphasizing its departure. Simultaneously, the voiceover laments the injustice of having to visit a specialty store to access these publications. Throughout every scenario, the voiceover reveals the protagonist's reaction to his situation – confusion, dismay, disquiet – in tones that teeter on hysteria: "I'm getting confused, sort of mixed up. I don't know my reality from their fantasy. I've been starting to say MP when I'm talking about my Congressman ... What can I do? When I look, I see you ... Where is me? Where am I?" His bewilderment speaks to the lack of control felt by cultural producers and their audiences.

While making light of the power difference between Canada and the United States, as well as the dominance of American culture in Canada, Steele and Tomczak underline the assumption that there are very real differences between the two nations. *White Dawn* suggests that Canadian culture and, by proxy, Canada itself would be at a disadvantage under free trade. Employing humour and parody in this experimental reflection on trade liberalization, the video illuminates the fears of many Canadians that CUSFTA would devastate their culture. Throughout, it refers to well-known examples of Canadian culture in film, music, and literature. The video highlights the tensions surrounding the production and protection of national culture, revealing the significant investment in this issue that many artists experienced. As the voiceover concludes, "I just never thought it would come to this. I never thought it would go quite this far. The mighty eagle trod asunder by an animal many consider to be nothing but an overgrown rat, the beaver. I'm surprised." Ending with a reference to these national symbols, *White Dawn* underscores the dominant narrative of US cultural products in Canada and, in turn, emphasizes the lack of power felt by Canadians.

The Winning of the North

The Winning of the North, by Eva Manly, connects CUSFTA to the process of colonialism in Canada.[25] Created in 1989, the same year that CUSFTA was implemented, it runs for ten minutes and uses historical treaty negotiations as an allegory for the free trade talks. It evokes the seizure of Indigenous land and autonomy through agreements made in bad faith. The subtext implies that Canada itself could potentially experience similar damage as a result of CUSFTA.

Structured around a loosely defined story presented in what the artist describes as a "playful" manner, *The Winning of the North* focuses on power relations and the way in which power is exercised.[26] In fact, it is very much open to interpretation: "The connections are made implicit rather than explicit," Manly explains.[27] Set in the present day, it depicts a symbolic encounter between two men who meet outdoors in a nondescript suburban neighbourhood. Their encounter is conveyed through simple actions that make the plotline easy to understand. They never speak, and the soundtrack consists entirely of instrumental and popular music.

The video begins with a man walking along a sidewalk. Wearing a white shirt and a leather jacket, he carries a briefcase. Noticing a man sitting at a bus stop, he looks nervous and ducks away. The seated man, who wears a beige trench coat and a black hat, holds a black briefcase. Sitting alone, he reaches into a nearby garbage bin, pulls out a copy of CUSFTA, and starts to read it. The first man reappears, now dressed in a black hat and a black cape with a prominent cross. His costume indicates that he is a clergyman, suggesting that colonial states hide their true intentions behind a veneer of altruism. Sitting beside the second man, he reads over his shoulder for a while. Eventually, he opens his briefcase and shows its contents to the other man, though they are not visible to us. Next, both walk down the street, with the man in black leading the man in beige, who carries the CUSFTA text.

They stop near a raised sewer grate and two tree stumps, which serve as impromptu seats. Sitting down, they face each other, using the manhole cover as a table. The man with the cross removes some buns and a bottle of wine from his briefcase. He pours a large glass for his companion and a second for himself, which they consume. Then, the two men tape four lengths of red ribbon to the manhole cover, creating a small grid. At this point, the man in the trench coat removes his coat and hat and shakes out his long hair. We see that he is wearing a black beaded outfit, clearly Indigenous. Opening his briefcase, he removes several doughnuts and places them on the table. Using the doughnuts and four hot cross buns (marked with an "X" on top), the men begin a serious game of tic-tac-toe. Throughout, the CUSFTA document leans against their makeshift game board, clearly visible. Through this juxtaposition, the treaty talks are conflated with the CUSFTA negotiations. The religious figure makes the first play and subsequently wins the game. The Indigenous man bows his head in sorrow, while the other places his hand on his heart, almost as if giving a blessing, seeming to indicate a paternalistic relationship between the two. Representing trade negotiations as a game refers to their arbitrary nature and also seems to suggest an unequal historical power dynamic between Indigenous peoples and settlers. The game has further significance, given that colonial powers did not enter into treaties in good faith and commonly failed to honour their commitments, resulting in disputes that persist to this day.

The video concludes with textual intertitles that ask viewers to choose between two possible endings or even to script their own. The scrolling text reads, "Viewers are invited to see the video as an unfinished production in whose completion they can participate by: 1. Choosing from two suggested scenes and scripting them, 2. Suggesting their own additional scenes."[28] In the first suggested scene, the Bureau of Indian Affairs in Washington DC is made responsible for the administration of CUSFTA, reaffirming the agreement as a colonizing instrument that would render settler Canadians as Indigenous, to be overseen by the bureau. The second suggested scene is a tongue-in-cheek proposal that CUSFTA should replace "a great Canadian institution," the Eaton's catalogue – footage of a small outhouse in a farmer's field hints at where the document might be best used. The video closes with another call for resolution, asking the presumed settler audience to send their suggested endings to Manly. Whether anyone did is unclear, but this element of the work speaks to ongoing engagement and continued conversation. As a result, *The Winning of the North* can be read as a limited call to participate in discussions of free trade, as well as an improvised means of polling opinions on CUSFTA.

The Winning of the North plays on the colonization or enslavement of white people, a trope that has a long history in racist colonial discourse, where it is presented as the supreme injustice. Arguing that settler states work to produce the nation as a white possession, Aileen Moreton-Robinson (Goenpul) explains this process as predicated on the erasure of Indigenous peoples: "The regulatory mechanisms of these nation-states are extremely busy reaffirming and reproducing this possessiveness through a process of perpetual Indigenous dispossession, ranging from the refusal of Indigenous sovereignty to overregulated piecemeal concessions."[29] Similarly, Eve Tuck (Unangax̂) and K. Wayne Yang contend that settler-colonial society is grounded in the obliteration of Indigenous presence. "In order for the settlers to make a place their home," they write, "they must destroy and disappear the Indigenous peoples that live there."[30] Further, Tuck and Yang explain, "Everything within a settler colonial society strains to destroy or assimilate the Native in order to disappear them from the land – this is how a society can have multiple simultaneous and conflicting messages about Indigenous peoples."[31] *The Winning of the North*, which warns white settlers about potentially being colonized under free trade, must be understood within the framework of setter colonialism.

Similar national narratives have been advanced in twentieth-century Quebec, for example, where francophone populations were constructed as inherently native, thus legitimizing their possession of land and claims of nationhood, which sought to render them as indigenous. Examining the rise of the separatist movement in 1960s Montreal, which accused English Canada of imperialism, historian Sean Mills argues, "In order to imagine themselves as the indigenous population, Quebec liberationists needed to ignore the existence, both past and present, of Aboriginal communities in the province."[32] Similarly, *The Winning of the North* speaks to the hegemony of whiteness and the pervasiveness of white settler claims to belonging through declarations of nativism (this is also true of *Trade Winds*, by Clive Robertson).

Quebec nationalist claims to nativeness still reverberate today. As writer Emilie Nicolas remarks, contemporary national themes elide the histories and contributions of those who are seen as non-native. To what end, Nicolas questions:

> Pourquoi a-t-on *besoin* de se représenter comme naïfs? À quoi sert-il de faire de la place à l'autre *que* comme une métaphore de soi? Quelle est la fonction de l'effacement? Qu'est-ce qui est rendu possible par cette idée que la « diversité » est toujours nouvelle? À *qui* sert le déni? Répondre à ces questions, c'est commencer à comprendre pourquoi la voie du changement est parsemée d'embûches.[33]

Nicolas argues that the myth of an "old stock" Quebec inflicts significant damage, retrenching discussions of diversity as a contemporary issue, perpetuating the dominance of white settler populations. As Nicolas explains, "On efface des siècles de contributions politiques, militantes et intellectuelles des femmes autochtones et racisées toute en consolidant le mythe d'un Québec 'pur laine' et homogène, où la diversité ethnique est toute nouvelle et donc étrangère, voire 'd'intégration.'"[34] Manly's mobilization of Indigenous experiences in *The Winning of the North* acts as a warning to white settlers that they too may be subject to colonization under free trade. At the same time, it omits the violence inflicted on Indigenous people by settler colonialism, suggesting that the implementation of free trade and the impact of colonization on Indigenous populations are equivalents. In this, it can be seen as yet another settler move to innocence, as identified by Tuck and Yang: "strategies or positionings that attempt to relieve the settler of feelings of guilt or responsibility without giving up land or power or privilege, without having to change much at all."[35] To put it another way, the video is a "nuanced move to innocence," which entails the "homogenizing of various experiences of oppression as colonization."[36]

Ultimately, Manly sees the trade deal in a negative light and suggests that like Indigenous peoples, settler Canadians will lose their "power to exercise their right to self-determination."[37] In evoking this threat to Canadian independence, she seemingly has settler Canada in mind by implying that the colonization of (white) Canada is somehow equivalent to (or more unjust than) that of Indigenous North America. Here, colonialism again serves cultural nationalism, bringing to mind the complexities raised by exhibitions of Indigenous visual and material culture deployed by settler states, as examined in Chapter 4.

The simple story in *The Winning of the North* presents CUSFTA as one claim on the land in a long history of claims, while emphasizing the legacies of colonialism that underwrite current political systems. There are, however, significant problems with its use of historic Indigenous-settler treaties to comment on the free trade negotiations—and this metaphor is now at odds with how we understand the dynamics of CUSFTA. Patterning the Canada-US relationship after that between Indigenous peoples and colonial powers taps into the lengthy tradition of co-opting Indigenous people and their histories for settler purposes. In this case, the video suggests that settlers will resist free trade once they discover that it is a form of colonization, thus inadvertently implying a racial order that legitimizes the colonization of Indigenous peoples but not white settlers (while also seemingly inferring that the former did not resist colonization). The use of Indigenous stories speaks to the long-standing asymmetrical relationship between Canadian nationalist narratives and Indigenous culture, resulting in the settler co-optation of Indigenous histories and the minimization of violence against Indigenous communities while delegitimizing their claims to the land. In this respect, settler narratives are more pervasive and insidious than state narratives. These analogies dismiss the power imbalance between Indigenous and settler populations. However, they are clearly a means by which free trade was understood in the period. Such analogies are not limited to *The Winning of the North.* Robertson's *Trade Winds* also makes a connection to Indigenous histories in criticizing free trade. These works seem to imply a racial order that legitimizes the colonization of Indigenous peoples while warning white settlers that they must avoid a similar fate at all costs. Tuck and Yang make clear that such settler moves to innocence "rescue settler futurity" by frustrating decolonization efforts and stabilizing settler-colonial narratives.[38]

Trade Winds (Canada) Ltd

Trade Winds begins on a windy and overcast day, with the artists Robertson and Leeming rowing a small metal skiff onto the Kiamika Reservoir in Quebec. Facing the camera as he plies the oars, Robertson speaks frankly to the viewer (Figure 16). In dramatic prose, he describes his and Leeming's surprise at the announcement of NAFTA: "The Canadian summer of '92 promised fast food from the Olympics and added fibre from the constitutional drama. Out here [in Canada], all was calm. Until, like a gust of

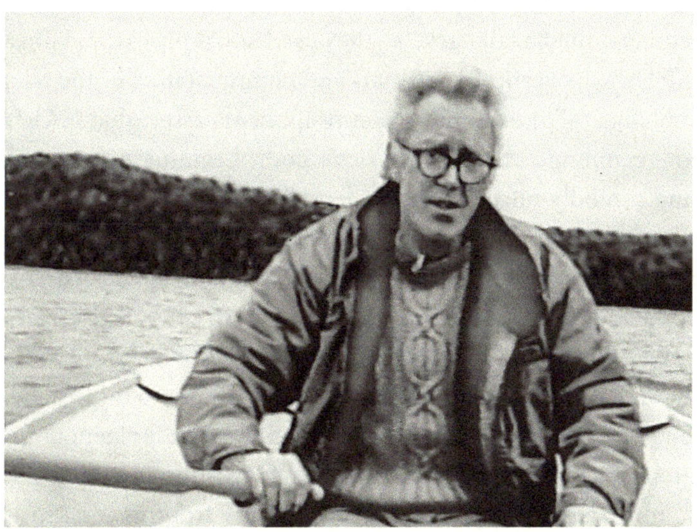

FIGURE 16 Clive Robertson, *Trade Winds (Canada) Ltd,* 1992, video still. Courtesy of Clive Robertson and Vtape.

wind out of nowhere, we heard the news."[39] Robertson contextualizes the NAFTA announcement by intercutting media clips from prominent sources such as the *National,* the CBC's flagship news program. The clips reveal the extent to which the media were dominated by the public controversy surrounding the trade agreement.

In one clip, reporter Keith Bow discusses clashing editorials in the *Toronto Star* and the *Globe and Mail,* which disagree on NAFTA. Subsequent footage gives examples of the rhetoric regarding NAFTA, including a comment from the Canadian trade minister, Michael Wilson, who states at a Toronto press conference that "Canadians have every right to be optimistic." He adds that NAFTA "will put money in people's pockets, so it isn't just a trade deal, it's a prosperity deal as well." The video touches on claims that the agreement will have environmental benefits. William Reilly, a representative of the US Environmental Protection Agency, boasts that NAFTA is "the most environmentally sensitive, the greenest trade agreement ever negotiated anywhere." The news clips also show that NAFTA was not universally endorsed by the Canadian public – Bow describes it as a "deal [that] still needs selling." Thus, the video makes clear that free trade was initially not broadly accepted.

Leeming and Robertson intended *Trade Winds* to act as a vehicle for "immediate ... media talkback," so they used it to reply to the claims made for NAFTA by government officials and commentators in the television and film clips.[40] For example, when proponents assert that NAFTA will raise the economic status of Mexico's poor, Leeming offers a rebuttal, speaking candidly into the camera lens: "But trade itself has little to do with the redistribution of wealth ... Though it's being promoted as a new imperative, globalization of trade and its accompanying social destruction has a long and repetitive history" (Figure 17). To support this reasoning, *Trade Winds* includes footage from the 1972 National Film Board documentary *The Other Side of the Ledger,* which delved into the history of the Hudson's Bay Company (HBC) and its relations with Indigenous peoples. The film took an Indigenous perspective, suggesting that the company's wealth and trade monopoly stemmed unfairly from its long history of support from the British Crown and participation in white settler expansion across the lands now known as Canada. *The Other Side of the Ledger*

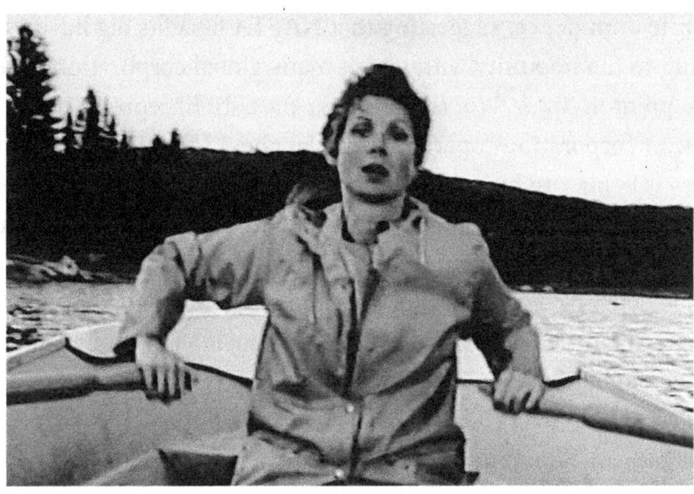

FIGURE 17 Artist Frances Leeming rowing on the Kiamika Reservoir. Clive Robertson, *Trade Winds (Canada) Ltd,* 1992, video still. Courtesy of Clive Robertson and Vtape.

shows a confrontation between Howard Adams of the Saskatchewan Métis Association and Robert Cook, a divisional manager at the HBC. Their public exchange uncovers the HBC exploitation of Indigenous people by charging exorbitantly high prices at the company store and forcing Indigenous people on reserves to sign over their government money directly to the store. Robertson sums up the situation succinctly: "Capital is by intent and definition a mean master." By pointing to capitalist settler-colonial practices, he seems to suggest (like Manly) that free trade would enable the American colonization of (settler) Canada. Again, the use of Indigenous-settler relationships as a metaphor to understand free trade exemplifies settler moves to innocence that help themselves to Indigenous histories while disempowering Indigenous agency and obscuring the ongoing reality of settler colonialism.

Further emphasizing the idea of colonization and loss of sovereignty, *Trade Winds* refers to different instances where the United States sought to exercise or asserted dominance over Canada. These include reference to US-Canada relations in the nineteenth century when the United States moved to annex Canada (at the time a British colony). The video then shifts chronologically to the present and provides information about US corporate dominance, suggesting that NAFTA benefits big business and pointing to the impunity with which many global corporations operate. At one point in *Trade Winds,* the writer Barbara Ehrenreich argues that American corporations operate carte blanche: "There is a sense that the country is being run by, maybe I shouldn't say run, I mean plundered, by a little group at the top." The video does not limit itself to business-oriented news sources. To demonstrate that NAFTA had made its way into the public lexicon, it includes footage of comedian Jay Leno conducting his signature stand-up routine as host of the *Tonight Show.* Joking about the premise that borders would be opened via free trade, Leno also speaks to public confusion over the details of the agreement and its potential impact: "Does anybody understand this free trade agreement? This is supposed to help Americans get jobs ... All it means now is that ... a worker in a GM plant in Mexico can now get a better deal on a Ford, built in Canada by Canadians." His comment mirrors the anxieties felt in all three countries that free trade would somehow disadvantage them while benefiting the others.

Altogether, *Trade Winds* suggests that the NAFTA announcement should be a moment to pose questions about how the economy functions and whose priorities are considered. Leeming asks, "Why must our economy be determined by private instead of public interests?" She continues, "Though we may not know the minute details of how our country's economy works, we all experience its effects. The current free flow of capital and globalization of trade has little to do with guaranteeing jobs, social programs, pensions or our cultural needs." As she calls for a "true global redistribution of wealth," clouds gather on an ominously dark horizon, accompanied by the sounds of an approaching storm. After advocating for regional alternatives to corporate free trade to ensure economic equality, Leeming and Robertson row back to the shore to seek shelter. Through a multilayered approach, *Trade Winds* portrays NAFTA as part of a well-entrenched pattern in which trade policy inevitably takes priority over social justice. By employing media footage in a critical examination of free trade rhetoric, it contributes to a reading of NAFTA against North American histories while pointing out affinities between colonialism and capitalism.

The videos by Steele and Tomczak, Manly, and Robertson all address free trade in terms of US cultural imperialism. They affirm the perceived power of the United States and the corresponding weakness of Canada, making the case for protectionist measures to support Canadian cultural production. Manly and Robertson draw parallels between the colonization of Indigenous peoples and the potential colonization of white Canadian settlers under free trade. From the standpoint of 2025, these narratives can seem jarring because they are grounded in settler moves to innocence. They demonstrate that white settlers are not accustomed to thinking of themselves as colonized or colonizable, but as colonizers – holders of power in a racial, cultural, and economic relationship. The videos point to Indigenous peoples and colonialism seemingly as a warning to settler Canadians that they could lose their land and culture, that they, too, could be colonized. Thus, cultural nationalism plays on fears of racial confusion as the artists co-opt Indigenous experiences, while excluding Indigenous voices and solidarity with Indigenous peoples, in order to make a point about settler culture. In other words, they position settlers as indigenous to the territory while slowly writing actual Indigenous people out of the story and off the land.

New Narratives

By the turn of the millennium, videos that dealt with free trade had largely abandoned the theme of cultural nationalism and commonly engaged with a range of experimental narrative structures. We can trace the use of video as a documentary and activist force, utilized to capture the protests that erupted around globalization and free trade. Additionally, though video continued to invoke Indigenous historical examples as a way of understanding free trade, it did so in ways that advanced Indigenous perspectives not bounded by settler states.

Debates about globalization were inextricably linked to free trade. At the time, protests against trade liberalization and deregulation were often described as anti-globalization but can more accurately be understood as advocating for a different form of global connectivity, which art historians J. Keri Cronin and Kirsty Robertson suggest is best captured in the term "alter-globalization."[41] During the late 1990s and into the first years of the twenty-first century, alter-globalization protests were staged around the world, including several in North American cities. They tended to coincide with key political meetings aimed at consolidating the global economic system, such as the 1999 World Trade Organization meetings in Seattle and the Third Summit of the Americas held in Quebec City in April 2001. These protests and others became widely known through images of police in riot gear employing tear gas to disperse the crowd. As Cronin and Robertson write, confrontations between activists and police "were often marked by the use of tear-gas and pepper spray, rubber bullets, and increasingly technologized riot gear versus generally unarmed protesters holding posters, large-scale papier maché [sic] puppets, making music, chanting, shouting, and generally performing the chaotic politics of affinity groups (small groups sharing a common purpose within the larger framework of the protest)."[42] The 2010 photographic work *Liberty Lost (G20, Toronto)* by activist artists Carole Condé + Karl Beveridge responded to the G20 meetings that year in Toronto and encapsulated this description (Figure 18). The photograph shows tear gas, police in riot

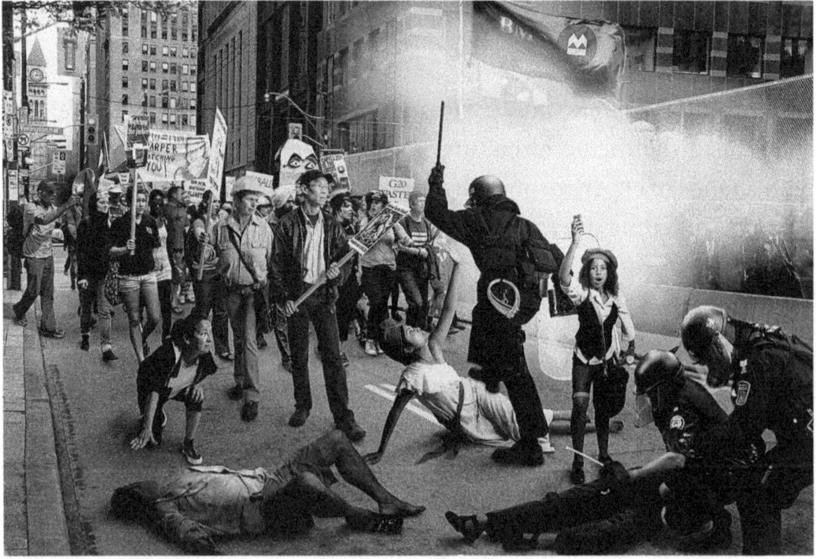

FIGURE 18 Carole Condé + Karl Beveridge, *Liberty Lost (G20, Toronto)*, 2010, photograph. Courtesy Carole Condé + Karl Beveridge.

gear, barricades and fences, and protesters with signs and papier mâché objects. To drive home its point, it borrows a few figures from *Liberty Leading the People (July 28, 1830)*, a famous allegorical work by French painter Eugène Delacroix, but whereas his Liberty triumphantly leads the people to victory in the revolution of 1830, her counterpart in *Liberty Lost* is trampled underfoot by a police officer, who raises his baton to strike her.

Alter-globalization protests were notably reflected in video art production.[43] Video functions on multiple levels: as a form of art expression and historical documentation, it provides a second life to the protests and is an accessible, creative form of activism itself. Moreover, filming during protests provides a level of protection for the activists. Cronin and Robertson state that protest is filmed "for posterity and protection (one is less likely to be beaten, arrested, or otherwise abused if the action is being recorded)."[44] Protesters shot video to track the demonstrations and their own actions, as well as their perspectives. In addition, filming police behaviour could be useful for documenting arrests, police aggression, and other efforts to interfere with the right to convene and demonstrate. This use also speaks to the evidentiary status associated with video and photo-based media more broadly. According to John Fiske, video is "an instrument of both communication and surveillance. It can be used by the power bloc to monitor the comings and goings of the people, but equally its cameras can be turned 180 social degrees, to show the doings of the power bloc to the people."[45] In this spirit, artists employ video to create works that document protest and foreground protesters. At the turn of the millennium, the creative structures of video allowed them to playfully and poignantly intercede into the dominant discourse about free trade.

Two short videos from 2001, *Packin'* by John Greyson and *Like a Nice Rubber Gas Mask* by Malcolm Rogge, make powerful statements about the potential of art as a form of activism.[46] Both responded to the protests at the April 2001 Summit of the Americas in Quebec City. Comprised of three days of meetings between leaders from North and South America, the summit was the site for negotiations toward a proposed Free Trade Area of the Americas (FTAA), which had been announced in 1995 as a means of uniting all the nations of the Americas (with the exception of Cuba) through the elimination of barriers to trade. The summit was to have been the occasion when heads of state and delegates agreed to a draft document, but the process subsequently stalled, and by 2005 – the initial deadline for its implementation – the FTAA had failed. The summit was marked by a large complement of peaceful protesters, who objected to neoliberal globalization and the extreme security measures in Quebec City.

Packin' and *Like a Nice Rubber Gas Mask* exemplify the new approaches to free trade in video works. They employ humour to great effect and move beyond the focus on cultural nationalism. Both were part of a larger compilation of thirteen videos assembled by the Blah Blah Blah Collective.[47] The collective took its name from a widely publicized remark by Prime Minister Jean Chrétien, who dismissed protesters at the summit as misguided pleasure seekers. Chrétien scoffed to the media, "They say to themselves, 'Let's go spend the weekend in Quebec City; we'll have fun; we'll protest and blah, blah, blah.'"[48] In the face of such scorn for citizens' rights, the collective stipulated that funds generated by screenings of its video compilation would go to offsetting the legal fees of protesters who were arrested in Quebec City.[49] The videos addressed the history of free trade's implementation, recording the significant public backlash to the agreements. They engaged with the large-scale demonstrations, which brought diverse communities together in resistance to neoliberalism.

Packin'

Through a tongue-in-cheek documentation of the crotches of cops and politicians, *Packin'* focuses on the heavy police presence in Quebec City. In his artist statement, director John Greyson describes the four-minute work: "Bored crotches, nervous crotches, violent crotches: a unique view on the overwhelming police presence that tear-gassed a city."[50] These phallic references speak to patriarchy and power. The Quebec summit was notorious for its numbers of police officers – "the largest police deployment in Canadian history" – and included security measures that transformed the city, such as chain-link fencing and concrete barriers, as well as water cannons, tear gas, smoke bombs, and rubber bullets.[51] The crotches in *Packin'* are interspersed with text panels commenting on the police presence and on government, as well as the patriarchal nature of power (Figure 19).

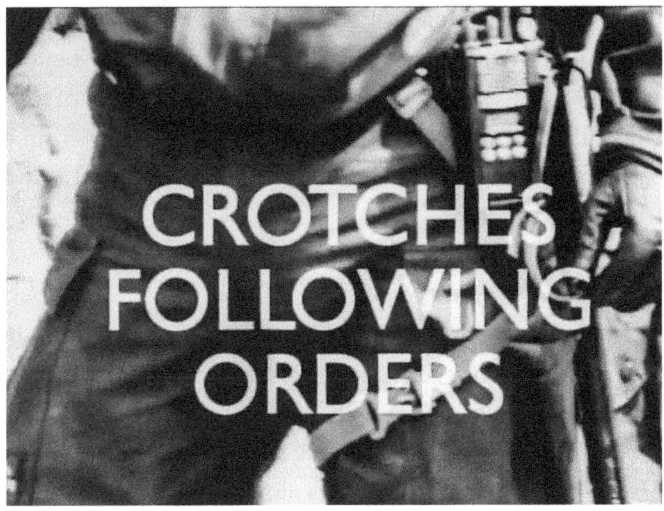

FIGURE 19 John Greyson, *Packin,'* 2001, video still. Courtesy of John Greyson.

Intertitles describe the crotches as national crotches, provincial crotches, undercover crotches, corporate crotches, canine crotches, crotches following orders, and more. The fast pace of the video can be disorienting, as the text frames quickly scroll up the screen, intercut with shots of the protest landscape, including police, politicians, and chain-link fencing. Greyson queers the state apparatus, revealing its heteronormativity and highlighting the connections between body and power. Rather than defending national culture, Greyson concentrates on the power accorded to police and politicians, suggesting that free trade is advanced by hegemonic forces. Unlike in the videos from the late twentieth century, his criticism of free trade is implicit rather than explicit. According to Jan Allen's analysis, "*Packin'* recalls that the sexual body is the habitation of first order and an underacknowledged force in the economy of power."[52] Laura U. Marks writes that Greyson "uses bodies against reification, re-embodying the police and the politicians whose power resides in their disembodiment, in their representation of abstract power."[53] I suggest that Greyson's approach evidences artists' ongoing investment in the struggle against free trade, while simultaneously demonstrating a shift in critique. The videos from this period oppose larger structures of which free trade agreements were but a symptom. No longer tied to anxieties around the nation-state and the new North America, *Packin'* acknowledges the influence of neoliberalism and the disempowerment of citizens in the face of militarized police control. It shows that artists positioned free trade within existing power structures – through a broader social criticism of the system in which free trade functions.

Like a Nice Rubber Gas Mask

Malcolm Rogge also approaches the Quebec City protests with humour, in *Like a Nice Rubber Gas Mask,* a title that references the creative attire of the protesters who came to town for the summit. Four minutes and thirty seconds long, it parodies street fashion segments on television programs by interviewing the activists about what they are wearing. The protesters are not wearing clothes with designer or corporate labels. Emphasizing this absence, in a nod to red-carpet media coverage that is notorious for the question "Who are you wearing?," *Like a Nice Rubber Gas Mask* asks protesters to describe their outfits. One replies, "The look is red. Red is the hot colour of the season. Everybody is wearing it." The video comments on the conspicuous consumption of consumer goods by emphasizing the absence of corporate labels. In fact, many of the "fashion" items are repurposed from conventional uses. For example, many people wear goggles to protect their eyes from tear gas. One comments, "Goggles are in. Day or night, swimming, non-swimming. Any time of the day." An old-fashioned gas mask is "retro." Some demonstrators wear red clown noses, and many use wit as a protest tactic. Costumes reinforce the nonviolent nature of the gathering. In another encounter, a protester attired in kitchen gear is asked, "Hey you, with the colander. Any words for fashion in 2001?" The swift reply is, "Well your biggest fashion statement is going to be the wooden spoon, to stir shit up!" Rogge employs a popular culture media format to focus on the demonstrators. Like *Packin,'* his video is an implicit endorsement of the anti-free-trade stance, using levity to catch viewers' attention while also speaking to larger capitalist systems of consumption. His approach humanizes the protesters, refuting the newspaper articles that focused on the violence and portrayed the activists as homogeneous groups of anarchists.

Both *Packin'* and *Like a Nice Rubber Gas Mask* demonstrate the differing ways that video can speak back to power while capturing the nature of protest and the efforts of protesters. Marks's comment on the body, quoted above, seems equally applicable to *Like a Nice Rubber Gas Mask*, where a strategic focus on the body provides "an imaginative tool that ever so briefly cuts through the smirking surface of power."[54] The attention to resistance through those who enacted it on the streets advances a nuanced understanding of what took place during the protests, complicating media representations and bringing new aspects of free trade histories to light. The two videos also reveal the efforts of artists to oppose free trade and how video was able to capture that opposition and effectively communicate alternative narratives. They rely on humour to intercede with and disarm viewers, highlighting the peaceful nature of the protesters and the armed militaristic control they encountered. In turning attention to the activists, the works confirm that, as Fiske notes, video "still allows, on occasion, those who are normally monitored to monitor the monitors."[55] Thus, we can see video art as enabling the artist to leverage power, disseminating new and counterhegemonic narratives about both the protests and the broader issues of free trade and neoliberalism.

The Original Summit: Journey to the Sacred Uprising

Created in 2002 by Rebeka Tabobondung and Adrian Kahgee, *The Original Summit: Journey to the Sacred Uprising* explores globalization, sovereignty, and colonialism in relation to Indigenous communities.[56] A forty-three-minute work, it provides another means of understanding the shift in the approach to free trade and can be seen as talkback to the videos of Manly and Robertson, which employed Indigenous themes but did not include Indigenous people or world views. A documentary, it deals with the Americas as a whole, a pointed reminder that the national boundaries of Canada, the United States, and other American countries were imposed upon Indigenous land.[57] *The Original Summit* proposes that Indigenous perspectives are vital to understanding globalization in North America and asks its critics to consider a new world order that prioritizes Indigenous world views. It uses the 2001 protests in Quebec City as a starting point for connecting resistance to globalization to broader conversations about the rights of Indigenous peoples and the need for Indigenous communities to unite across the hemisphere. It underscores again the function of video as an ongoing productive space for opposition through art.

A complex and multilayered work, *The Original Summit* is structured around interviews with notable Indigenous elders, writers, and activists, such as Lillian McGregor, Fernando Hernandez, Wendy Thomas, Ovide Mercredi, and Rodney Bobiwash.[58] The interviews are interspersed with the Haudenosaunee creation story, an Anishinabek prayer, and footage of works created by Indigenous artists Maria Hupfield and Travis Shilling.[59] In addition to the protests at Quebec City, the video highlights other protests in the Americas, such as against the murder of Dudley George, an unarmed man killed by the Ontario Provincial Police during a confrontation with the Stoney Point Ojibway at Ipperwash Provincial Park in 1995. Protest footage also covers the disappearance of Kimy Pernía Domicó, a leader of the Indigenous Embera Katio in Colombia, who was kidnapped by paramilitaries for his opposition to the Urra Dam project, revealing the very real dangers faced by Indigenous activists throughout the Americas.

The Original Summit suggests a connection between capitalism, colonialism, and the exploitation of Indigenous populations. Through the comments of interviewees it details the "contact" experience of Indigenous groups in North America, beginning with Jacques Cartier's voyage along the north shore of the St. Lawrence River in the sixteenth century. Cartier relied heavily on the help of the Stadacona people but repaid that debt by kidnapping several Stadaconans and taking them to France, showing extreme disregard for their lives. Interviews contextualize contentious contact histories as central in shaping settler-Indigenous relations, even to the present day. As McGregor, a respected elder from the Nokomis community, points out, many settlers know very little about the treatment of Indigenous peoples. Summing up the purpose of settler moves to innocence, she states, "This group of people that we welcomed to our shores four hundred years ago still think that they were the first ones that lived here." Here, she accentuates the naturalization of settler colonialism and the ways in which it works to rhetorically and physically erase Indigenous populations, undercutting their sovereignty and ties to the land.

During his interview for *The Original Summit,* Ward Churchill states that contemporary processes of globalization further diminish Indigenous ways of life and world views: "One of the projections of the present globalization initiative is to ... incorporate every aspect of the resource profile of the planet into one integrated whole coordinated for consumption for particular purposes by a particular race, and manipulated and handled by a preferred vendor corporation." The film touches on the experience of colonialism for Indigenous people since first contact, noting the imposition of Christianity, government systems, and education systems, all of which have eliminated or reduced Indigenous ways of life. Tabobondung and Kahgee also include concerns from South America. They interview Hernandez, an activist associated with Food for Chiapas, who discusses the 1994 Zapatista uprising in the southern Mexican state, a largely Indigenous movement. Hernandez says the ongoing struggle of the Zapatistas is explicitly connected to the spread of globalization.

Bobiwash, director of the Centre for World Indigenous Studies, argues that globalization is merely a novel type of colonialism: "It's really just a new and more sophisticated form of colonization. And really for Indigenous people what it represents is the end of colonization. Because ... they're taking the very last things that we have." Here, he refers to Indigenous culture, providing a counterpoint to the late-twentieth-century videos and the state-orchestrated exhibitions of the early twenty-first century, all of which positioned Indigenous culture within settler cultural nationalism. The former employed Indigenous culture to suggest that CUSFTA and NAFTA endangered "Canadian" culture. Bobiwash emphasizes the importance of stories, songs, and language to the maintenance of Indigenous culture, because stories can function as a means of resistance. *The Original Summit* can thus be read as a work of activism for its inclusion of the Haudenosaunee creation story, chronicling the origins of Turtle Island. Bobiwash also identifies corporate involvement in the diminishing of Indigenous culture. Addressing the impact of transnational corporations such as Coca-Cola, Nike, and IBM, he argues that they abet state imperialism: "They all want to control the narrative, the ways that we tell our stories, the ways that we give meaning to our lives." Maintaining cultural control and articulating Indigenous world views occurs through language, story, and song.

The environment is a key focus of *The Original Summit*, which proposes that Indigenous ties to the land are central to environmental protection. Several speakers assert the need for Western society to recognize Indigenous knowledge. Thomas, a community activist associated with the First Nations Technical Institute in Ontario, argues that environmental activists should inform themselves of Indigenous connections to the land: "They ... have to see that Indigenous knowledge and Indigenous science is important to their work." Cooperation between Indigenous and non-Indigenous groups will prove essential to maintaining the environment, she suggests: "There has to be an alliance ... They have to look to the people who [know the land and] ... have been living there for thousands of years." Here, the video stresses the importance of valuing Indigenous ways of knowing and being, pointing to the intimate knowledge that Indigenous peoples hold about the environment.

One woman, unidentified in the documentary, maintains that settler activists embrace solidarity only at certain moments of struggle. "When we fight for nature and the protection of nature," she states, "there is solidarity for us. But when Indigenous people fight to change the establishment, the structure of power, and to achieve power, they are afraid of us." Ultimately, she points to the difficulties that Indigenous groups have encountered in their attempts to enact change. This stands out in contrast to the narratives of Manly and Robertson, where there is no solidarity, just co-optation for the artists' own purposes. Manly and Robertson seem not to argue for the protection of Indigenous cultures and lands but for Canadian culture and lands. Conversely, *The Original Summit* makes the point that a true recognition of traditional Indigenous values requires activists to take on different priorities, and for the Governments of Canada, the United States, and Mexico to engage in different economic strategies. Bobiwash states that people need to struggle *with* Indigenous peoples as allies, not on behalf of Indigenous peoples.

Tabobondung and Kahgee see the FTAA as part of a larger movement to subordinate Indigenous rights to economic globalization. *The Original Summit* roots its discussion in earlier moments of settler-Indigenous contact, emphasizing that the 2001 Quebec City summit is part of a long history of settler state claims to power over land. It calls for Indigenous peoples of the Americas to form alliances with each other, as well as with non-Indigenous people, and proposes a hemispheric unity that differs entirely from the version offered by the FTAA. Speakers express the hope that the potential of Indigenous solidarity in the Americas will be fulfilled. They are united in their aim to put individuals and the land before governments and corporations. As Bobiwash clarifies, this need is vital: "We have to unite the Americas. We have to somehow come up with a project which will tear down that wall of shame ... that separates Latin America and North America." Here, the video makes clear the need to decolonize to achieve more equitable futures. It suggests a vision for a unified North America that is altogether different from that of the fine art exhibitions put on by the three NAFTA governments. Its expansive temporal scope presents new ways of thinking through free trade.

Tacet

Tacet (Anthems of the Member Nations of the North American Free Trade Agreement: Canada, United States of America, Mexican United States) is a 2005 video by Antonia Hirsch. Like *The Original Summit,* it is not based in cultural nationalism.[60] Foregrounding the banality and endurance of national narratives under free trade, it can be read as a subtle response to cultural nationalism and to the claims for harmonious North American integration offered by the state-sponsored exhibitions. Its title makes specific reference to NAFTA, uniting Canada, the United States, and Mexico. Seizing on an emblem of national difference, it employs the anthems of the three countries to explore complex relationships under increased economic integration of the continent. As political scientist and historian Benedict Anderson says, signifiers such as flags and anthems are central to modern nationalist projects: "The internal logic of a world of nations, understood at one level as a world of fundamentally similar, co-operating and rivalrous entities, also meant that nation states were required to display, for one another, their parallel differences."[61] In *Tacet,* however, Hirsch posits a power struggle between national and transnational interests. Curator Heather Anderson notes that "the specific reference to the NAFTA alliance foregrounds our global age in which trade agreements and corporate power often supersede national policies and

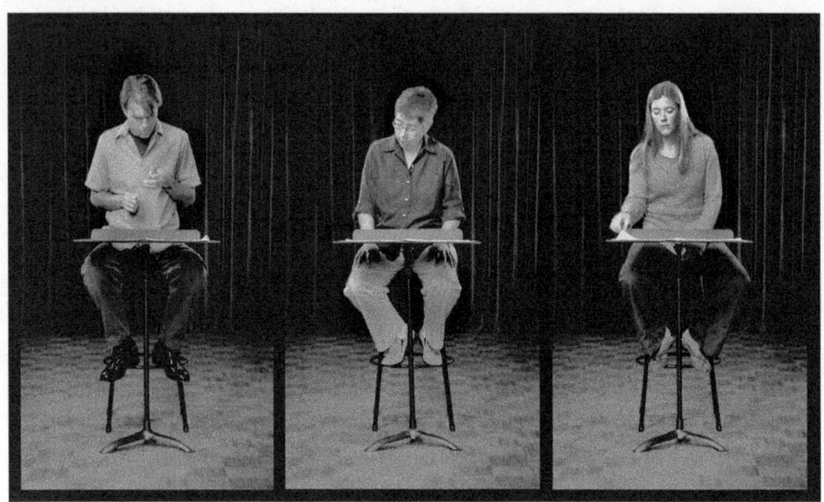

FIGURE 20 Antonia Hirsch, *Tacet (Anthems of the Member Nations of the North American Free Trade Agreement: Canada, United States of America, Mexican United States),* 2005, 3-channel HD video installation, stereo audio, dimensions variable, individual image sizes: w 97 cm x h 180 cm © Antonia Hirsch, 2005.

interests."[62] Thus, *Tacet* points to the nation-state's insecurity in the face of neoliberalism and global corporations.

Two minutes and forty-five seconds long, *Tacet* is a three-channel video installation in which three orchestra conductors silently sight-read from several pages of sheet music. Each sits alone in front of a black curtain in an identical room with a parquet floor (Figure 20). They are also similarly located within the camera frame and shot in full body portrait, as they sit on tall black stools at their music stands. The action consists solely of the conductors working their way through their musical scores, which, as the title of the video indicates, are the anthems of either Canada, Mexico, or the United States. Anderson describes the individualized nature of each person's reading process: "Each of the conductors interprets the anthem's score in a personal and physical manner, highlighting how the imagined collectivity of the nation state becomes embodied on an individual and symbolic level."[63] Our attention is wholly occupied by their embodied experience of conducting the music.

However, nothing in the video specifies which conductor is reading which anthem, as we hear no music and sound is virtually absent. The title, *Tacet,* provides a clue to this element of the work. "Tacet" is a musical term that indicates silence, a period in which an instrument or voice does not sound. Here, Hirsch references the famous 1952 conceptual work by John Cage, *4'33,*" which is entirely comprised of tacet.[64] While the conductors read their scores, the lack of music draws our attention to their gestures and movements. Hirsch explains, "When mentally conjuring the sounds of an orchestra, the readers' involuntary movements, changes in breathing, or rustle of paper, manifest their sense of the music's rhythm, volume, or a particularly dramatic moment in the score."[65] They are relatively restrained in the process of sight-reading, so movements are subtle and limited to facial expressions, a slight sway of the body to the beat of the song, or understated hand and arm gestures. From time to time, one turns a page, the crackling of paper assuming prominence due to the absence of any other sound. By structuring the work around these well-known anthems but without vocals or music, the artist asks viewers to draw on their own knowledge of the songs and their meanings. In this way, Hirsch creates a reference that plays on the ubiquity and dominance of national signifiers.

Tacet reveals the contradictions inherent in the economic unification of North America, despite a common adherence to national narratives of difference. Anderson explains that as "a symbol of each nation state, the anthems evoke these democracies' imagined collectivity and idealism."[66] However, a core contradiction lies within any nationalist project – the simultaneous but conflicting desires for authenticity and modernity. Nationalism, says Anderson, holds a "complex appeal to a vanished or imagined past and its ambitions for a limitless future."[67] Hirsch comments on the artificiality of national signifiers, because we cannot tell which anthem is which – they blend together, unified in their silence. Hirsch explains, "*Tacet* explores how the collective fiction of the nation state is individually embodied and critiques conventional models aiming to harmonize divergent voices."[68] This also brings to mind the fact that national narratives typically silence difference – and often, specific communities – within the nation-state.

Tacet raises awareness of the artificiality of national boundaries and the difficult negotiation of nationalist projects in the presumed moment of post-nationalism. Hirsch intended to comment on the idealism and democracy at the heart of the North American countries. Although nations are central to structures of liberal democracy, whether they will endure under transnational agreements such as NAFTA remains to be seen. In fact, Hirsch questions their longevity as the dominant method of global organization, also inferring that the ideals of democracy may be at risk. "Globalization has given rise to economically-driven state alliances such as NAFTA," she observes, "thereby calling into question the relevance of the nation state – together with its democratic institutions."[69] *Tacet* rebukes nationalisms and in highlighting national anthems draws attention to the banal structures of the nation-state. The uncertain unity of North America as presented in Hirsch's work brings to mind the North American projects advanced through large government-sponsored exhibitions that were discussed in Chapter 3. Ultimately, I submit that Hirsch's work underscores the complexities and ambivalence in video artists' responses to free trade.

Contemporary Artists' Engagement with Free Trade

The videos explored in this chapter exemplify the "new documentary" style and demonstrate artists' ongoing engagement with free trade. Although cultural nationalism was important initially, it was eventually displaced by other themes. This change opened up discussion of the contexts in which free trade is deployed and included videos that concentrated on large-scale protest demonstrations. Others spoke back to metaphors of settler-Indigenous relations in North America to foreground Indigenous perspectives, a development that can be seen as a first step toward the "necessarily unsettling" work of decolonization. Tuck and Yang comment that this "must involve the repatriation of land simultaneous to the recognition of how land and relations to land have always already been differently understood and enacted; that is, all of the land, and not just symbolically."[70] Of course, narratives around free trade do not follow a linear progression, as shown by *Tacet,* which subtly criticizes economic integration while revealing that nation-states still have a firm grip on our understanding of the world.

Further work remains to be done to fully capture the extent of artists' engagement with free trade, including in media beyond video. Some of this work can also be read as espousing the ethics and approach of "new documentary" in advancing social critique. For but one example, consider *State Dinner*, a 2005 installation by Halifax-based artist Peter Dykhuis, which confirms that free trade continued to weigh on the minds of artists (Figures 21 and 22). His response to the 1994 implementation of NAFTA took shape in an installation featuring a lowbrow multiple – the disposable paper plate.[71] He chose Royal Chinet plates, with their recognizable blue-and-grey floral border, as the basis for the work. Realized over a decade after NAFTA's implementation,[72] *State Dinner* comments on the complexities of mapping place through nation, region, and trade zone, emphasizing the discrete parts of the territory encompassed by the trade alliance, while inverting the pomp and circumstance typically afforded to state diplomacy.

The installation features ninety-five plates mounted on the wall and arranged in a grid. Each one sports a simple outline map of a province, territory, or state in Canada, the United States, or Mexico, carefully rendered

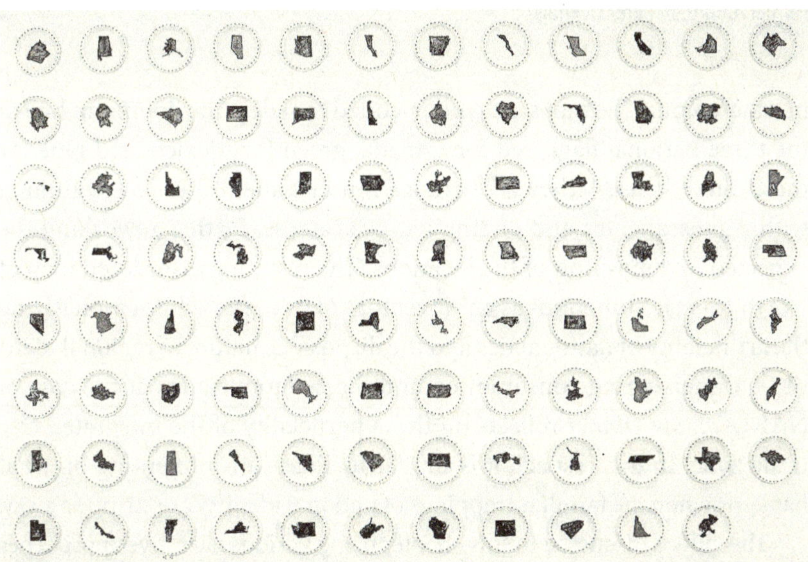

FIGURE 21 Peter Dykhuis, *State Dinner*, 2005, 114 inches x 173 inches installed, water colour on Royal Chinet paper plates. The photo shows the 2007 installation at Saint Mary's University Art Gallery, Halifax. Photograph by Steve Farmer. Courtesy Peter Dykhuis.

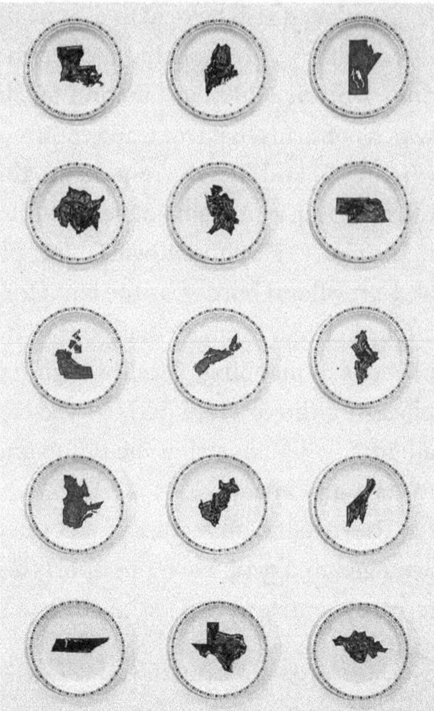

FIGURE 22 Peter Dykhuis, *State Dinner,* detail, 2005. Each plate is 10.5 inches in diameter. The photo shows the 2007 installation at Saint Mary's University Art Gallery, Halifax. Photograph by Steve Farmer. Courtesy Peter Dykhuis.

in watercolour. The maps are colour-coded to reflect the dominant hue of the three national flags; red for Canada, green for Mexico, and blue for the United States.[73] They are arranged in alphabetical order, beginning with Aguascalientes and ending with Zacatecas, further reworking the expected juxtaposition of the locations. The resulting disordered map of North America functions as an "inventory of its parts," while emphasizing the artificiality of national ties and the disposable nature of regional identity.[74] Underscoring consumption and the economic aims at the core of NAFTA, *State Dinner* reflects on the superficiality of the integrated free trade zone. In this respect, it is similar to *Tacet* in commenting on what happens when the familiar trappings of national identity are stripped away.

The videos discussed in this chapter bring various narrative approaches to bear on free trade, employing media talkback, documentary, and performance. Despite their formal and aesthetic differences, they address the complexities of the formation of North America, as established by free trade. Notably, they speak to key threads in discussions of culture and free trade – including activism and public resistance, American cultural imperialism, and new regional formations. Together, they chronicle the changing ways that Canadian activist artists grappled with North American integration throughout the period of my study, stressing key issues of neoliberal expansion. They illuminate the tensions regarding the production and protection of national culture under free trade, revealing the significant investment of many artists in these issues. The fact that such a varied body of work exists tells us a lot about the complicated relationship between culture and trade and also shows the effectiveness of video in critical exploration and dissent. Artists capitalized on video as a means to engage with ideas of identity, including national belonging and regional integration. Their work provides valuable insights into a moment when dominant understandings of Canada in relation to North America were changing.

Epilogue
Art and the Invention of North America

Free trade agreements radically reshaped the economies and public conceptions of the western hemisphere at the end of the twentieth century. A pivotal aspect of this process was the promotion of an integrated North America and positive linkages between Canada, Mexico, and the United States. Pointing to the often unacknowledged political and economic forces underpinning this narrative, literary scholar Rachel Adams sees North America as "a place that few would call home, a concept that is more the invention of politicians and economists than the product of its inhabitants' collective imagination."[1] In her view, NAFTA was a "watershed moment in the invention of North America," which signalled a "newfound continental sensibility."[2] The magnitude of this development necessitated government management to affirm the new economic and political order. "Government wants to manage these big picture realities rather than be managed by them," according to political scientist Daniel Drache.[3] Therefore, we need to read cultural initiatives – particularly those funded by the governments of the three countries – as a means of mediating identities and alliances.

Although Canada and the United States already had a close relationship prior to the free trade era, it changed with the advent of CUSFTA and NAFTA, causing considerable concern among Canadians. Closer economic integration raised the spectre of US cultural imperialism, a threat that was widely cited in the struggle against free trade and the call to support Canadian cultural products and producers. In response, governments turned to art shows to encourage mutual understanding, counter parochialism, and advance the new North America.

Canada's relationship with Mexico also changed, as that country was realigned to become part of North America. This process, according to political scientist Edgar J. Dosman, "fundamentally altered the political geography of the Western Hemisphere" and resulted in Mexico's "strategic reorientation vis-à-vis Latin America."[4] For example, from the perspective of Brazil, which vied for political and economic power during the same period, Mexico's decision to enter into NAFTA showed that "it had rejected the historic Latin American integration project initiated in 1960 with the Latin American Free Trade Agreement and had chosen instead to become part of North America, within the inner US geopolitical orbit."[5] This step resulted in the bifurcation of the western hemisphere into North and South America. Mexico's inclusion in North America, Dosman argues, meant that "'Latin America' no longer existed – in fact, the term disappeared in the official Brazilian category of regions."[6] Although it is perhaps hyperbolic to suggest that Latin America ceased to exist, Dosman's comments underscore the malleability of regional formations.

Prior to NAFTA, Canada had only a very limited relationship with Mexico, but that changed as well. The new North America necessitated stronger ties between the two countries, something that played out through art exhibitions. Notably, art associated with national myths – such as the work of Emily Carr – was employed to naturalize the connections between the three North American countries. This versatility of national signifiers is not surprising, given the historic elasticity of national myths and symbols. As curator Brian Wallis explains, "Such representations are not just reactive (that is, depictions of an existing state of being), they are also purposefully creative and they can generate new social and political formations."[7] Art possesses narrative potential, the ability to introduce, reinforce, or destabilize ideas about regional formations.

The artworks, exhibitions, and cultural initiatives examined in this book demonstrate the important role that culture played in framing, promoting, and in some cases rejecting the new North American identity. In many of the state-sponsored shows, art became a tool of governments, a means of educating citizens about geopolitical changes. By instigating and investing in exhibitions through which to gain visibility and build connections, Ottawa furthered Canada's economic and political interests. Some critics regarded this use of culture as a means of papering over conflict. Poet Rubén Martínez calls art used to foster ties between the NAFTA countries "free trade art." For Martínez, it aimed "to create a conflict-free image for a country in order to seduce investors and promote cultural tourism."[8] The trilateral online exhibition *Panoramas,* discussed in Chapter 3, exemplifies Martínez's definition. At the same time, artists who opposed free trade could use their work to express its tensions and conflict rather than trying to conceal them. Free trade was attacked in many ways, from the photograph *Free Expression* by Carole Condé + Karl Beveridge discussed in the Introduction to the video *White Dawn* by Lisa Steele and Kim Tomczak, which is examined in Chapter 6.

Thus, culture sat uneasily in the context of free trade, and this book seeks to emphasize the nuance and contradictions of its instrumentalization. Regardless of whether it promoted or condemned free trade, a paradox overhung its use: though culture was integral to the new narratives of North America, it was largely exempt from the trade agreements that made them essential. The government mobilization of culture was often overt; with the exception of 49th Parallel, which took a more furtive tone, Ottawa's use of Canadian art was no secret. Even so, audiences may not necessarily have been aware of it and may have known nothing of the circumstances of its creation, funding, or how it supported government priorities. *Trading on Art* seeks to showcase the broader use of culture by government, in contrast to its much-lauded cultural exemption that supposedly kept art "off the table."

Free trade lurked in the background of just about everything many artists did from the 1980s into the new century, dominating other issues such as censorship, copyright, and funding for the arts, which also came to the fore. The prevalence of free trade concerns can be seen not just in the work that artists made and the markets in which they sold it but also in their organizing. A case in point is the Independent Artists' Union (IAU), a visual arts labour body that was active in Ontario between 1983 and 1989 and that positioned free trade as a central issue for artists.[9] IAU newsletters and records show that though the primary aim was to advocate

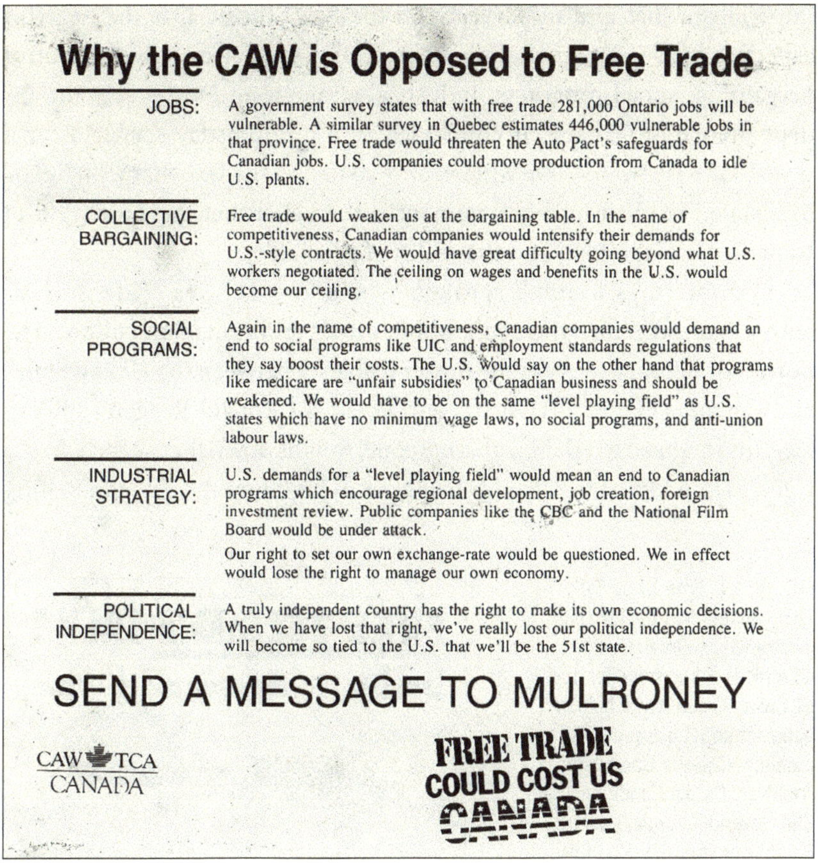

Why the CAW is Opposed to Free Trade

JOBS: A government survey states that with free trade 281,000 Ontario jobs will be vulnerable. A similar survey in Quebec estimates 446,000 vulnerable jobs in that province. Free trade would threaten the Auto Pact's safeguards for Canadian jobs. U.S. companies could move production from Canada to idle U.S. plants.

COLLECTIVE BARGAINING: Free trade would weaken us at the bargaining table. In the name of competitiveness, Canadian companies would intensify their demands for U.S.-style contracts. We would have great difficulty going beyond what U.S. workers negotiated. The ceiling on wages and benefits in the U.S. would become our ceiling.

SOCIAL PROGRAMS: Again in the name of competitiveness, Canadian companies would demand an end to social programs like UIC and employment standards regulations that they say boost their costs. The U.S. would say on the other hand that programs like medicare are "unfair subsidies" to Canadian business and should be weakened. We would have to be on the same "level playing field" as U.S. states which have no minimum wage laws, no social programs, and anti-union labour laws.

INDUSTRIAL STRATEGY: U.S. demands for a "level playing field" would mean an end to Canadian programs which encourage regional development, job creation, foreign investment review. Public companies like the CBC and the National Film Board would be under attack.

Our right to set our own exchange-rate would be questioned. We in effect would lose the right to manage our own economy.

POLITICAL INDEPENDENCE: A truly independent country has the right to make its own economic decisions. When we have lost that right, we've really lost our political independence. We will become so tied to the U.S. that we'll be the 51st state.

SEND A MESSAGE TO MULRONEY

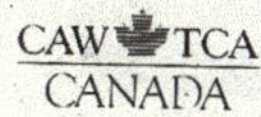

FREE TRADE COULD COST US CANADA

FIGURE 23 Canadian Auto Workers ad in the Independent Artists' Union newsletter. Queen's University Archives, Carole Condé and Karl Beveridge fonds, Layout IAU/CAR TO, 1988, layout page.

for improvements in artists' material conditions, such as through the "living wage," free trade was a constant concern in various dimensions of the union's work.

At a granular level, it was literally on the agenda at union meetings – notes from an August 1986 meeting detail the need to "get our arts off the free trade table."[10] The IAU newsletter reveals the union's links to organized labour. For instance, the Canadian Auto Workers (CAW) placed an ad in its pages, advocating against CUSFTA with the frank title "Why the CAW Is Opposed to Free Trade" (Figure 23). Echoing the fear of US cultural imperialism that was so pervasive at the time, the ad lists the negative aspects of CUSFTA, including its potential impact on jobs, collective bargaining, social programs, industrial strategy, and ultimately the independence of Canada. It concludes with a doomsday scenario for a post-CUSFTA world: "We will become so tied to the U.S. that we'll be the 51st state." Explicit in this statement is the belief that the extinction of Canada itself is not beyond the realm of possibility.

IAU meetings featured speakers who addressed free trade, such as author Susan Crean, who spoke about artists and Canadian culture. The poster for her talk conveys the power disparity between the United States and Canada (Figure 24). At the left, President Ronald Reagan's smiling face, his forehead overlaid with a barcode, weighs down the balance. At the right, Prime Minister Brian Mulroney rises high into the air, a drenching

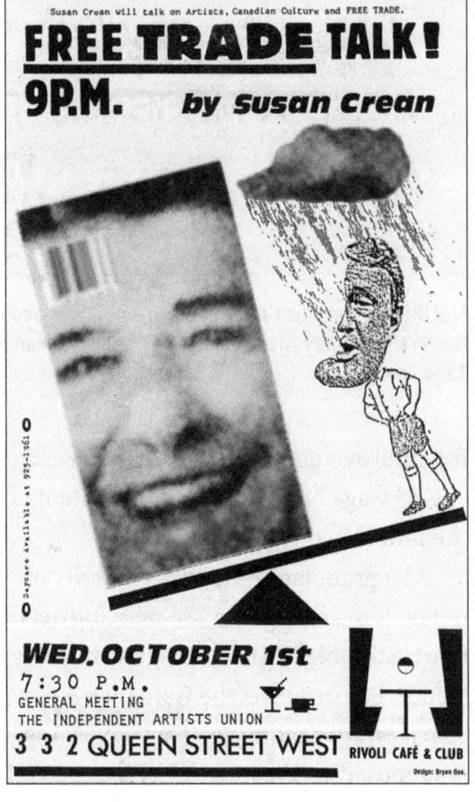

FIGURE 24 *Free Trade Talk!* This undated IAU poster and illustration by Bryan Gee advertises a free trade lecture by Susan Crean, to be held in conjunction with a general meeting. Queen's University Archives, Carole Condé and Karl Beveridge fonds, Posters, Pamphlets (Archives), 1965–2010, F2665. Courtesy Queen's University Archives/Bryan Gee.

shower of acid rain (a hot-button topic at the time) emphasizing his perceived disadvantage in negotiations. This common trope – that the all-powerful United States would push for, and inevitably acquire, a trade agreement to suit itself and to disadvantage Canada – also appeared in the video art covered in Chapter 6.

Similar rhetoric is found in other IAU publications. One simple black-and-white flyer that promoted a living wage for artists stated, "No clearer example exists to demonstrate our mutual concerns than the specter of free trade. Free trade sheds a clear light on the fact that a healthy economy and a healthy culture are dependent on one another. The Canada we know, and the Canada we desire to create, depends on our solidarity."[11] A pamphlet conveyed much the same message: "With the advent of serious Free Trade negotiations, Canadians have become increasingly aware of the vital importance of creating and maintaining a strong culture."[12] And a drawing by IAU member Scott Marsden depicted Canadian culture wrung into a US media machine (Figure 25).[13]

In its campaign to improve artists' material conditions, the IAU built broad alliances and developed connections within and outside of the cultural sector, engaging with various community groups and political leaders. Free trade was highly contested at the time, and IAU anxieties about cultural sovereignty paralleled discussions in the realm of politics. For example, NDP MP Lynn McDonald warned in October 1985 that "those responsible for free trade bargaining have demonstrated no real commitment to the cultural sector ... I am very concerned that any cultural autonomy we have developed may be seriously compromised during these negotiations."[14] A public forum on free trade and the arts was held in Toronto in November 1985.[15] Documentation of the event highlighted the anti-free-trade rhetoric that characterized it:

> Those attending the meeting came away knowing that Free Trade poses a great threat to Canadians. Canadians risk losing control over our own media, our production resources, our distribution networks for books and films. The events and experiences that cement us as a nation will be replaced by those of a continental culture. Canadianism would be a regional variant of a North American (read U.S.) culture.[16]

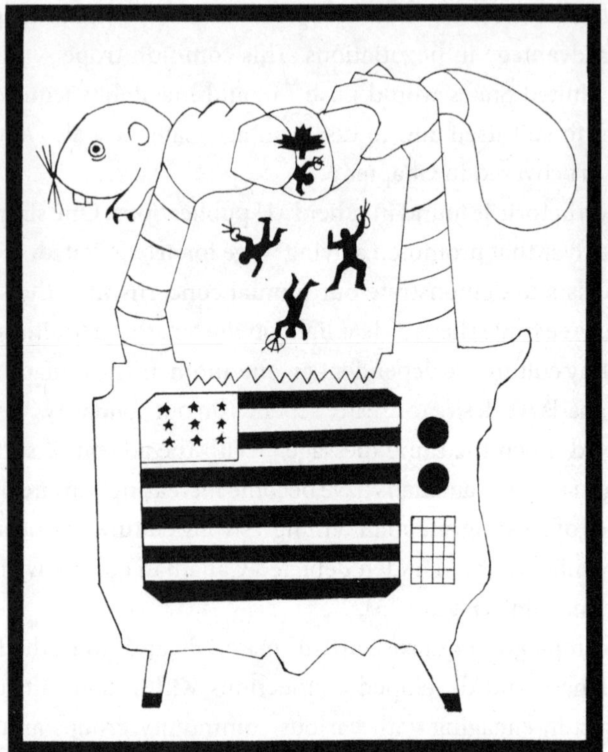

FIGURE 25 This untitled 1988 drawing by Scott Marsden appeared in an IAU pamphlet titled *Adopt an Artist?* Anti-Free Trade Project, Artist Union. Queen's University Archives, Carole Condé and Karl Beveridge fonds, New Members – Info Package, *Adopt an Artist?* undated pamphlet. Courtesy Queen's University Archives/ Scott Marsden.

Here, the creation of a North American identity was nothing more than camouflage for US cultural dominance.

In 1986, artist and IAU member Clive Robertson spoke in Vancouver at a conference on artists' living conditions. He prophesied the demise of Canada's cultural industries, which he contended would lead to artists becoming the remaining "protectors of cultural sovereignty."[17] In a letter to the *Ottawa Citizen*, IAU representative Jim Miller argued for the role of artists in maintaining Canadian culture. Echoing Robertson's prediction that artists would be the last bulwark against the tide of US culture and were thus in need of government support, Miller suggested that Canadian culture was under threat due to free trade and that "the well-being of Canadian culture is crucially important to the continued health of our country."[18] Here, the union positioned artists as a core component of Canadian national distinctiveness and presented culture as a valuable resource for the nation.

The IAU struggled against free trade on multiple fronts, pointing out that the issue was a crucial one and thus of concern to artists, that opposing it could be a means of encouraging support for Canadian artists, and that combining with other unions and coalitions could help the IAU to forge broader networks of support.[19] To further its ends, the IAU joined with the provincial Coalition Against Free Trade (CAFT), which included other cultural organizations such as ACTRA and the Playwrights Union.[20] Through this association, IAU members contributed to public demonstrations, such as the "Free Trade's No Picnic" event staged by the CAFT in Toronto on 28 June 1987.[21] As well as urging its members to attend, the IAU contributed "visually to the picnic spectacle."[22] Other IAU locals expressed their opposition to free trade. In tandem with CAW Local 199, the Niagara IAU local joined the Canadian Labour Congress campaign, offering "visual and written material about the union," and its members marched on City Hall with NDP MP Marion Dewar.[23]

When Toronto held its Labour Day Parade in 1986, the IAU seized the opportunity to educate the public (Figure 26). Its members joined the procession, bearing signs that promoted Canadian culture and discouraged free trade. The IAU newsletter reported on the union's float: "In the parade we all performed an agit-prop performance consisting of a Brian Mulroney dressed as a used-car salesperson and a magic Free Trade table. He performed a disappearing act by making Canadian cultural icons disappear under an American flag into the free trade table's depths."[24] The IAU engagement with free trade demonstrates the degree to which the issue had permeated public consciousness and that it was a rallying point for artists, who took on the role of activists, moving beyond the production of artworks.

Beyond assessing policy, then, we need to understand the larger changes brought about by free trade and how cultural production mediated

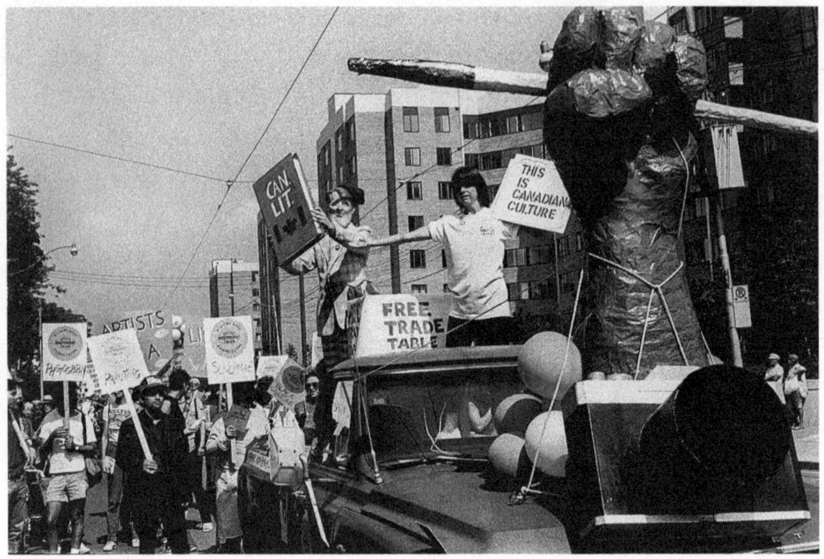

FIGURE 26 IAU free trade performance at Toronto's Labour Day Parade, 1986. Wearing a plaid suit, an activist dressed as Brian Mulroney lifts a book labelled "Can. Lit." above the Free Trade table. Photograph by Vid Ingelevics. Queen's University Archives, Carole Condé and Karl Beveridge fonds, IAU Photos, Untitled (Labour Day parade).

these changes, both positively and negatively. In this book, I have shown that many artists critically examined topics of trade liberalization. Although the videos discussed in Chapter 6 did not necessarily have as wide an audience as the state-sponsored exhibitions, they were nevertheless an equally important component of the negotiation of identities that took place in Canadian and North American society during the free trade era. Similarly, artists at the inSite festival played a role in critically examining issues at the border and, through their artwork, in presenting these issues to public audiences. My examination of state-sponsored arts initiatives in Chapters 1, 2, 3, and 4 speaks to the need to critically examine the evolution and transformation of national representations under globalization. Free trade was never *only* about trade, and exhibitions were never *only* about policy. Free trade reached into all aspects of social and cultural life.

In the late twentieth century, the process of integrating North America seemed unrelenting and inescapable. This was intentional, led by governments that wished to highlight a cohesive culture across the continent in support of new trading relationships, a trend that continued with attempts to create a hemispheric free trade zone under the FTAA. The negotiations were highly contested, as the civil society demonstrations against globalization make clear. Following events such as 9/11 and the failure of the FTAA negotiations, a push against integration began in government policy. The realities of the twenty-first century reveal that North American integration was a moment in time rather than an inevitable trajectory, as governments turned back toward the barriers that separate countries. "If, in the 1990s, the contour of North America was organized around a grand commercial project driven by neo-liberal deregulation and deep market access," states Drache, "in this new century, security and immigration have overtaken the once seemingly unstoppable dynamic of NAFTA as the driver of the North American community."[25] Thus, the rhetoric of community and collaboration that typified the rise of free trade was time-specific rather than ongoing.

In 2006, the Canadian government flagged its disinclination to pursue further integration of the Americas by cutting funding to the Canadian Foundation for the Americas (FOCAL). The sole Canadian think-tank that was dedicated to promoting the country's interests in the Americas, FOCAL had made significant contributions to furthering Canadian trade in the region and to shaping government policy. It was established by an act of Cabinet in 1990, and its goal was to "enhance co-operation and dialogue, create new linkages, and strengthen existing ties between countries of the hemisphere through policy analysis and discussion."[26] After Stephen Harper's Conservative government cut its funding in 2006, FOCAL persevered despite its severe financial limitations and decreasing support, but on 14 June 2011 it announced that it would cease operation by the end of September and would transfer its ongoing research projects and archives to other institutions.[27]

A further blow to hemispheric initiatives came on 15 June 2013, when Harper shuffled his Cabinet and did away with the dedicated minister of state for the Americas, transferring the responsibility to the foreign affairs minister. Justifying this move, political scientist Jean Daudelin argued that Ottawa was no longer interested in the Americas: the "government considers its agenda in the Americas ... basically complete. The core of their agenda was the trade file, and we've signed agreements with basically all the countries that are basically interested."[28] Although the government continued to claim that Latin America and the Caribbean were still a priority, it was obvious that less time and effort would be expended on both. Carlo Dade, former FOCAL executive director, maintained that Ottawa was now more interested in new trade opportunities in regions such as Southeast Asia.[29] Although Canada did make small bilateral trade deals, such as with Colombia in 2008 (implemented 2011), they were accompanied by much less fanfare. By no means did free trade disappear, but it became more focused on trade and less on the social and cultural contexts of globalization. Or, to put it another way, it became naturalized and inevitable, even if the culture around it did not.

Cultural diplomacy also waned under the Harper Conservatives. In 2008, as noted earlier, the government eliminated Trade Routes (run by the Department of Canadian Heritage) and PromArt (a program of the Department of Foreign Affairs and International Trade), showing that it no longer saw cultural diplomacy as a priority.[30] With $9.0 and $4.7 million budgets, respectively, the two programs had allowed the Canadian government to support the circulation of Canadian culture abroad, and arts groups across the country loudly protested their demise.[31] Dade tied this shift to the climate of austerity that followed the financial crisis of 2008. Due to funding shortages, he wrote in 2011, "any government would be cutting cultural diplomacy."[32] He also stated that the public approved of the cuts: "The only thing lower down the list than public diplomacy for this government is cultural diplomacy and in that they've captured the mood of the majority of Canadians."[33] Other factors contributed to the abandonment of continental integration, such as US concerns around immigration, vocal opposition to NAFTA under the Trump administration, and ongoing "buy American" policies.

Cultural diplomacy did not reappear on the government agenda until 2017, following the election of the Trudeau Liberals. In that year, the Standing Senate Committee on Foreign Affairs and International Trade undertook a study of the utilization and impact of Canadian culture and arts in foreign policy and diplomacy. This was a landmark study because, though cultural diplomacy had been identified as the "third pillar" of Canadian foreign policy, by the Chrétien government in 1995, it had received inconsistent government attention over the ensuing two decades. In 2019, the Senate committee released its report, *Cultural Diplomacy at the Front Stage of Canada's Foreign Policy,* which recommended that the government should develop a comprehensive cultural diplomacy strategy and cited the need to establish a robust policy framework to manage the roles and responsibilities of the multiple players and agencies involved.[34] Notably, the report boldly called for cultural diplomacy to serve a more prominent role in effecting foreign policy. Yet, at the time of writing, how the government will take up these recommendations remains unclear.

NAFTA, of course, made a dramatic reappearance in public consciousness when it became a campaign issue for Donald Trump in 2016. Once elected, Trump oversaw its revision into a new agreement that was implemented in 2020, which in Canada is referred to as the Canada-United States-Mexico Agreement, or CUSMA.[35] In the United States, it is known as the United States-Mexico-Canada Agreement, or USMCA, and in Mexico as the Tratado entre México, Estados Unidos y Canadá, or T-MEC. Tellingly, "North American" has been removed from its title, and relations between the three parties have been rebalanced back to the national. The deal is focused on trade; the ancillary activities around NAFTA – the creation and promotion of a North American imaginary – are a thing of the past.

The development of CUSMA falls outside the scope of this book because the deal was not accompanied by extensive cultural programming and did not spark broad public protest. There are many potential reasons for this. For one, North America had already been reconfigured in the 1990s, and art was no longer needed to make sense of the changes imposed by free trade. However, it is difficult to talk about the free trade era in absolute terms of success or failure. On the one hand, this book has demonstrated the prominence of narratives of the new North America and the widespread rhetoric that advanced cultural nationalism. On the other hand, both were very much rooted in their time and do not appear to have been lasting. Given the 2020 advent of CUSMA, it seems obvious that the image of an integrated North America gradually faded to insignificance as the years wore on.

As three decades have elapsed since the 1994 implementation of NAFTA, it seems an opportune moment to reflect on the swift and sweeping reorganization of North America under free trade and the fluctuations in the process of continental integration that occurred between 1989 and the first decade of the 2000s. Art and art shows offer great insight into the developments that gripped the continent at the time. They enable a critical assessment of the messages about geopolitical changes and offer up counternarratives that engage with and can directly affect how we continue to structure our world. Ultimately, though the free trade deals brought about an enduring economic restructuring, the use of art and culture in the service of neoliberalism could not achieve the same result for the continental mindset.

Notes

Introduction

1 Numerous other independent Canadian publications are visible, including *OWL, Canadian Dimension, This Magazine, Our Times,* and *Briarpatch*, among others.

2 For two exceptions, see Fox, *The Fence and the River;* and Carroll, *REMEX*. Examining the situation outside of North America, scholars have tackled art and trade more broadly, addressing free ports, for instance. See Steyerl, *Duty Free Art;* and Wakefield, "Arts and the Super-Rich," 167–86. More recently, curatorial projects in Canada have engaged with art and trade, notably *Trans-Pacific Transmissions: Video Art across the Pacific.* Curated by Haema Sivanesan at the Art Gallery of Greater Victoria in 2016, it addressed video art and the Trans-Pacific Partnership.

3 The constructed division between Anglo and Latin America is vital to the history of how the Americas have been conceptualized. It has also shaped scholarly production. Citing Walter Mignolo, scholar Ricardo D. Salvatore argues that "the 'idea of Latin America' is a construct with a protracted formative period, an accumulated excess of representation that has domesticated, through over-simplification, the radical diversity of its subject matter." This comment is made within Salvatore's larger discussion of the intellectual history of Latin America, during which he calls for a "Critical Hemispherism" in American studies to address US hegemony in knowledge production on Latin America. Salvatore underscores that hemispheric studies must foreground a critical agenda that is "inclusive of all the Americas and ... critical of the boundaries, foundations, and historical presuppositions of earlier programs of hemispheric knowledge." See Salvatore, "On Knowledge Asymmetries," 365, 383. For further discussion of hemispheric American studies, see Sadowski-Smith and Fox, "Theorizing the Hemisphere," 5–38; and Levander and Levine, *Hemispheric American Studies.*

4 Heidrich and Macdonald, "Introduction," 4.

5 Gutiérrez Haces, "Mexico-Canada Relations," 197; McKercher, "Locating Latin America," 42.

6 Poitras, *Inventing North America.*

7 "The Canada-U.S. Free Trade Agreement."

8 As I discuss in Chapter 3, scholars have noted the Canadian state's equivocal relationship with Mexico, characterizing its engagement as "half-hearted" and stressing the centrality of the United States to the continent's dynamics (Heidrich and Macdonald, "Introduction," 4). Other work emphasizes Mexico's changing place in the western hemisphere, noting this has to do with tensions between the state's connections to North America and Latin America. See Ochoa Bilbao and Schiavon, "Is Mexico a North American?," 113.

9 Anderson follows Ernest Gellner, who argues that nationalism "*invents* nations where they do not exist." Benedict Anderson, *Imagined Communities,* 6 (emphasis in original).

10 Goff, "Canada's Cultural Exemption," 563. For an overview of the cultural exemption and cultural policy implications of the free trade agreements, including CUSFTA and NAFTA, see Gagné, "The Evolution," 298–312; Dymond and Hart, "Abundant Paradox," 15–33; Neathery-Castro, "Canada as Multilateral Player," 76–91; and Mulcahy, "Cultural Imperialism," 181–206. Gagné also discusses Quebec's cultural identity in relation to the exemption and continental integration. See his "L'identité québécoise et l'intégration continentale," 45–68.

11 Government of Canada, "The Canada-US Free Trade Agreement," 292. Note that article 2005 details four "limited exceptions" – tariffs on inputs and products of cultural industries, sales of foreign-owned enterprises involved in cultural activities, copyright on broadcasts by distant stations and retransmissions, and advertising in magazines or newspapers.

12 The framework was introduced in North American Cultural Diplomacy Initiative, "Cultural Diplomacy and Trade."

13 A great deal of scholarship assesses the complexity of definitions of culture, including prominent contributions by Williams, "The Analysis of Culture," 48–56.

14 Goff, *Limits to Liberalization,* 18.

15 Goff, *Limits to Liberalization,* 18.

16 UNESCO, "The Convention on the Protection and Promotion of the Diversity of Cultural Expressions," n.d. (emphasis added), https://webarchive.unesco.org/20230614143248/http://en.unesco.org/creativity/convention. The convention enshrines the right of states to implement policies to protect cultural products domestically and internationally.

17 Goff, "NAFTA 2.0," 566.

18 Goff, "Canada's Cultural Exemption," 553.

19 Goff, "Canada's Cultural Exemption," 563.

20 Goff, "Canada's Cultural Exemption," 564.
21 Goff, "Canada's Cultural Exemption," 564.
22 Goff, "Trade and Culture," 547. Goff's article is part of a special issue addressing the topic of culture and trade.
23 I do not address the reception of exhibitions or how museums would have evaluated them. Instead, I concentrate on their structure and organization, the curatorial arguments they advanced, as well as the promotional campaigns that helped to distill their messages for broad publics. I also chart how exhibitions can become prominent meeting grounds for establishing and deepening international relationships.
24 Carole Condé + Karl Beveridge, "Shutdown (1991)," https://condebeveridge.ca/project/shutdown-1991/. The artists photographed the Inglis appliance factory in Toronto, which had recently closed.
25 The naturalization of this economic zone resulted in rhetoric that attests to the close relationship between Canada and Mexico, such that a 2017 Senate of Canada report utilizes the language of neighbours to refer to the North American states and mentions a "North American neighbourhood." Canada, Standing Senate Committee on Foreign Affairs and International Trade, "North American Neighbours."
26 In 1965, the Canada-U.S. Automotive Products Agreement, known as the Auto Pact, established a North American market for vehicles and parts. Thus, the Auto Pact created an integrated market in North America that significantly assisted the Canadian automotive industry. See Globerman and Storer, "Canada-U.S. Free Trade," 423–52.
27 Orme, *Understanding NAFTA*, xiii, 313.
28 Crean, Edwards, and Hebb, "Intellectual Property."
29 Galperin, "Cultural Industries."
30 Kirsty Robertson, "Crude Culture," 18.
31 Serra was the lead negotiator for Mexico during the NAFTA talks in the 1990s.
32 Quoted in García Canclini, "North Americans or Latin Americans?," 143.
33 Launched at the Metropolitan Museum of Art in 1990, *Mexico: Splendors of Thirty Centuries* relocated to the San Antonio Museum of Art in 1991 and closed at the Los Angeles County Museum of Art the same year. It was accompanied by a significant and extensive publication with a foreword written by Mexican poet and Nobel laureate Octavio Paz. See *Mexico: Splendors of Thirty Centuries.*
34 Three significant dates relate to the establishment of the Mexican nation-state: the beginning of the War of Independence on 16 September 1810; the signing of the Act of Independence on 28 September 1821; and the promulgation of the First Federal Constitution of Mexico on 4 October 1824. I cite 1810 because it is widely referenced by the government and population of Mexico and 16 September is the date on which the Mexican state officially commemorates its independence.
35 Wallis, "Selling Nations," 279.

36 The alter-globalization debates were inextricably linked to free trade. I employ the term "alter-globalization" because it more accurately reflects the aims of these protesters than the label "anti-globalization." Those who participated in the movement were not entirely against globalization; instead, they united to argue for a different form of it. See J. Keri Cronin and Kirsty Robertson, "Imagining Resistance: An Introduction," in *Imagining Resistance: Visual Culture and Activism in Canada,* ed. J. Keri Cronin and Kirsty Robertson (Waterloo: Wilfrid Laurier University Press, 2011), 17, 21.

37 Konrad and Nicol, *Beyond Walls,* xiii.

38 NAFTA was a campaign issue for Donald Trump in 2016, who even stated that he would scrap it if elected. As president, however, he opened negotiations with Canada and Mexico in 2017. Other developments in the changing landscape of Canadian free trade include renewed interest in the Trans-Pacific Partnership (referred to as TPP-11), which moved ahead without the participation of the United States and became the Comprehensive and Progressive Agreement for Trans-Pacific Partnership.

39 This agreement went into force in 2020.

40 A fractious North America is exacerbated by struggles at its borders – both the highly fortified Mexico-US border and relatively recently, the Canada-US border, which is experiencing an influx of asylum seekers from the United States. In the summer of 2017, an unprecedented number of them, predominately Haitians, began crossing from New York into Quebec.

41 Catharine Tunney, "No NAFTA without Cultural Exemption and a Dispute Settlement Clause, Trudeau Vows," *CBC News,* 4 September 2018, https://www.cbc.ca/news/politics/trudeau-cultural-exemption-1.4806919.

42 Goff addresses the uncertainty surrounding NAFTA's cultural exemption in the renegotiation process that resulted in CUSMA. See Goff, "NAFTA 2.0," 563–71.

43 See Janyce McGregor, "Canada to Apply USMCA Cultural Exemption to Trade in Digital Media," *CBC News,* 17 October 2018, https://www.cbc.ca/news/politics/usmca-nafta-cultural-exemption-1.4865113.

Chapter 1: Mexican Art in Canada

1 Clifford, "Introduction," 8.

2 Springer, "Birds of a Feather," 32.

3 Armony, "Latin American Communities," 7.

4 In the last decade, the Universities Art Association of Canada annual conference has made a concerted effort to include Latin American art. Recent scholarship addressing the Canadian dimensions of Latin American art includes Argonza, *Vues transversales;* Robin and Suescun Pozas, *Latin America Made in Canada;* and Hernandez and Robin, "Introduction to the Dialogues on Latin American Art(ists) from/in Canada: Expanding Narratives, Territories, and Perspectives," 75–79.

5 Robin, "Mapping the Presence," 36.

6 Robin, "Mapping the Presence," 47. The author also argues for the presence of Latin American art in Canada and reflects on her experiences teaching Latin American visual culture in Robin, "Colores de Latinoamérica."

7 The Department of External Affairs was renamed the Department of Foreign Affairs and International Trade in 1995. In 2013, it merged with the Canadian International Development Agency and became the Department of Foreign Affairs, Trade and Development. Its current name, Global Affairs Canada, dates from 2015. In this book, I employ the period-appropriate name for the department.

8 In the mid-twentieth century, the NGC was a federal institution under the jurisdiction of the Department of Citizenship and Immigration. In 1990, it was established as an arm's-length Crown corporation. The government wanted to employ art to engage with countries of strategic interest, but the NGC had different priorities, seeking to circulate Canadian art to centres of artistic excellence. As a result, the gallery and the government had a close but sometimes contentious relationship. Complicating matters was the gallery's changing formal link with government over the twentieth century. For a discussion of how these dynamics played out in Canada's relationship with Brazil, see Robertson et al., "'More a Diplomatic,'" 60–88.

9 For but one example, we can look to historic connections between Canadian and Mexican artists, such as those fostered by Leonard and Reva Brooks in San Miguel de Allende, Mexico. See Virtue, *Leonard and Reva Brooks.*

10 This book does not consider exhibitions of Mexican art that were offered by Canadian commercial galleries, regional museums, or artist-run centres. Nonetheless, a few commercial shows did come to the fore, providing avenues for future scholarship. Compared to those of the NGC, they may have been more consumer-friendly and oriented toward a broader public, as some were held in retail spaces rather than in museums. One series of shows, sponsored by an airline, had notable links to tourism and travel. The exhibitions include a 1948 example described as "a small show of Mexican paintings," which was presented at Eaton's department store on College Street in Toronto. In 1953, an untitled show of works by José Clemente Orozco was displayed in Toronto (institution unknown). In 1956, Canadian Pacific Air Lines circulated an untitled exhibition of Mexican paintings among Hudson's Bay department stores across Canada. See H.O. McCurry to Howard Gamble, 8 January 1954, National Gallery of Canada Archives (NGCA), Correspondence, Exhibitions – Mexican Art Ex. (Proposed), 1948–1954; G.W.G. McConachie to Donald W. Buchanan, 13 June 1956, NGCA, Correspondence, Exhibitions – Mexican Art Ex. (Proposed), 1948–1954.

11 For an in-depth assessment, see Smith, "Exhibiting Mexican Art," 67–84.

12 The three painters were engaged by the Mexican government (under José Vasconcelos) in the 1920s to promote the Mexican Revolution, leading to the country's celebrated muralism. Rankin, "A Revolutionary Mural," 104.

13 "Insight into Mexican Life Is Afforded by Art Exhibit," *Ottawa Journal,* 17 July 1943, NGCA, National Gallery of Canada fonds, Clippings, Exhibitions – Mexican Art Today, 1943.

14 Cooper, Heine, and Thakur, "Introduction," 22.

15 These included, for instance, the major show *Mexican Arts,* a survey of 1,200 objects curated by René d'Harnoncourt (later the director of the Museum of Modern Art, New York), which was circulated from 1930 to 1932 by the American Federation of the Arts. See Indych-López, *Muralism without Walls.*

16 The NGC records do not mention Amor's involvement but rather emphasize the role of the Mexican state, specifically that of the Dirección General de Educación Extraescolar y Estética. For a discussion of Clifford and Amor's relationship and work on the first installation of the show in Philadelphia, see Kaplan, "Mexican Art Today," 264–88.

17 H.O. McCurry to A.S. Grigsby, 10 September 1943, NGCA, Exhibitions – Mexican Art Today, file 2; John Grierson to H.O. McCurry, 20 May 1943, NGCA, Exhibitions – Mexican Art Today, file 1.

18 "Sees Opening of Mexican Exhibit Education for Both Countries," *Montreal Gazette,* 10 September 1943, NGCA, Clippings, Exhibitions – Mexican Art Today, 1943.

19 J.F.C. Wright, "Mexican Art on Exhibition at Gallery Starting July 22," *Ottawa Citizen,* 17 July 1943, NGCA, Clippings, Exhibitions – Mexican Art Today, 1943.

20 "Color in Mexican Works Is Magnificently Vital," *Telegram* (Toronto), 16 October 1943, NGCA, Clippings, Exhibitions – Mexican Art Today, 1943.

21 "Mexico's Consul-General Opens Fine Art Display," *Ottawa Citizen,* 23 July 1943, NGCA, Clippings, Exhibitions – Mexican Art Today, 1943; "To Open Exhibition Tonight of Mexican Art at Gallery," *Ottawa Citizen,* 22 July 1943, NGCA, Clippings, Exhibitions – Mexican Art Today, 1943.

22 "Many See Exhibit of Mexican Art," *Ottawa Journal,* 23 July 1943, NGCA, Clippings, Exhibitions – Mexican Art Today, 1943.

23 "Address Given by Sr. C.A. Calderón, Consul-General of Mexico in Canada, upon the Opening of the Exhibition of 'Mexican Art TO-day' in the National Gallery of Canada, Ottawa on July 22nd 1943," NGCA, Exhibitions – Mexican Art Today, 1943, file 1.

24 Wright, "Mexican Art on Exhibition."

25 McKercher, "Locating Latin America," 30.

26 "To Open Exhibition Tonight."

27 "To Open Exhibition Tonight."

28 H.O. McCurry to Martin Baldwin, 19 August 1952, NGCA, Exhibitions – Mexican Art Ex. (Proposed), 1948–1954; Fernando Gamboa to Arthur Blanchette, 28 September 1951, NGCA, Correspondence, 1948–1954, Exhibitions – Mexican Art Ex. (Proposed).

29 I thank Adriana Ortega Orozco for bringing this touring exhibition to my attention.
30 Davis, "The Wembley Controversy," 68. As Davis points out, control over the selections of Canadian art circulated to Wembley was the subject of a dispute between the Royal Canadian Academy and the NGC. For information on the gallery's efforts to advance Canadian art internationally in concert with the Canadian ministry of foreign affairs, see Brison and Jessup, "*Terre Sauvage*," 495–535. The authors explain that the Wembley exhibition was the NGC's "curatorial debut on the international stage" and one in which the gallery advanced its "interpretive role in the collection and management of the country's art" (523).
31 In 1951, NGC director H.O. McCurry described Mexico's lack of interest in Canadian art: "The proposed exchange of exhibitions between Canada and Mexico has been under discussion ever since I was there in 1947 and we never seem to get any further, largely I think because the Mexicans are not specially interested in exchanging exhibitions with us, although they did assure me that it was one of their most cherished hopes." By 1954 McCurry decided to cease attempts to secure this exchange or even a show of Mexican art. H.O. McCurry to A.F. Key, 13 August 1951; H.O. McCurry to Paul Malone, 15 February 1954, both in NGCA, Correspondence, 1948–1954, Exhibitions – Mexican Art Ex. (Proposed).
32 Pearl McCarthy, "Mexican Painting Coming to City," *Globe and Mail,* 2 October 1943, NGCA, Clippings, Exhibitions – Mexican Art Today, 1943.
33 McCarthy, "Mexican Painting Coming."
34 Similar rhetoric around Mexican art occurred in the United States and other international locations in this period.
35 "Mexican Films to Be Shown," *Star* (Montreal), 14 September 1943, NGCA, Clippings, Exhibitions – Mexican Art Today, 1943.
36 "Mexican Art Will Be Shown," *Star* (Montreal), 9 September 1943, NGCA, Clippings, Exhibitions – Mexican Art Today, 1943.
37 "Mexican Art Will Be Shown."
38 These coincided with developing state relationships. In 1959, Mexican president Adolfo López Mateos made an official visit to Canada, where he met Prime Minister John Diefenbaker in Ottawa. As Jason Gregory Zorbas notes, this was Mateos's first state visit, an indication of the Mexican government's significant interest in connecting with Canada. Zorbas, "Diefenbaker, Latin America and the Caribbean," 98.
39 Miguel Salas Anzures to Donald W. Buchanan, 15 February 1960, NGCA, Exhibitions – Mexican Exchange Exhibition (Mexico to Canada), vol. 1; Jacques Asselin to Salas Anzures, 7 January 1960, NGCA, Exhibitions – Mexican Exchange Exhibition (Mexico to Canada), vol. 1.
40 "Remarks by the Minister, the Hon. Ellen Fairclough," 6 January 1961, NGCA, Exhibitions – Mexican Exchange Exhibition (Mexico to Canada), vol. 3; Charles F.

Comfort to Ellen Fairclough, 22 December 1960, NGCA, Exhibitions – Mexican Exchange Exhibition (Mexico to Canada), vol. 3.

41 "Preface," n.p.

42 In 1967, Canada used the anniversary of Confederation to position itself internationally, especially via Montreal's Expo 67. Notably, Fernando Gamboa, a key figure who organized numerous displays of Mexican culture abroad, including Mexico's pavilion in Venice in 1950, was also involved in coordinating the Mexican pavilion at Expo 67, which featured, among other things, a mural by Rufino Tamayo.

43 "Preface," n.p.

44 *Cartographies* was curated by Ivo Mesquita and organized by the Winnipeg Art Gallery (WAG). The impetus for this show is unknown. Nonetheless, it is clear that the WAG played an essential role in introducing Latin American art to Canada during the late 1980s and early 1990s. This occurred through its Curator in Residence program, a significant effort to engage with and present Latin American art that notably drew on Latin American expertise. Mesquita was the first curator to participate in the program, taking up residence at the WAG in 1988. His work at the gallery resulted in *Cartographies,* which toured five venues internationally between 1993 and 1995. Despite its success, the WAG's efforts to promote Latin American art were not sustained beyond the late 1990s. Areas for future research include determining whether its interest in Latin American art was connected to patterns of migration from Latin America.

45 Théberge and Cogeval, "Foreword," 7.

46 Randall and Konrad, "Introduction," 7.

47 Chasteen, *Born in Flood and Fire,* 221.

48 Paul Gessell, "Kahlo Gets Star Billing at Mexican Art Show," *Ottawa Citizen,* 5 November 1999, NGCA, Montreal Museum of Fine Arts, Exhibitions – Mexican Modern Art, 1998, vol. 2.

49 Paul Gessell, "Trading Paintings: Canada and Mexico Exhibit Exchange Includes Top Paintings of 20th Century," *Ottawa Citizen,* 22 May 1999, NGCA, Montreal Museum of Fine Arts, Exhibitions – Mexican Modern Art, 1998, vol. 2.

50 Lozano, "Mexican Modern Art," 27.

51 Lozano, "Mexican Modern Art," 12.

52 Quoted in National Gallery of Canada, "Sol y Vida."

53 Ramírez, "Beyond 'the Fantastic,'" 240.

54 Debroise, "Mexican Art on Display," 30.

55 Debroise, "Mexican Art on Display," 22, 32.

56 Blake Gopnik, "Minus Murals, It's No Show of Mexican Art: As a Snapshot of the Country's Modernism, This Exhibition Falls Far Short of the Mark," *Globe and Mail,*

25 November 1999, NGCA, Montreal Museum of Fine Arts, Exhibitions – Mexican Modern Art, 1998, vol. 2.

57 Gopnik, "Minus Murals."

58 Goldman, *Contemporary Mexican Painting*, xxi.

59 Wallis, "Selling Nations," 272.

60 Cogeval and Aquin, untitled, *Moi et ma circonstance*, n.p.

61 Cogeval and Aquin, untitled, *Moi et ma circonstance*, n.p.

62 Abaroa, "Mobility," 31, 33.

63 Bartra, "I and My Circumstances," 102.

64 "Mexico as Muse: Photographs 1923–1986 at the National Gallery of Canada," press release, 28 January 2000, NGCA, Exhibitions – Mexico as Muse, 1999, vol. 1.

65 "Mexico as Muse Panels, 2nd Edit," 22 November 1999, NGCA, Exhibitions – Mexico as Muse, 1999, vol. 1.

66 Dorota Kozinska, "Join Us on a Personal Tour of a Blockbuster Show at the Museum of Fine Arts," *Montreal Gazette*, 20 November 1999, NGCA, Exhibitions – Mexican Modern Art, 1998, Montreal Museum of Fine Arts, vol. 2.

67 Untitled, *Night Shift*, Winter 1999, NGCA, Exhibitions – Mexican Modern Art, 1998, Montreal Museum of Fine Arts, vol. 2.

68 Kozinska, "Join Us."

69 Paul Gessell, "Impressive Show Perfectly Captures the Spirit of Mexico: Modern Art Retrospective May Travel to Mexico after Gallery Run," *Ottawa Citizen*, 24 February 2000, NGCA, Montreal Museum of Fine Arts, Exhibitions – Mexican Modern Art, 1998, vol. 2.

70 Wallis, "Selling Nations," 265.

71 Berger, "Goodwill Ambassadors," 107.

72 Placement média, Montreal Museum of Fine Arts Archives (MMFAA), Fonds L'arte Moderne Mexicain, 1999, 610-86-673.

73 Matérial promotion, MMFAA, Fonds L'arte Moderne Mexicain, 1999, 610-86-672.

74 Gómez-Peña, "The Multicultural Paradigm," 190.

75 Henry Lehmann, "Modernist Mexico: Blockbuster Show Is a Rare Glimpse at a Rich Modernism Born of Folk Craft, Revolution and High Art," *The Gazette*, 6 November 1999, J2, NGCA, Montreal Museum of Fine Arts, Exhibitions — Mexican Modern Art, 1998, vol. 2.

76 "Concours 'Pasión,'" MMFAA, Fonds L'arte Moderne Mexicain, 1999, 610-86-672.

77 "Communications, Special Events," NGCA, Exhibitions – Mexican Modern Art, 1998, vol. 3.

78 Théberge and Cogeval, "Foreword," 7. Notably, this rhetoric also picks up on "good neighbour" discourse, a reference to the US Good Neighbor Policy, a strategy of

cooperation and trade between the United States and Latin America announced by President Franklin Delano Roosevelt in 1933. Dina Berger characterizes this period as the "era of the good neighbor," a time "when friendship and cooperation toward Latin America replaced U.S. interventionism by the mid to late 1930s." Berger, "Goodwill Ambassadors," 107.

79 Lindauer, *Devouring Frida*, 3.

80 Lindauer, *Devouring Frida*, xi, 1, 12.

81 Lindauer, *Devouring Frida*, 174.

82 Goldman, "Metropolitan Splendors," 25.

83 José Springer, "A Tale of Cultural Exchange," NGCA, Clippings, Exhibitions – Mexican Modern Art, 1998.

84 Théberge and Cogeval, "Foreword," 7.

85 "Communications and Special Events," Mexican Modern Art TV script, NGCA, Exhibitions – Mexican Modern Art, 1998, vol. 3.

86 See Hinsley, "The World as Marketplace," 344–65.

87 Yúdice, *The Expediency of Culture*, 240.

88 Marie Claire Morin to Robert W. Armstrong, 29 October 1999, NGCA, Exhibitions – Mexican Modern Art, 1998, "Sponsorship," vol. 2.

89 "Memorandum: Mexican Modern Art, 1900–1950," 28 October 1999, NGCA, Exhibitions – Mexican Modern Art, 1998, "Sponsorship," vol. 2.

90 Théberge and Cogeval, "Foreword," 7.

91 Hain, "Message from the Sponsor," 5.

92 Cogeval and Aquin, untitled, *Moi et ma circonstance*, n.p.

93 Emily Tolot to Marie Clarie Morin, 15 February 2000, NGCA, "Communications, Special Events," Correspondence, Exhibitions – Mexican Modern Art, 1998, vol. 8.

94 Tolot to Morin.

95 Paul Gessell, "Trading Paintings: Canada and Mexico Exhibit Exchange Includes Top Paintings of 20th Century," *Ottawa Citizen*, 22 May 1999, NGCA, Montreal Museum of Fine Arts, Exhibitions – Mexican Modern Art, 1998, vol. 2.

96 National Gallery of Canada, "Terre Sauvage: Canadian Landscape Painting and the Group of Seven Premieres in Mexico," press release, 25 August 1999, accessed 31 July 2013. http://www.gallery.ca/en/about/439.php.

97 See, for example, Dawn, *National Visions*.

98 Jessup, "Art for a Nation?," 189.

99 See Bowen's large-scale photomural *The Black Canadians (after Cooke)*, which consisted of archival imagery and was installed on the facade of the NGC in 2023–24.

100 "Briefing Notes for Minister Sheila Copps, Canada in Mexico: A Salute to the Millennium," NGCA, Exhibitions – Mexican Modern Art, 1998, vol. 1.

101 Paul Gessell notes that Culham was instrumental in securing the exhibition (stating "When Culham heard about the exhibition, she decided it must come to Mexico") and that she undertook significant fundraising to secure corporate support. Paul Gessell, "Sponsors Upstage Art at Show Gala: Commerce Beats Culture at Opening That Ignores the Art," *Ottawa Citizen,* 28 August 1999, NGCA, Montreal Museum of Fine Arts, Exhibitions – Mexican Modern Art, 1998, vol. 2.

102 Paul Gessell, "Trading Paintings."

103 National Gallery of Canada, "Terre Sauvage."

104 Gessell, "Sponsors Upstage Art."

105 Gessell, "Sponsors Upstage Art."

106 Autonomy and separation are not absolute in an arm's-length system, but they are more prevalent than when the arts are directly managed by the state. In a comparative study of state art funding models, Kevin Mulcahy asserts that Canada's arm's-length approach allows it to function as an "'enabler' state." As such, it fits a model of funding in which the state transfers financial resources to specialized organizations that though "subject to the cultural policy ... as far as the artistic side of their operations is concerned, the institutions are autonomous." In Canada, however, culture also falls under provincial jurisdiction. Mulcahy, "Cultural Patronage," 252, 254. Anna Rosser Upchurch traces the historic connections between John Maynard Keynes's ideas about autonomous government and the arm's-length policy model, including notions of distance from government and professional standards via peer review. See Upchurch, "Keynes's Legacy," 69–80.

107 This occurred in 1995, though the extent to which the policy was taken up has been disputed. See Government of Canada, *Canada in the World.*

108 Haskell, *The Ephemeral Museum,* 2.

109 Wallis, "Selling Nations," 279.

110 "Sees Opening of Mexican Exhibit Educational for Both Countries," *Montreal Gazette,* 10 September 1943, NGCA, Clippings, Exhibitions – Mexican Art Today, 1943.

Chapter 2: Canadian Art at 49th Parallel

1 An earlier version of this chapter was published as Smith, "Bridging the 49th Parallel," 95–125.

2 Although many circumstances and developments underpin the so-called special relationship, I suggest that whiteness and settler colonialism provide a foundation for the closeness between Canada and the United States. Srdjan Vucetic addresses the privileging of special relationships among a core group of "English speaking peoples" internationally, which he terms the "Anglosphere" – Britain, Canada, the United States, Australia, and New Zealand. See Vucetic, *The Anglosphere,* 2. For a

discussion of the special relationship's history, see Azzi, *Reconcilable Differences;* Thompson and Randall, *Canada and the United States;* Hillmer and Granatstein, *For Better or for Worse;* Bothwell, *Your Country, My Country;* Lennox, *At Home and Abroad;* McKercher, *Camelot and Canada;* and Muirhead, "From Special Relationship," 439–62.

3 Despite its widespread usage as a moniker for the Canada-US border, the forty-ninth parallel matches the border line only in British Columbia, Alberta, Saskatchewan, and Manitoba.

4 Nancy Tousley, "Government Advised to Close N.Y. Gallery," *Calgary Herald,* 30 March 1985.

5 "49th Parallel/49e Parallele: Centre for Canadian Contemporary Art, Position Paper," 1, NGCA, 49th Parallel fonds, 49th Parallel – Opening, box 36, file 1.

6 "Canada's Art Child Christened," *Globe and Mail,* 23 March 1981.

7 "Basic Background," 4, NGCA, 49th Parallel fonds, 49th Parallel – Opening, box 36, file 1.

8 In a catalogue first published in 1970, art historian Dennis Reid identified the Group of Seven's aim to promote "a Canadian art for Canadians." This stance, Reid explained, dovetailed with the aims of the NGC during the tenure of Director Eric Brown (1912–39). Lynda Jessup later addressed the gallery's ongoing promotion of the group in an article initially published in *Fuse Magazine.* See Reid, "Introduction"; and Jessup, "Art for a Nation?," 187–92.

9 Martha Langford argues against understanding Snow's work as a critical commentary on Canadian nationalism. See Langford, *Michael Snow,* 29–30.

10 According to a *Globe and Mail* article, Plamondon had the idea for the gallery in 1977. See J.B. Mays, "Controversy Flares around the 49th Parallel," *Globe and Mail,* 20 March 1982.

11 Quoted in J.S. Hage, "49th Parallel: Canada Opens Showcase Gallery in New York," *Ottawa Citizen,* 11 April 1981.

12 External Affairs also engaged in visual art through its support of discrete exhibitions staged by partners, including the NGC. For example, it supported *OKanada,* a prominent show of contemporary art presented at the Akademie der Künste in West Berlin in 1982–83. The show was accompanied by a rich program of events encompassing historical and contemporary art, architecture, film, and literature to which the Canada Council and, to a lesser extent, the German government also contributed. *OKanada* was deemed unsuccessful, however, due to dismal attendance and a lack of positive response from German art critics. Wayne, "Does Canada Have?," 35.

13 In the 1980s, Canada directed significant attention to its cultural centres. At this time, Canada House in London underwent renovation. Additionally, plans were announced to expand Canadian cultural offerings in cities including Mexico City,

Tokyo, and Washington DC. See L.B. Bowen, "Canada House Is Home to Art," *Toronto Star*, 20 June 1981.

14 Georges Bogardi, "Gallery for Canadian Artists Set for N.Y.," *Montreal Gazette*, 17 January 1981.

15 Wayne, "Does Canada Have?," 36.

16 Cooper, "Introduction," 5. Simon L. Mark explains that Quebec's cultural diplomacy activities can be traced to the Quiet Revolution and the province's desire for recognition of its cultural distinctiveness at home and abroad. See Mark, "Rethinking Cultural Diplomacy," 62–83.

17 Cultural and Public Information Bureau, "International Cultural Relations," first draft, October 1984, 22, NGCA, 49th Parallel fonds, box 36, "49th Parallel - Restructuring (1984)," file 2.

18 Wayne, "Does Canada Have?" 35.

19 "Bio of Guy Plamondon & Robert Handforth," 19, NGCA, 49th Parallel fonds, 49th Parallel - Opening, box 36, file 1.

20 "Consulate General New York Cultural Affairs Programme, Establishment of a Canadian Art Centre," 14 February 1978, NGCA, 49th Parallel fonds, 49th Parallel – Opening, box 36, file 1.

21 "Consulate General." The document lists the individuals who were contacted about the project, as well as their cities of origin. Interestingly, it also cites an agreement in principle with US secretary of state John Roberts, indicating the high-level nature of the conversations.

22 "Consulate General," 23.

23 "Consulate General," 1.

24 "Consulate General," 1. Here, his comments reflected Canadian fears of US cultural imperialism in the 1980s and 1990s, anxieties that also came to the fore in cultural production, particularly video art, which is discussed in Chapter 6. Additionally, these concerns permeated the arts scene and are evidenced in artist organizing activities, such as those of the Independent Artists' Union, which are detailed in the Epilogue.

25 Department of External Affairs, "New York Show-Case for Canadian Artists," press release, 13 February 1981, NGCA, 49th Parallel fonds, 49th Parallel - Opening, box 36, file 1.

26 Canadian Consulate General, "Canada to Open Unique Soho Art Centre 49th Parallel: Centre for Contemporary Canadian Art, First Canadian Cultural Facility in the United States," 20 March 1981, NGCA, 49th Parallel fonds, 49th Parallel – Opening, box 36, file 1.

27 "Bio of Guy Plamondon & Robert Handforth," 21.

28 L.B. Bowen, "Ottawa Opens Art Gallery in New York," *Toronto Star*, 22 March 1981.

29 Tousley, “Government Advised to Close.”
30 The rent for the gallery ($5,400 a month) was widely mentioned in the press at the time. Hage, “49th Parallel.”
31 “Consulate General,” 8, 16.
32 Catherine Anka, “Showcase of Avant Garde Scene Acquires Taste for Canadian Art,” *Ottawa Citizen,* 26 March 1983.
33 Quoted in “Canadians Open Gallery in SoHo,” *New York Times,* 29 March 1981 (emphasis added).
34 Quoted in Bogardi, “Gallery for Canadian Artists.”
35 This inability would prove an ongoing issue for the gallery. Anka, “Showcase of Avant Garde Scene.”
36 In a 1991 document on the future of 49th Parallel, the undersecretary of state for external affairs explained the gallery’s historic position on sales: “Since the gallery is, for practical and other reasons, a creature of the Canadian consulate, NYC, the regulations of the U.S. State Department and the federal and New York State tax authorities would not permit the gallery to conduct direct commercial operations while enjoying tax-free status.” “Future of the 49th Parallel Gallery, NYC,” 19 December 1991, 2, NGCA, 49th Parallel fonds, box 37, Susan Whitney – Correspondence, file 2.
37 C. Corbeil, “Canada Sets Up Visual Art Gallery in New York,” *Globe and Mail,* 5 February 1981.
38 Other top contenders included “Canada Space/Espace Canada” and “Studio Canada.” “Name for New Cdn Art Facility in NYork,” 22 January 1981, NGCA, 49th Parallel fonds, box 36, 49th Parallel – Opening, file 1.
39 “Name for New.”
40 Hsiio-Yen Shihto to Guy Plamondon, 24 February 1981 (emphasis added), NGCA, 49th Parallel fonds, box 1, Michael Snow Exhibition (21 March–11 April 1981), file 1.
41 Quoted in A.M. Ashley, “Hearing Told of Canada’s ‘Cultural Poverty,’” *Ottawa Citizen,* 16 April 1981.
42 The critical reception was poor. A review in *Arts Canada,* for instance, critiqued the choice of Snow, as well as the fact that no attempt was made to position his oeuvre in a new way. See Christ, “Michael Snow.”
43 *Blind, Plus Tard,* and *Scope* were loaned by the NGC. *Next* (1980) was loaned by the Anthology Film Archives, New York.
44 Bronson, “The Humiliation,” 33–34.
45 Bronson, “The Humiliation,” 31.
46 Robertson, *Policy Matters,* iv.
47 Robertson, *Policy Matters,* iv.
48 Skoggard, “The 49th Parallel,” 17.

49 Quoted in Mays, "Controversy Flares."
50 Seven individuals were initially appointed for a two-year term, including Alvin Balkind, Claude Bouchard, Eric Cameron, Thérèse Dion, Chantal Pontbriand, Jeffrey Spalding, and Elke Town. See "Department of External Affairs – Communique," 29 August 1983, NGCA, box 37, Consulting Committee – General, file 5.
51 Skoggard, "The 49th Parallel: After," 33.
52 Early in Morin's tenure, however, the gallery faced charges that it was too focused on Montreal and Toronto to the exclusion of Vancouver.
53 The exhibition received mixed reviews from critics. It featured work by Simon Cerigo, David Craven, Stephen Lack, Marcus Leatherdale, John Massey, Dorothea Rockburne, Jana Sterbak, Robert Walker, and Krzysztof Wodiczko.
54 Quoted in Wayne, "Does Canada Have?," 38–39.
55 Morin also did outreach for the gallery and the Canadian arts community. For instance, she and a 49th Parallel staff member ran a Canadian booth at the Chicago International Art Exposition at Navy Pier in 1986. In a memorandum documenting her work, she reported that she amassed "a variety of books, catalogues, journals and brochures [representing Canadian visual art], the majority of which were given away." France Morin to Under-Secretary of State for External Affairs (Ottawa), Memorandum, 30 May 1986, NGCA, box 40, Chicago Art Fair – 1986 (Participation In), file 10.
56 In contrast, it singled out Canada House in London for praise.
57 Quoted in L. Black, "Gallery Threatened," Canadian Press, 1985, NGCA, 49th Parallel fonds, box 34, Spring 1985 – Canadian Press (Political), file 54.
58 Quoted in Tousley, "Government Advised to Close."
59 Quoted in Black, "Gallery Threatened."
60 Quoted in M. Landsberg, "The Bubbling Presence at Canada's Art Embassy," *Globe and Mail,* 19 October 1985. An overview of the arts promotion strategies of Australia, France, Germany, Britain, Italy, Japan, and Sweden is provided in Appendix E of "New York City as the World's Art Capital and Its Relevance for Canadian Art and Artists," 6 January 1988, 10–12, NGCA, 49th Parallel fonds, box 36, 49th Parallel – Restructuring (1987), file 5.
61 Political scientist Andrew Cooper noted the department's increasing interest in marshalling cultural diplomacy initiatives in support of foreign trade. Quoted in Wayne, "Does Canada Have?," 39.
62 The Woods Gordon Report was very clear in this regard: "The positive influence of cultural activity in terms of trade has largely to be taken as an act of faith ... Thus, in terms of generating direct, hard benefits, cultural centres generate a nice warm feeling, but not much more." Woods Gordon, "Department of External Affairs Assessment of the Concept of Cultural Centres," draft report, July 1984, 22, NGCA, 49th Parallel fonds, box 36, 49th Parallel – Restructuring (1984), file 2.

63 This closeness stood in sharp contrast to the Pierre Trudeau government's relationship with Reagan, which was notoriously acrimonious.
64 This perception is evidenced, for instance, in the enormous controversy roused by the NGC's 1989 purchase of *Voice of Fire,* a 1967 painting by US artist Barnett Newman. Its $1.8 million price tag generated outrage.
65 Summarizing the reorganization of the gallery in 1991, Undersecretary of State for External Affairs Janet Bax explained that the shift to a non-profit corporation with a board of directors was meant, in part, to spur greater private-sector funding. Janet Bax (Undersecretary of State for External Affairs) to Glen Cumming, 19 December 1991, NGCA, 49th Parallel fonds, box 38, Janet Bax – Correspondence, file 1.
66 In a move that attests to her credentials and connections within the New York art scene, Morin subsequently took up a curatorial position at the New Museum, where she worked until 1994.
67 I. Vincent, "Canadian Gallery in New York Launching a Major Assault," *Globe and Mail,* 9 December 1989.
68 This reorganization also had an impact on the type of art that was shown in the gallery. As Ellen Cunningham writes, programming during the last three years focused largely on painting. Cunningham, "Taking a Bite," 91.
69 "49th Parallel Report," 13 March 1990, NGCA, 49th Parallel fonds, box 37, 49th Parallel – Restructuring (1988–1990), file 1.
70 Olga Korper, "Letter to the Editor," *C Magazine* 24 (1990): 71.
71 K. Taylor, "Gallery Official Upbeat Despite Low Sales," *Globe and Mail,* 8 April 1991.
72 As late as 1 April 1992, ideas were circulating on how to prevent the closure. See Glen Cumming to Janet Bax, fax, 1 April 1992, NGCA, 49th Parallel fonds, box 38, "Janet Bax – Correspondence," file 1.
73 A task force appointed by Minister of External Affairs Joe Clark identified this issue in a 1989 report, which asserted that "many of the problems of the 49th Parallel in the past have stemmed from a confusion of objectives. The primary interest of the Department of External Affairs has been in promoting Canada's image and [contacts] abroad. This has not always been consistent with the development of living Canadian artists and their reputations in international art circles." "Draft Report, Task Force on the Future of the 49th Parallel Gallery," n.d., 3, NGCA, 49th Parallel fonds, box 36, 49th Parallel – Restructuring (1984), file 2.
74 Tracing the history of cultural institutions abroad, Gregory Paschalidis argues that their roles as centres for cultural diplomacy were apparent between the Second World War and the end of the Cold War. He suggests that in response to nation-branding efforts in the 1990s, they took on a different role as sites of cultural capitalism. See Paschalidis, "Exporting National Culture," 275–89.
75 Janet Bax made this point about 49th Parallel's partnership with PADAC. In 1991, near the end of the trial relationship with PADAC, she cited the depressed art market,

the fact that the gallery did not privilege repeat exhibitions (essential to building an audience for an artist's work), and its complicated tax-free status, which precluded sales, and concluded that "it is difficult to fairly assess the success of the three year experiment." Janet Bax to Glen Cumming, 19 December 1991, NGCA, 49th Parallel fonds, box 38, Janet Bax – Correspondence, file 1. Anguish over measuring cultural impact continues; for example, the problem was mentioned in the lead-up to the UNESCO World Conference on Cultural Policies and Sustainable Development MONDIACULT 2022. A background document states, "Measuring and strengthening evidence on the impact of culture on sustainable development remains critical to inform public policymaking" and notes that "culture-related data remains fragmented and scattered across diverse institutions." UNESCO, "Background Document," 10.

76 Schneider, "Cultural Diplomacy," 196.

77 Global Affairs Canada and the University of Southern California's Center on Public Diplomacy organized a workshop titled *Diplometrics* in April 2016 to address how to measure the results of public diplomacy and advocacy activities. See "PD & Advocacy for Effective Results."

78 The committee explored the uses and impact of Canadian culture and arts in Canadian foreign policy and diplomacy, and other related matters. Its report, "Cultural Diplomacy at the Front Stage of Canada's Foreign Policy," was released in 2019. See Canada, Standing Senate Committee on Foreign Affairs and International Trade, "Cultural Diplomacy."

79 For a full list of speakers, see Canada, Standing Senate Committee on Foreign Affairs and International Trade, "Studies and Bills – Study on the Impact and Utilization of Canadian Culture and Arts in Canadian Foreign Policy and Diplomacy, and Other Related Matters."

80 Sterbak, "Testimony" (emphasis added).

Chapter 3: Exhibiting the Continent

1 Clarkson, *Does North America Exist?,* 38.

2 Clarkson, *Does North America Exist?,* 12.

3 Gutiérrez Haces, "Mexico-Canada Relations," 197.

4 Heidrich and Macdonald, "Introduction," 4.

5 McKercher, "Locating Latin America," 42.

6 Ochoa Bilbao and Schiavon, "Is Mexico a North American?," 113.

7 Orme, *Understanding NAFTA,* 302.

8 Reviewing Canada's engagement with Latin America since the twentieth century, McKercher notes a pattern of ongoing "discovery" with respect to Canada, explaining that the state is continually "realizing and recognizing Canada's place in the hemisphere." McKercher, "Locating Latin America," 49.

9 Clarkson, *Does North America Exist?*, 38; Randall and Konrad, "Introduction," 7.

10 The authors demonstrate that, among Mexicans, North American identity ranks most highly in the northern part of the country, which most benefited from NAFTA. Ochoa Bilbao and Schiavon, "Is Mexico a North American?," 114, 117–18, 120.

11 Ochoa Bilbao and Schiavon, "Is Mexico a North American?," 114, 122.

12 Poitras, *Inventing North America*, 167.

13 In discussing changes to normative understandings of North America, I use the term regionalism to refer to both intranational regions and transnational regions, underscoring the mutability of land-based identities.

14 That same year, the twenty-seventh G8 summit took place in Genoa, which was read as the peak of the alter-globalization movement (of which free trade was an integral part). Kirsty Robertson, *Tear Gas Epiphanies*, 328n12.

15 Heinrich and Macdonald argue that the failure of the FTAA "marked a period of decline in Canada-Latin American relations." Heinrich and Macdonald, "Introduction," 12.

16 For a history of the FTAA negotiations, tracing their supposed inevitability in the 1990s to their failure in the 2000s, see Nelson, *A History of the FTAA*.

17 "Smithsonian American Art Museum Participates in First Ever Collaborative International Virtual Exhibition," press release, 27 March 2001, Smithsonian American Art Museum (SAAM) and the Renwick Gallery. My discussion of *Panoramas* expands on arguments put forth in Smith, "Visualizing the 'New,'" 130–49; and Smith, "Cross-Border Identifications," 187–205.

18 The video conference did not succeed in connecting Mexico with the United States and Canada. The press provided various explanations for this lapse, including scheduling, connection failure, and issues with the cables at the Museo Nacional de Arte (MUNAL). See Verónica Vega, "El arte de Norteamérica, en una exposición virtual," *unomásuno*, 4 April 2001, 26C, SAAM, Curatorial Office, Exhibition Records, 1981–2001, "Panoramas Publicity." Mexico's absence was widely noted in Mexican press coverage, with emphasis on the irony of the situation, given that the exhibition was promoted as technologically innovative. For example, *Reforma* newspaper wrote, "La oficina de prensa del INBA dio a conocer que la falla en la transmisión se debió 'a problemas técnicos causados por ruido eléctrico en el ambiente', en contraste con uno de los conceptos más mencionados en los discursos de los funcionarios 'la tecnología del siglo 21.'" (The INBA press office announced that the transmission failure was due to "technical problems caused by electrical interference," in contrast to one of the concepts most mentioned in the speeches of the officials: "21st century technology.") Gómez, "Presentan sin México," 3C.

19 This high-profile event on 3 April 2001 was attended by political and cultural figures from the three North American states, including Copps; Gordon D. Giffin, the American ambassador to Canada; and Sari Bermudez, president of Mexico's national

council for culture and the arts. Press Room, Virtual Museum of Canada, "Launching of the Virtual Exhibit Panoramas: The North American Landscape in Art," 3 April 2001, accessed 28 July 2013, http://www.virtualmuseum.ca/English//Pressroom/p-04-01-1.html.

20 Virtual trilateral art exhibition (emphasis added), SAAM, Curatorial Office, Exhibition Records, 1981–2001, "Panoramas email."

21 Carmen Bancalari to Rebecca Brown et al., 12 March 2001, SAAM, Curatorial Office, Exhibition Records, 1981–2001, "Panoramas email."

22 In March 2006, the Smithsonian American Art Museum and the Canadian Heritage Information Network agreed to extend *Panoramas* for another five years, with Smithsonian staff noting they were pleased that it "continues to be well-used." "Amendment to the Articles of Agreement," 14 March 2006, SAAM, Curatorial Office, Exhibition Records, 1981–2001, "C.H.I.N. Project"; Rachel M. Allen to Danielle Boily, 17 March 2006, SAAM, Curatorial Office, Exhibition Records, 1981–2001.

23 In 2013, a Virtual Museum of Canada representative informed me that *Panoramas* was being evaluated and could potentially be modified to become compliant with accessibility standards so that it could be relaunched in the future. Wendy Thomas to Sarah E.K. Smith, personal correspondence, 17 June 2013.

24 Here, it is worth noting other digital exhibitions of the period. The formal agreement for *Panoramas* states that it was built on international partnerships established with the *Virtual Museum of the Americas,* launched in 1999 by the Canadian Heritage Information Network in relation to the 1998 conference "Museums and Sustainable Communities." "Trilateral Cultural Collaboration, Virtual Exhibition Agreement," 15 November 2000, 2, SAAM, Curatorial Office, Exhibition Records, 1981–2001, "C.H.I.N. Project."

25 In 2014, the VMC was transferred to the Canadian Museum of History. See Virtual Museum of Canada, "About Us."

26 When the SAAM began work on the exhibition, it was known as the National Museum of American Art. See Smithsonian American Art Museum, "Museum History," https://americanart.si.edu/about/history; Morley Walker, "WAG Joins International On-line Virtual Exhibit," *Winnipeg Free Press,* 4 April 2001, D7; Wasney, "Panoramas," 7; and McAlear, "WAG Chosen," 3.

27 Diego Cevallos, "Art-North America: Internet Displays Works from NAFTA Nations," *Inter Press Service,* 11 May 2001.

28 "Trilateral Cultural Collaboration, Virtual Exhibition Agreement," 15 November 2000, 2.

29 Danielle Boily to Adel Pax, J. Gimenez, and S. Valdes, 8 June 2000, SAAM, Curatorial Office, Exhibition Records, 1981–2001, "C.H.I.N. Project."

30 McAlear, "WAG Chosen," 3.

31 Mitchell, "Imperial Landscape," 29–30.

32 Mitchell, "Imperial Landscape," 27–28.
33 "North American Virtual Exhibition Project Canada-US-Mexico," draft, 9 February 2000, Canadian Heritage (CH), Virtual Museum of Canada (VMC), Executive Produced Exhibitions – Panoramas: The North American Landscape in Art, 80 B 4220-P1, vol. 1.
34 Elizabeth Broun to Lawrence Small, n.d., SAAM, Curatorial Office, Exhibition Records, 1981–2001, "State Dept Info."
35 This seems to have affected some of the participating institutions. The National Gallery of Canada was initially secured as the main Canadian institutional partner when the exhibition was first conceived. After discussions, however, the NGC withdrew due to a disagreement over the focus of the show. The gallery favoured a concentration on visual literacy, whereas US funding required that the exhibition take a socio-historical approach. Subsequently, the Winnipeg Art Gallery was invited to replace the NGC.
36 Balfe, "Artworks as Symbols," 5.
37 Balfe, "Artworks as Symbols," 5.
38 Balfe, "Artworks as Symbols," 24–25.
39 Cull, *Public Diplomacy: Foundations,* 5. Cull defines public diplomacy as "an international actor's attempt to manage the international environment through engagement with a foreign public." He offers a typology of public diplomacy that encompasses listening, advocacy, exchange, cultural diplomacy, and international broadcasting. Cull, *Public Diplomacy: Lessons,* 10, 12.
40 Museums are one of these actors, giving rise to recent scholarship on museums and diplomacy. See Brison and Smith, "The Global Engagement"; Kong, *Museums, International Exhibitions;* Priewe, *Museum Diplomacy;* Grincheva, *Global Trends;* and Smith and Priewe, *Museum Diplomacy.*
41 Although this makes the exhibition seem almost propagandistic, I suggest it was both conceived and enacted as public diplomacy out of a mutual interest in genuine cultural exchange among the partners. In *Public Diplomacy: Foundations,* 13, Cull discusses the qualitative difference between public diplomacy and propaganda. Garth S. Jowett and Victoria O'Donnell define propaganda as emphasizing power and manipulation to achieve a certain effect. Jowett and O'Donnell, *Propaganda and Persuasion,* 6.
42 Goff, "Cultural Diplomacy," 421.
43 Broun to Small, n.d.
44 Other documentation puts the US contribution at $72,000. Broun to Small, n.d.
45 The Government of Canada's average exchange rate for the year 2000 was C$1.48 = US$1. Government of Canada, "Average Exchange Rates for 2000," https://www.canada.ca/en/revenue-agency/services/forms-publications/previous-year-forms-publications/archived-rc4152/archived-average-exchange-rates-2000.html.

46 A comparison of total funds devoted to cultural diplomacy initiatives across Canada, Mexico, and the United States during this period is beyond the scope of the present study.

47 "Memorandum to Madame Eillen Sarkar, Canada-US-Mexico Trilateral Landscapes Exhibit," n.d., CH, VMC, Executive Produced Exhibitions – Panoramas: The North American Landscape in Art, 80 B 4220-P1, vol. 1.

48 "Smithsonian National Museum of American Art, Virtual Exhibition Conference Call, Summary," 27 March 2000, SAAM, Curatorial Office, Exhibition Records, 1981–2001, "Conference Calls CHIN."

49 Denny Gelinas to Michelle d'Auray, 12 January 2000, CH, VMC, Executive Produced Exhibitions – Panoramas: The North American Landscape in Art, 80 B 4220-P1, vol. 1.

50 Speaking to the differing perspectives on cultural protections at the *Panoramas* launch in Mexico in 2001, Gerardo Estrada of the Secretaría de Relaciones Exteriores (a former director of the INBA), was reported to have stated publicly, "Las medidas proteccionistas, usuales en el intercambio comercial, no operan en el terreno de la cultura." (Protectionist measures, which are common in trade, do not operate in the field of culture.) This speaks to the Mexican government's view that cultural protections were not necessary, which contrasted sharply with that of Canada. Quoted in C. Silva, "El proteccionismo, insostenible en el campo cultural," *Milenio,* 4 April 2001, 45C, SAAM, Curatorial Office, Exhibition Records, 1981–2001, "Panoramas Publicity."

51 "Smithsonian National Museum of American Art, Virtual Exhibition Conference Call, Summary," 27 March 2000.

52 "Landscapes Exhibit, Summary," 21 July 2000, SAAM, Curatorial Office, Exhibition Records, 1981–2001, "Conference Calls CHIN."

53 Elizabeth Broun to Rick Johnson, 24 August 2000, SAAM, Curatorial Office, Exhibition Records, 1981–2001, "Budget Info – CHIN."

54 Jeana Foley to Elizabeth Broun, 7 June 2000, SAAM, Correspondence, Curatorial Office, Exhibition Records, 1981–2001, "C.H.I.N. Project."

55 Jeana Foley to Elizabeth Broun, 8 June 2000, SAAM, Correspondence, Curatorial Office, Exhibition Records, 1981–2001, "C.H.I.N. Project."

56 Danielle Boily to Adel Pax, J. Gimenez, and S. Valdes, 8 June 2000.

57 "Trilateral Cultural Collaboration, Virtual Exhibition Agreement," 15 November 2000, 1, SAAM, Curatorial Office, Exhibition Records, 1981–2001, "C.H.I.N. Project."

58 Quoted in U.S. Department of State, "Collaborate on U.S. Role in Trilateral Art Exhibition for the Web," notice to the press, 27 March 2001, http://2001-2009.state.gov/r/pa/prs/ps/2001/1709.htm.

59 Cull, *Public Diplomacy: Lessons,* 13.

60 "Possible Educational Directions for Landscape," n.d., SAAM, Curatorial Office, Exhibition Records, 1981–2001, "Tom Thomson."

61 Quoted in Walker, "WAG Joins," D7.

62 Rebecca Brown to Jeana Foley, Danielle Boily, and William Gooding, 6 March 2001, SAAM, Curatorial Office, Exhibition Records, 1981–2001, Correspondence, "Panoramas email."

63 Jeana Foley to Rebecca Brown, 1 March 2001, SAAM, Curatorial Office, Exhibition Records, 1981–2001, Correspondence, "Panoramas email."

64 Carmen Bancalari to Jeana Foley, 2 March 2001, SAAM, Curatorial Office, Exhibition Records, 1981–2001, Correspondence, "Panoramas email."

65 Cara Ross to Danielle Boily et al., 15 August 2000, CH, VMC, Executive Produced Exhibitions – Panoramas: The North American Landscape in Art, 80 B 4220-P1, vol. 2.

66 McAlear, "WAG Chosen," 3.

67 Quoted in Cevallos, "Art-North America."

68 Quoted in U.S. Department of State, "Collaborate on U.S. Role."

69 Vega, "El arte de Norteamérica," 26C.

70 Quoted in "Smithsonian American Art Museum Participates."

71 "Sole Source Justification, SAAM Purchase Order Request," 5 April 2001, SAAM, Curatorial Office, Exhibition Records, 1981–2001, "Contracts and POS for Panorama."

72 "Sole Source Justification," 5 April 2001; SAAM Purchase Order Request (Jeana Foley, Woody Dowling), 20 March 2001, SAAM, Curatorial Office, Exhibition Records, 1981–2001, "Contracts and POS for Panorama."

73 "Sole Source Justification," 5 April 2001.

74 Virtual Museum of Canada, Canadian Heritage Information Network, "Panoramas." This is no longer available online. Now Digital Museums Canada, VMC has shifted its focus to supporting online projects rather than hosting them. See Digital Museums Canada, "Digital Museums Canada Decommissions."

75 The tours were as follows: Georges Bédard: Peaks in the Great Canadian North; *Achelous and Hercules* by Thomas Hart Benton; *Storm King on the Hudson* by Samuel Colman; *I Baptize Thee* by William H. Johnson; Female Imagery and Landscape; *Early Snow* by Tom Thomson; North American Landscapes in Video; and North American Landscapes in Panorama.

76 Virtual Museum of Canada, Canadian Heritage Information Network, "Panoramas: The North American Landscape in Art – The Artist's Perspective," accessed 20 December 2018, http://www.virtualmuseum.ca/edu/ViewLoitCollection.do?method=preview&lang=EN&id=4991.

77 Virtual Museum of Canada, Canadian Heritage Information Network, "Suggested Activities."

78 In 2013, when *Panoramas* was taken down, a VMC representative told me that the teaching resources would remain accessible and that the VMC "may retain the

Learning Object Collections ... as part of the Teachers' Centre of the VMC, in an effort to ensure that this rich content continues to be available and accessible to all Canadians." Thomas to Smith, personal correspondence, 17 June 2013.

79 "Educational Component, Panoramas Education Project Prospectus," n.d., CH, VMC, Executive Produced Exhibitions – Panoramas: The North American Landscape in Art, 80 B 4220-P3, vol. 1.

80 Mousseau, "Panoramas Extends," 4; Roberta W. Rubinoff to Marnie A. Butvin, 26 February 2001, SAAM, Curatorial Office, Exhibition Records, 1981–2001, Correspondence, "Contracts and POS for Panorama."

81 Quoted in Mousseau, "Panoramas Extends," 4.

82 Walker, "WAG Joins," D7.

83 Karen Kisiow to Peter M. Liba, 30 January 2001, Winnipeg Art Gallery Archives (WAGA), Exhibition Files, Panoramas: The North American Landscape in Art, Correspondence.

84 Donna McAlear, "Panoramas Exhibition," 22 January 2001, WAGA, Exhibition Files, Panoramas: The North American Landscape in Art, Email correspondence.

85 Walker, "WAG Joins," D7; "Basic Fields List," 12 February 2001, WAGA, Exhibition Files, Panoramas: The North American Landscape in Art.

86 "Basic Fields List," 12 February 2001, WAGA, Exhibition Files, Panoramas: The North American Landscape in Art.

87 Ibid.

88 Tricia Wasney, "Selections from Panoramas: The North American Landscape in Art," WAGA, Exhibition Files, Panoramas: The North American Landscape in Art.

89 Wasney, "Selections."

90 At the MUNAL launch event in Mexico City, press coverage stated that there was a lack of awareness of the strong historical ties between the three states: "El discurso de Susan Wood señalaba que si bien mucha gente sabe que el comercio trilateral entre los integrantes del TL-CAN alcanza los 640 mil millones de dólares por año, y que Norteamérica es uno de los mercados económicos más grandes del mundo, no se tienen presentes los fuertes lazos históricos que mantienen unidas a estas culturas." (Susan Wood's speech noted that while many people know that trilateral trade between the NAFTA partners totals $640 billion annually, and that North America is one of the largest economic markets in the world, the strong historical ties that bind these cultures together are often overlooked.) Silva, "El proteccionismo," 45C.

91 McAlear, "WAG Chosen," 3.

92 *Carr, O'Keeffe, Kahlo: Places of Their Own, Highlights from the Exhibition,* exhibition pamphlet, 2001, McMichael Canadian Art Collection Archives (MCACA), McMichael Documents.

93 *Carr, O'Keeffe, Kahlo.*

94 Paul Gessell, "Kahlo Gets Star Billing at Mexican Art Show," *Ottawa Citizen,* 5 November 1999, NGCA, Montreal Museum of Fine Arts, Exhibitions – Mexican Modern Art, 1998, vol. 2.

95 Layne Christensen, "Artists Fiercely Devoted to Their Homelands," *Vancouver Courier,* 3 July 2002, 23.

96 Kirsty Robertson, *Tear Gas Epiphanies,* 223. The Vancouver opening of the show was marked by protests related to British Columbia premier Gordon Campbell's presence at the event, which raised the ire of groups who objected to his government's cuts to social programs. Of the protest, Robertson explains, "Although the gender of the artists came up ... the link to NAFTA did not, except indirectly." Robertson, *Tear Gas Epiphanies,* 225. For a review of the show, see Hadani Ditmars, "Arts Abroad: In a Notable Constellation, Canada Embraces Its Star," *New York Times,* 16 July 2002.

97 Udall, *Carr, O'Keeffe, Kahlo,* 2.

98 "Carr, O'Keeffe, Kahlo: Places of Their Own," in-house exhibition description, MCACA, McMichael Documents

99 Gessell, "Kahlo Gets Star Billing."

100 Ditmars, "Arts Abroad."

101 Udall, *Carr, O'Keeffe, Kahlo,* 1–2.

102 Udall, *Carr, O'Keeffe, Kahlo,* 3.

103 Udall, *Carr, O'Keeffe, Kahlo,* 1.

104 This composition changed slightly at each venue on the tour due to availability of loans. Varga, "Untitled," 42; Duchamp, "What's the Story?"; Sponsorship package, "Executive Summary," 2, "Carr, O'Keeffe, Kahlo: Places of Their Own," MCACA, McMichael Documents.

105 Sponsorship package, "Executive Summary," 2.

106 "Exhibition Wall Text," n.d., National Museum of Women in the Arts Archives, Curatorial Exhibition Design and Exhibition Files, Carr, O'Keeffe, Kahlo: Places of Their Own.

107 Sutherland, "Indigenismo and the Limits," 77, 81. Sutherland adds that the movement "entailed the dehumanization of living indigenous peoples whose bodies and cultures were transformed into 'raw material for the creation of art.'" For more on Kahlo's appropriation of Indigenous dress, see Aragon, "Uninhabited Dresses," 517–49.

108 In recent years, there have been many discussions of Kahlo's appropriation of Indigenous culture. See, for example, Cheran, "An Indigenous Perspective"; and Chris Gonzalez, "Frida Kahlo and Appropriation of Indigenous Cultures," Oregon Public Broadcasting, 28 February 2022, https://www.opb.org/article/2022/02/28/frida-kahlo-and-cultural-appropriation.

109 For an analysis of *Klee Wyck* and "the intricacies of [Carr's] colonizing and appropriative moments, acts, and practices of identification," see Stewart, "Cultural Appropriations," 70; for the book itself, see Carr, *Klee Wyck.*
110 Moray, "Emily Carr," 60–61.
111 Crosby, "The Construction," 278, 279.
112 Crosby, "The Construction," 279.
113 Media ad, MCACA, McMichael Documents.
114 Gregson, "Carr, O'Keeffe, Kahlo," 65.
115 Quoted in Christensen, "Artists Fiercely Devoted," 23; Udall, "Carr, O'Keeffe, Kahlo," 3.
116 Michael O'Sullivan, "Three Women, One Journey," *Washington Post,* 15 February 2002.
117 Cusack, "Introduction: Art, Nation and Gender," 6.
118 Cusack, "Introduction: Art, Nation and Gender," 7.
119 Udall, "Carr, O'Keeffe, Kahlo," 2–3.
120 Sarah Milroy, "Three Sisters of Modernism," *Globe and Mail,* 30 June 2001, http://www.theglobeandmail.com/arts/three-sisters-of-modernism/article762149/?page=all.
121 McMichael Canadian Art Collection, untitled summary (emphasis added), https://mcmichael.com/event/carr-okeeffe-kahlo-places-of-their-own/.
122 Exhibitions held in public museums in Canada benefit from federal funding through the Canada Council for the Arts. However, in this chapter I focus on additional state funding as a means of gauging government support for the exhibitions I examine.
123 *Panoramas: The North American Landscape in Art* Post-Mortem Conference Call, 18 April 2001, SAAM, Curatorial Office, Exhibition Records, 1981–2001, "Conference Calls CHIN."
124 Gessell, "Kahlo Gets Star Billing."
125 The VMC developed *Perspectives* with the assistance of the MCAC, as well as several other institutional partners in Canada, Mexico, and the United States. Due to accessibility requirements, the show is no longer available online. Additional educational information was previously accessible through the VMC Teachers' Centre, which is now closed. Virtual Museum of Canada, "Perspectives."
126 Roth et al., "Foreword," 6.
127 Robert L. Pincus, "Four Museums Team Up for 'Baja to Vancouver,'" *San Diego Union-Tribune,* 27 May 2003.
128 Clarkson, *Does North America Exist?,* 38.
129 Vancouver Art Gallery, "Baja to Vancouver: The West Coast and Contemporary Art," press release, 10 May 2004, accessed 31 July 2013, http://www.vanartgallery.bc.ca/media_room/pdf/B2V.pdf.

130 Rugoff, "Baja to Vancouver," 13.
131 Roth et al., "Foreword," 6.
132 Roth et al., "Foreword," 6.
133 The press did not mention that there was no institutional partner from Mexico.
134 Christopher Knight, "Coastal Confluence," *Los Angeles Times,* 1 February 2004, http://articles.latimes.com/2004/feb/01/entertainment/ca-knight1.
135 D.K. Row, "Best of the West," *Oregonian,* 11 November 2003, E4.
136 Rugoff, "Baja to Vancouver"; Will K. Shilling, "West Coast's Best Exhibit in *Baja to Vancouver,*" *San Diego City Beat,* 21 January 2004.
137 Roth et al., "Foreword," 6.
138 "Baja to Vancouver: The West Coast," artdaily.org, http://artdaily.com/news/8528/Baja-to-Vancouver--br--The-West-Coast#Ue_pBxbvxmA.
139 Roth et al., "Foreword," 6.
140 Quoted in Shilling, "West Coast's Best Exhibit."
141 Rugoff, "Baja to Vancouver," 19.
142 Richard Florida, "The Buffalo Mega-Region: Bigger Than We Know," *Buffalo News,* 15 June 2008, http://www.creativeclass.com/rfcgdb/articles/The%20Buffalo%20Mega-Region%20%20Bigger%20Than%20We%20Know.pdf.
143 Florida, "The Buffalo Mega-Region."
144 Orme, *Understanding NAFTA,* 303.
145 Orme, *Understanding NAFTA,* 302.
146 Courchene, "FTA at 15," 10.
147 Rugoff, "Baja to Vancouver," 16.
148 Moser, "Every Building."
149 Augaitis, "Stan Douglas," 44.
150 Moser, "Every Building."
151 Jen Graves, "'Baja to Vancouver' Exhibit Transcends Regionalism," *Tacoma (WA) News Tribune,* 12 October 2003, D4.
152 "Baja to Vancouver," *La Jolla Light,* 20 November 2003; Robert L. Pincus, "Farce-Sighted: Many of the Artistic Eyes in 'Baja to Vancouver' See a World to Be Parodied," *San Diego Union-Tribune,* 29 January 2004, 40.
153 Kamps, "Torolab," 112.
154 Rugoff, "Baja to Vancouver," 19.
155 Quoted in Knight, "Coastal Confluence."
156 Graves, "'Baja to Vancouver,'" D4.
157 Two contributions to rethinking the prominence of the nation in art history are Jessup, Morton, and Robertson, *Negotiations in a Vacant Lot;* and Langford, *Narratives Unfolding.*
158 For more on neoliberalism, see Harvey, *A Brief History.*

159 Palumbo-Liu, “Hybridities and Histories,” 253.
160 Palumbo-Liu, “Hybridities and Histories,” 254.
161 Palumbo-Liu, “Hybridities and Histories,” 252.
162 García Canclini, “Redefinitions,” 160.
163 García Canclini, “Redefinitions,” 160.
164 Poitras, *Inventing North America,* 167.
165 Hobsbawm, “Inventing Traditions,” 1, 12.
166 Tuck and Yang, “Decolonization Is Not,” 5.
167 Kirsty Robertson, *Tear Gas Epiphanies,* 328n12.

Chapter 4: Settler State Claims to Indigeneity

1 Nadia Myre, dir., *Rethinking Anthem,* 2008, http://www.nadiamyre.net/time-based#/rethinking-anthem-2008/.
2 Rice, “Rethinking Anthem.”
3 For a discussion of ways in which Ottawa claims territory and denies Indigenous sovereignty, see the Yellowhead Institute’s report “Land Back: A Yellowhead Institute Red Paper,” October 2019, https://redpaper.yellowheadinstitute.org/wp-content/uploads/2019/10/red-paper-report-final.pdf.
4 Artist Alan Michelson, a Mohawk member of the Six Nations of the Grand River, engages with the complexities of Akwesasne Mohawk territory in *Third Bank of the River,* an etched glass installation displayed at the US port of entry at Massena, New York, in 2009. The work echoes the form of the Two Row, a historic Iroquois wampum belt marking respectful co-existence with Dutch settlers, distinct in its alternating rows: two purple and three white. *Third Bank* presents views of the St. Lawrence River shorelines, highlighting the borders and boundaries between Akwesasne Mohawk territory, Canada, and the United States. Michelson’s work asserts Indigenous sovereignty and the contemporary significance of the wampum belt as a diplomatic form. See Michelson, “Third Bank of the River”; and Stirrup, “Bridging the Third Bank,” 163–85.
5 For more on the movement, see its homepage at https://landback.org.
6 Veracini, *Settler Colonialism,* 95.
7 Wolfe, “Settler Colonialism,” 389.
8 Moreton-Robinson, *The White Possessive,* 15, 18.
9 Moreton-Robinson, *The White Possessive,* 75.
10 Tuck and Yang, “Decolonization Is Not,” 10.
11 Such narratives are explored by Eva Mackey in *The House of Difference.*
12 The museum has been organized in various ways through the nineteenth to twenty-first centuries. Recent key moments include the disbanding of the National Museums Corporation of Canada in 1990, which led to the creation of the Canadian Museum

of Civilization Corporation – providing more distance from the government. In 2013, the museum was renamed the Canadian Museum of History, marking a shift from a broad focus on "human cultural achievements and human behaviour ... with special but not exclusive reference to Canada" to a narrower focus on Canadian social and political history. The current mandate is to "enhance Canadians' knowledge, understanding and appreciation of events, experiences, people and objects that reflect and have shaped Canada's history and identity, and also to enhance their awareness of world history and cultures." Aronczyk and Brady, "Branding History," 178. The authors discuss the partisan rebranding of the museum in 2013. See also Canadian Museum of History, "About – History Timeline," https://www.historymuseum.ca/about/history-timeline/#tabs; Canadian Museum of Civilization Corporation, "Summary of the Corporate Plan," 2; and Canadian Museum of History, "About – Mandate, Vision and Values."

13 *First Peoples of Canada: Treasures from the Collections of the Canadian Museum of Civilization,* brochure, Canadian Museum of History Archives (CMHA), Ancient Peoples of Canada, 2010-I0001, Agreement, 2005–2006.

14 Canadian Museum of Civilization, "International Exhibition of Aboriginal Masterworks Begins a Three-Continent Tour," press release, 15 April 2009, Canadian Museum of History, http://www.civilization.ca/media/news/international-exhibition-of-aboriginal-masterworks-begins-a-three-continent-tour. The phrasing "Canadian Aboriginal artifacts" implies that Indigenous peoples are a Canadian possession, naturalizing an understanding of Indigenous artifacts as subsumed by and belonging to the Canadian government and thus thwarting Indigenous sovereignty. This wording reinforces the national framing of *First Peoples of Canada.* See also "Aboriginal Treasures Are Beijing-Bound," press release, 13 March 2007, CMHA, First Peoples of Canada, 2010-I0020, vol. 3.

15 The exhibition was presented at the Art Museum of the Imperial City but staged by the National Museum of China. See Tim Wieclawski, "Museum Enters the Games," *Metro News,* 13 March 2008; and "Aboriginal Treasures Are Beijing-Bound."

16 "Aboriginal Treasures Are Beijing-Bound."

17 Canadian Museum of Civilization, "International Exhibition."

18 Canadian Museum of Civilization, "International Exhibition."

19 Canadian Museum of Civilization, "Exhibition of Canadian Aboriginal Masterworks to Open in Mexico City," press release, 8 October 2010, Canadian Museum of History, http://www.civilization.ca/media/news/exhibition-of-canadian-aboriginal-masterworks-to-open-in-mexico-city.

20 CMHA, Nicholette Prince fonds, E2011.2, Chinese Connection, B7 F1, "First Peoples of Canada: Masterworks from the Canadian Museum of Civilization," 12 March 2008.

21 Phillips, "Show Times," 121 (emphasis in original).

22 Phillips, "Show Times," 121.

23 Government of Canada, Canadian Heritage, "2008–10 Canadian Heritage Cultural Activities."

24 The Canada-China relationship was affected by domestic developments between 2006 and 2009. Under the Harper Conservatives, relations cooled considerably due to Canada's withdrawal from multilateralism and its advance of specific bilateral relationships. See Nossal and Sarson, "About Face," 152.

25 Nossal and Sarson, "About Face," 148, 157; quoted in Evans, "China Choices," 258–59. Ottawa changed its approach in 2007, with Harper travelling to China in 2009 in a bid to restart the relationship. In 2012, negotiations between Canada and China resulted in the signing of a foreign investment promotion and protection agreement, after which China announced that it would be interested in a free trade agreement with Canada. See Peter Goodspeed, "Canada's Policy Pivot on China; Trade Mission; Harper to Meet Upcoming Chinese Leaders," *National Post,* 7 February 2012; Jeffrey Simpson, "The Lure of China – Yet Canada Hesitates on Free Trade," *Globe and Mail,* 15 March 2013; "5 Things to Know about the Canada-China Investment Treaty," *CBC News,* 27 October 2012, http://www.cbc.ca/news/politics/story/2012/10/27/pol-the-house-fippa-with-china.html; Canadian Museum of Civilization, "Treasures from China"; and Government of Canada, Canadian Heritage, "2008–10 Canadian Heritage Cultural Activities."

26 This show was also grounded in a partnership between Canadian and Chinese institutions: "The National Museum of China selected the artifacts and the Canadian Museum of Civilization curated the exhibition." See Canadian Museum of Civilization, "Treasures from China."

27 Canadian Museum of Civilization, "Treasures from China."

28 Quoted in Wallis, "Selling Nations," 272.

29 Canadian Museum of Civilization, "Museums on the Move."

30 See current scholarship on museum diplomacy including Brison and Smith, "The Global Engagement"; Kong, *Museums, International Exhibitions;* Priewe, *Museum Diplomacy;* Grincheva, *Global Trends;* and Smith and Priewe, *Museum Diplomacy.*

31 Lu and Rabinovitch, "Foreword," 5.

32 Canadian Museum of Civilization, "Museums on the Move."

33 "Internal Memorandum from the Exhibitions Planning Officer Exhibitions and Programs," 29 June 2007, CMHA, Ancient Peoples of Canada.

34 "Aboriginal Treasures Are Beijing-Bound."

35 "Exhibitions and Programmes, Report of Presentation to the Executive Committee," CMHA, Chantal Amyot, First Peoples of Canada, 2010-I0020, vol. 4.

36 “Exhibition Exchange Agreement of the Exhibitions Treasures from Beijing: Collections from the National Museum of China and Ancient Peoples of Canada: Collections from the Canadian Museum of Civilization,” 9 December 2005, CMHA, Ancient Peoples of Canada, 2010-I0001, Agreement, 2005–2006.

37 The online exhibition did a great deal to redress the limitations of presenting Indigenous peoples as “ancient,” with its emphasis on the continuity of Indigenous communities and voice given to members of those communities. The online show is still accessible. See “First Peoples of Canada Canadian Museum of Civilization,” online exhibition, accessed 13 November 2023, https://www.historymuseum.ca/cmc/exhibitions/aborig/fp/fpint01e.html.

38 “First Peoples of Canada,” online exhibition.

39 There were several permutations of the title before the museum settled on *First Peoples of Canada: Masterworks from the Canadian Museum of Civilization,* including “Ancient Peoples of Canada: Treasures from the Collections of the Canadian Museum of Civilization,” as well as “First Peoples of Canada: Treasures from the Collections of the Canadian Museum of Civilization.”

40 For Indigenous curatorial practices in connection with the Indians of Canada Pavilion at Expo 67, see Grussani and Phillips, “For We Have Waited,” 115–49.

41 Martin, “Anger and Reconciliation,” 115.

42 Rachelle Dickenson and Lee-Ann Martin, “Turning the Page on the Politics of Inclusion and Exclusion, 30 Years On,” *C Magazine,* 15 December 2019, https://cmagazine.com/articles/turning-the-page-on-the-politics-of-inclusion.

43 Phillips, “Show Times,” 131.

44 This history has significant links to the CMC, which was known for its support of Indigenous contemporary art and which hosted the exhibitions *The Spirit Sings: Artistic Traditions of Canada's First Peoples* and *INDIGENA: Perspectives of Indigenous Peoples on Five Hundred Years.* As curator Lee-Ann Martin notes, many of the same individuals were involved in these exhibitions, reports, and institutions: “‘INDIGENA’ was a logical extension of the Canadian Museum of Civilization's commitment to contemporary Indigenous art; the museum had opened three years earlier, and many of its staff members were participants on the Task Force on Museums and First Peoples.” Martin, “Anger and Reconciliation,” 115.

45 “Exhibitions and Programmes, Report of Presentation.”

46 Jean-Luc Pilon to Nicholette Prince, 21 December 2006, CMHA, Ancient Peoples of Canada, Correspondence.

47 Phillips, “Disrupting Past Paradigms,” 77.

48 Canadian Museum of Civilization, “International Exhibition” (emphasis added).

49 Chantal Amyot to David Morrison and Andrea Laforet, “Films on Contemporary Aboriginal Perspectives – Beijing,” email correspondence, 6 June 2008, CMHA, First Peoples of Canada, 2010-I0020, vol. 3.

50 Phillips, "Show Times," 123 (emphasis in original).
51 "Media Event Scenario," 12 March 2008, CMHA, Nicholette Prince fonds, E2011.2, Chinese Connection, B7 F1.
52 "Media Event Scenario," CMHA, First Peoples of Canada, 2010-I0020, vol. 3.
53 Institute of Ethnology and Anthropology, Chinese Academy of Social Sciences, "Canadian First Peoples' Masterworks."
54 Quoted in "Aboriginal Treasures Are Beijing-Bound," *Nation Talk,* 15 March 2008, http://nationtalk.ca/story/aboriginal-treasures-are-beijing-bound.
55 Quoted in "Aboriginal Treasures Are," *Nation Talk.*
56 Wieclawski, "Museum Enters the Games."
57 Nicolas Gauvin to [unknown], 16 May 2005, CMHA, Ancient Peoples of Canada, Correspondence.
58 Phillips, *Museums Pieces,* 83.
59 Kalant, *National Identity,* 129.
60 Canadian Museum of Civilization, "Exhibition Draws World Attention to Canada at Mexico's Centennial Celebrations," 26 November 2010, Canadian Museum of History, http://www.civilization.ca/media/news/exhibition-draws-world-attention-to-canada-at-mexicos-centennial-celebrations.
61 "Completely Renewed, the National Museum of Cultures to Be Reopened," *Art Daily,* n.d., accessed 27 July 2013, http://www.artdaily.org/index.asp?int_sec=11&int_new=41545&int_modo=1#.UfPo0RbvxmA; "Opening Ceremony: First Peoples of Canada Exhibit," CMHA, Nicholette Prince fonds, E2011.1, Mexico City, B6 F1; Government of Canada, "First Peoples of Canada."
62 *Los primeros pueblos de Canadá: Obras maestras del Museo Canadiense de las Civilizaciones,* brochure, CMHA, Nicholette Prince fonds, E2011.2, Mexico City, B6 F11.
63 *Los primeros pueblos.*
64 *Los primeros pueblos.*
65 "Opening Ceremony: First Peoples of Canada."
66 There is some irony in these efforts, given that Harper was simultaneously cutting funding and dismissing the arts at home. At a 2008 campaign event in Saskatoon, he infamously remarked that "ordinary" Canadians were not concerned with arts funding. As he told his listeners, "I think when ordinary working people come home, turn on the TV and see a gala of a bunch of people at, you know, a rich gala all subsidized by taxpayers claiming their subsidies aren't high enough when they know those subsidies have actually gone up – I'm not sure that's something that resonates with ordinary people." Bruce Campion-Smith, "Arts Uproar? Ordinary Folks Just Don't Care, Harper Says," *Toronto Star,* 24 September 2008. Harper's comment, which came amid federal funding cuts to arts and culture, was widely reported.
67 Lee Berthiaume, "Latin America, Caribbean Remain a Top Priority for Conservatives, John Baird Says," *Postmedia News,* 25 July 2013.

68 Canadian Museum of Civilization, "Exhibition Draws World Attention."

69 See Gobierno de México, "Etnografía del pueblo Kikapú (Kikaapoa) de Coahuila," https://www.gob.mx/inpi/es/articulos/etnografia-del-pueblo-kikapu-kikaapoa; and Tohono O'odham Nation, "Location," http://www.tonation-nsn.gov/location.

70 Government of Canada, "Canada-Mexico First Peoples Dialogue."

71 Government of Canada, "Canada-Mexico First Peoples Dialogue."

72 Government of Canada, "Canada-Mexico First Peoples Dialogue."

73 Fox, *The Fence and the River,* 35.

74 Heartney, "Native Identity," 39.

75 McMaster's significant curatorial work and contributions were recognized in 2022 with a Governor General's Award in Visual and Media Arts (Outstanding Contribution Award).

76 Baker, "Interventions," 17.

77 Baker, "Interventions," 15.

78 McMaster, "Introductions," 57.

79 West, "On the Edge," 11.

80 Marsh, "Bits and Pieces," 368, 348, 355.

81 McMaster, "Kent Monkman," 74; McMaster, "Hector Ruiz," 80; McMaster, "Steven Yazzie," 88.

82 Haworth, "Intersections," 92.

83 West, "On the Edge," 12.

84 In Toronto, *Remix* stimulated conversations about identity and Indigenous art practices. Debate was sparked by a *Globe and Mail* review of the show, where art critic and curator Sarah Milroy questioned the need for Indigenous-focused exhibitions in light of the success of numerous Indigenous artists. Her article generated a great deal of controversy, which the AGO addressed in a panel conversation on 23 August 2009. See Sarah Milroy, "Aboriginal Art Show Riddled with Clichés," *Globe and Mail,* 21 April 2009, http://www.theglobeandmail.com/arts/aboriginal-art-show-riddled-with-cliches/article4211394; and Art Gallery of Ontario, "Are We Past the Age?"

85 Heartney, "Native Identity," 38; Goodyear, "The Challenge of This," 7.

86 Tsouhlarakis, "About"; McMaster, "Anna Tsouhlarakis," 82.

87 Baker, "Interventions," 25.

88 Heartney, "Native Identity," 44.

89 Vizenor, "Native Cosmototemic Art," 42 (emphasis in original).

90 Consider, for example, the National Inquiry into Missing and Murdered Indigenous Women and Girls, the shooting death of Colten Boushie, and the discovery of unmarked graves of Indigenous children at residential schools. See National Inquiry into Missing and Murdered Indigenous Women and Girls, "Reclaiming Power and Place"; Guy Quenneville and Jason Warick, "Shouts of 'Murderer' in Courtroom after Gerald Stanley Acquitted in Colten Boushie Shooting," *CBC News,* 9 February

2018, https://www.cbc.ca/news/canada/saskatoon/gerald-stanley-colten-boushie-verdict-1.4526313; and Angela Sterritt and Courtney Dickson, "'This Is Heavy Truth': Tk'emlúps te Secwépemc Chief Says More to Be Done to Identify Unmarked Graves," *CBC News,* 15 July 2021, https://www.cbc.ca/news/canada/british-columbia/kamloops-residential-school-findings-1.6084185.

91 See Coulthard, *Red Skin, White Masks,* 108, 109; Simpson, *Mohawk Interruptus,* 193; and Daigle, "The Spectacle of Reconciliation," 706.

92 Coulthard, *Red Skin, White Masks,* 128. As Daigle points out, "Indigenous self-determination lies in the autonomy to remain unreconciled." Daigle, "The Spectacle of Reconciliation," 714.

93 Coulthard, *Red Skin, White Masks,* 127.

94 Simpson, *Mohawk Interruptus,* 21.

95 Daigle identifies as "Mushkegowuk (Cree), a member of Constance Lake First Nation in Treaty 9, and of French ancestry." Department of Geography and Planning, University of Toronto, "Michelle Daigle," https://www.geography.utoronto.ca/people/directories/all-faculty/michelle-daigle.

96 Daigle, "The Spectacle of Reconciliation," 706.

97 Ravensbergen, "Potluck Protocols"; Robinson, "Public Writing," 85–99; Robinson, *Hungry Listening.*

98 Robinson, *Hungry Listening,* 97.

99 Sandra Abma, "New Canadian Embassy Woos the French with Indigenous Art," *CBC News,* 23 June 2018, https://www.cbc.ca/news/canada/ottawa/paris-embassy-culture-canada-art-indigenous-1.4712383.

100 Canadian Cultural Centre Paris, "Maria Hupfield: The One Who Keeps On Giving," press release, n.d., https://canada-culture.org/wp-content/uploads/2018/07/frcommuniqué-maria-hupfieldenpress-release-maria-hupfield.pdf.

101 NoiseCat made these comments in relation to the centre's 2018–19 exhibition of Wasauksing First Nation performing artist Maria Hupfield's work. See NoiseCat, "How Canada Uses."

102 Ramírez, "Beyond 'the Fantastic,'" 228.

103 Kalant, *National Identity,* 88.

104 Kalant, *National Identity,* 136.

105 Rickard, "Rebecca Belmore," 68.

Chapter 5: Reading inSite against the Cultural Exemption

1 Although border art may appear at any international site, the genre itself has a specific connection to the Mexico-US border. Art production regarding this locale contends with its history, which began with the 1848 Treaty of Guadalupe Hidalgo following war between Mexico and the United States. Art from the Mexico-US border is also particularly prominent on the West Coast, and in the late twentieth

century, numerous artists produced works in and about the border zone between the cities of San Diego and Tijuana. As scholar Claire Fox explains, defining the genre of border art is problematic because "the term does not posit a shared political tendency, aesthetic project, or site of production." Fox, *The Fence and the River,* 44. Geographer Michael Dear and architect/artist Gustavo Leclerc add that the phrase "border art" automatically marginalizes the work because it categorizes it as peripheral. Dear and Leclerc, "Introduction," 14. Border art becomes particularly difficult to define when borders are understood conceptually. Artist Guillermo Gómez-Peña writes that "whenever and wherever two or more cultures meet – peacefully or violently – there is a border experience." Gómez-Peña, "The Multicultural Paradigm," 183.

2 Chávez, "Multi-Correct Politically," 5.

3 Avalos, "A Wag Dogging a Tale," 74.

4 I explore some of these ideas in Smith, "The Permeable Border," 91–106; Stirrup and Clarke, "Straddling Boundaries," 2.

5 Amihat-Szary, "The Geopolitical Meaning," 951–62.

6 Art Gallery of Windsor, "Border Cultures."

7 Fusco, *The Bodies,* 64. The word "inSite" has been treated in several ways throughout its history. For consistency, I refer to the festival generally as inSite but follow the lead of the exhibition catalogues in discussing its various iterations, with the result that the name will not necessarily be consistent throughout.

8 "inSITE_Archive Synopsis> Sinopsis," inSite Archive, inSITE94, Terry Allen – Cross the Razor.

9 "Javier Téllez," 72.

10 Chávez, "Multi-Correct Politically," 8.

11 Wallen, "Barrier or Bridge," 137.

12 Cruz, "Border Postcards," 71.

13 Chávez, "Multi-Correct Politically," 9.

14 Chávez, "Multi-Correct Politically," 9.

15 Herzog, "Global Tijuana," 136.

16 Chávez, "Multi-Correct Politically," 4.

17 Berelowitz, "Border Art since 1965," 149.

18 Baza and Davies, "Foreword," ix; Chávez, "Multi-Correct Politically," 4; Centro Cultural de la Raza, "Legacy," https://centrodelaraza.com/legacy.

19 Grynsztejn, "La Frontera/The Border," 25.

20 Arce, "Forms of Resistance," 161.

21 Controversy surrounded *Dos Ciudades,* in part due to the history of engagement with the border by the centro and artists' collectives such as BAW/TAF. The issue turned on who had the authority to speak about the border.

22 Berelowitz, "Border Art since 1965," 168; Chávez, "Multi-Correct Politically," 5.

23 The last large-scale festival version of inSite was held in 2005. However, inSite has participated in several ventures since then, including a 2007 conference and the creation of a bilingual and binational archive to document its history. More recently, it has established a website archiving the initiative, as well as *INSITE Journal* and a new platform for creative projects, titled *Common Places*. For more, see inSite: Art Practices in the Public Sphere, https://insiteart.org.

24 "Javier Téllez," 72; "Mauricio Dias and Walter Riedweg," 98.

25 Yúdice, *The Expediency of Culture*, 301.

26 Klein, "Performance, Post-Border," 31.

27 Yúdice, *The Expediency of Culture*, 297.

28 Berelowitz, "Border Art since 1965," 171.

29 Michael Krichman, conversation with author, San Diego, 20 May 2010.

30 Yúdice, *The Expediency of Culture*, 296–97. Berelowitz, however, says that the BAW/TAF collective had more legitimacy than other inSite artists. The work of its artists was "deeply rooted in the experience of the border, keenly attuned to its complex dynamics." Berelowitz, "Border Art since 1965," 162.

31 Notably, inSite had a higher profile in Mexico than in the United States. Louis Hock, an artist who participated in inSITE97, found that "whenever I travel in Mexico it always amazes me; I mean people know what inSite is ... It was clearly represented in the news media; it was clearly represented in the arts scene. People know what ... inSite is, or was. That's less true in the United States." Louis Hock, conversation with author, San Diego, 24 May 2010. Krichman agreed that inSite also had a much greater impact in Tijuana than in San Diego and in Mexico generally than in the United States. Tijuanan and Mexican audiences were more engaged with events, and the Mexican media provided more coverage. Krichman, conversation, 20 May 2010.

32 Krichman, conversation, 20 May 2010.

33 Jordan Crandall, conversation with author, San Diego, 13 May 2010.

34 Hock, conversation, 24 May 2010.

35 The association between inSite and Installation Gallery – as the non-profit organization and legal entity that ran inSite – continued throughout the festivals.

36 Leah Ollman, "'IN/SITE 92' a Comeback for Installation Art: Installation Gallery Makes a New Showing with an Innovative, Multi-Gallery Exhibit Concept," *Los Angeles Times*, 5 September 1992.

37 Stein, "Looking Backward," 418.

38 Quoted in Ollman, "'IN/SITE 92' a Comeback."

39 "Media Release/Notificación a la Prensa," inSite Archive, Version Materials, IN/SITE92.

40 "INSITE92 Participating Institutions/Instituciones participantes," inSite Archive, Version Materials, IN/SITE92.

41 "INSITE92 Participating Artists/Artistas participantes," inSite Archive, Version Materials, IN/SITE92.

42 "Installation 1992, IN/SITE92, Mesa College Art Gallery, San Diego, Collaboration by Lewis deSoto and James Luna, *Kísh Tétayawet Wampkísh (Dreamhouse),*" inSite Archive, Version Materials, IN/SITE92.

43 Robert L. Pincus, "A Bold Project Full of IN/SITE," *San Diego Union-Tribune,* 22 November 1992, E-1.

44 Pincus, "A Bold Project," E-1.

45 Pincus, "A Bold Project," E-1.

46 Krichman, conversation, 20 May 2010.

47 Krichman, conversation, 20 May 2010.

48 Stein, "Looking Backward," 418.

49 Ulf Rollof's work dealt with a community of children at Playas de Tijuana, but it did not comment on the border. Similarly, works by Carmela Castrejón Diego and Jean Lowe and Kim MacConnel gestured toward the differences between Mexico and the United States but did not specifically mention the border.

50 "inSITE94 Synopsis> Sinopsis," inSite Archive, Version Materials, inSITE94.

51 "inSITE94: An Introduction," inSite Archive, Version Materials, inSITE94.

52 Forsha, "Foreword," 7.

53 Forsha, "Foreword," 7.

54 Yard, "Tagged Turf," 34.

55 "inSITE94 Synopsis> Sinopsis."

56 "inSITE94: An Introduction."

57 Robert L. Pincus, "OUTSIDE THE LINES Transcending Borders, Vibrant Tijuana Artists Head for Creative Frontiers," *San Diego Union-Tribune,* 26 November 2001, D-1; Ann Jarmusch, "A Colonial Home Companion," *San Diego Union-Tribune,* 16 October 1994, H-22.

58 Jarmusch, "A Colonial Home," H-22.

59 Quoted in Stein, "Looking Backward," 420.

60 Quoted in Stein, "Looking Backward," 420.

61 Quoted in Stein, "Looking Backward," 420.

62 In 1997, Cuenca became executive director of inSite, alongside Krichman.

63 Stein, "Looking Backward," 419.

64 Quoted in Stein, "Looking Backward," 419.

65 Krichman, conversation, 20 May 2010.

66 For decades after the Mexican Revolution, the PRI formed the federal government, with PAN as the official opposition. The PRI monopoly on power was broken at the municipal level in 1947, eight years after PAN was founded, when Manuel Torres Serranía of PAN was elected mayor of Quiroga, Michoacán. PAN did not defeat the PRI at the federal level until the 2000 election.

67 Quoted in Stein, "Looking Backward," 419.
68 Krichman, conversation, 20 May 2010.
69 Krichman, conversation, 20 May 2010.
70 Krichman et al., "Acknowledgements," 11.
71 Krichman et al., "Acknowledgements," 11.
72 Krichman et al., "Acknowledgements," 11.
73 Medina, "A Line Is a Central Point," 55.
74 Stein, "Looking Backward," 420.
75 Krichman and Cuenca, "Preface/Prefacio," 8 (emphasis in original).
76 Bradley et al., "Private Time," 52.
77 This work is also identified in the archive and catalogue as *Toy an-Horse*.
78 Estrada and Haudenschild, "Forewords/Prólogos," 6.
79 Leah Ollman, "A New Frame for the Border; inSITE97 Examines the Relationship between the United States and Mexico through Numerous Site-Specific Projects," *Los Angeles Times*, 21 September 1997, 4.
80 Krichman and Cuenca, "Preface/Prefacio," 9.
81 "inSITE97 Synopsis> Sinopsis," inSite Archive, Version Materials, inSITE97.
82 Ollman, "A New Frame," 4.
83 Ollman, "A New Frame," 4.
84 Krichman and Cuenca, "Preface/Prefacio," 8.
85 Krichman, conversation, 20 May 2010.
86 "Francis Alÿs," 66.
87 Bradley et al., "Private Time," 58.
88 Bradley et al., "Private Time," 57.
89 Yúdice, *The Expediency of Culture*, 287–88.
90 "Louis Hock," 78.
91 The artist also discusses the work as a type of monument. See Insite, "Louis Hock."
92 Hock, conversation, 24 May 2010.
93 Insite, "Louis Hock."
94 Hock, conversation, 24 May 2010.
95 Hock, conversation, 24 May 2010. Hock specified that this happened about "a month or so" after the work had been installed. Insite, "Louis Hock."
96 Hock, conversation, 24 May 2010.
97 "inSITE2000: An Introduction," inSite Archive, Version Materials, inSITE2000.
98 "inSITE2000: An Introduction"; "inSITE2000 Curatorial Statement> Marco curatorial."
99 "Fact Sheet," inSite Archive, Version Materials, inSITE2000.
100 "inSITE2000: An Introduction."
101 Krichman and Cuenca, "Directors' Statement," 15.
102 Krichman and Cuenca, "Directors' Statement," 14.

103 Krichman, conversation, 20 May 2010.
104 "inSITE2000: An Introduction"; Krichman and Cuenca, "Directors' Statement," 15.
105 "inSITE2000: An Introduction."
106 "inSITE2000 Curatorial Statement."
107 "Residencies/Residencias," 60; "inSITE2000: An Introduction."
108 Crandall, conversation, 13 May 2010.
109 "inSITE2000: An Introduction."
110 "inSITE2000: An Introduction."
111 "Mônica Nador," 87–88.
112 "Krzysztof Wodiczko," 75, 77.
113 Crandall, conversation, 13 May 2010; "Jordan Crandall, Heat-Seeking," 48.
114 Crandall, conversation, 13 May 2010.
115 "A Note on Context," 6–7.
116 Yard, "A Dynamic Equilibrium," 12.
117 "Scenarios," 373.
118 Pedrosa, "Farsites," 22.
119 Pedrosa, "Farsites," 23.
120 Cuenca and Krichman, "Foreword/inSite," 6.
121 Quoted in Stein, "Looking Backward," 424.
122 "October 2003/Residencies," 25.
123 See "Unfolding Process," 50–65.
124 The game was accessible at Coco Fusco's website http://thing.net/~cocofusco/StartPage.html until 2020. Although it can no longer be played, the profiles of its four characters are still accessible at the webpage.
125 Ricardo Dominguez, conversation with author, San Diego, 10 May 2010.
126 Dominguez, conversation, 10 May 2010.
127 *Brinco* is an example of various art projects whose purpose is to help migrants, such as *Transborder Immigrant Tool* by artists Micha Cárdenas, Amy Sara Carroll, Ricardo Dominguez, Elle Mehrmand, and Brett Stalbaum, all of whom are members of the collective Electronic Disturbance Theater/b.a.n.g lab. A 2007 project, *Transborder Immigrant Tool* was a free mobile phone app that enabled users to employ the GPS as a compass, included information about specific aids for crossing the border, such as water or help stations, and also featured poetry. Another similar project is *Art Rebate/Arte reembolso* by Avalos, Sisco, and Hock, a 1993 conceptual project that gave ten-dollar bills to undocumented migrant workers in the San Diego region in acknowledgment of their contributions to the American economy through their labour and payment of sales taxes.
128 "Judi Werthein," 162.
129 Amy Isackson, "State-of-the-Art Shoes Aid Migrants," *BBC News,* 17 November 2005, http://news.bbc.co.uk/2/hi/americas/4445342.stm; "Judi Werthein," 162.

130 Grynsztejn, "La Frontera/The Border," 23.
131 Kropp and Dear, "Peopling Alta California," 79.
132 Canclini, "A Re-Imagined Public Art," 102.
133 Dominguez, conversation, 10 May 2010.
134 Dominguez, conversation, 10 May 2010.
135 Krichman, conversation, 20 May 2010.
136 Krichman, conversation, 20 May 2010.
137 Krichman, conversation, 20 May 2010. Friendship Park lies within Border Field State Park in California.
138 Dominguez, conversation, 10 May 2010.
139 Dominguez, conversation, 10 May 2010.
140 Quoted in Fox, *The Fence and the River*, 45.
141 "Alfredo Jaar," 242–43.
142 Crandall, conversation, 13 May 2010.
143 Crandall, conversation, 13 May 2010.
144 Louis Hock's water fountain could be considered an exception since it literally changed the border fence. Crandall's critique speaks to debates around the emancipatory potential of participatory art projects, often referred to as social practice or relational aesthetics, the latter a term coined by curator and critic Nicolas Bourriaud. In the early twenty-first century, art historians Claire Bishop and Grant Kester debated the impact of relational aesthetics. See Bishop, "Antagonism"; Bishop, "The Social Turn," 178–83; Claire Bishop, "Claire Bishop Responds," *Artforum* 44, 9 (2006): 23; Bishop, *Artificial Hells;* Bourriaud, *Relational Aesthetics;* Kester, "Another Turn," 22–23; Kester, *Conversation Pieces;* and Kester, *The One and the Many.*
145 Fusco, *The Bodies*, 64.
146 Krichman, conversation, 20 May 2010.
147 Yúdice, "Extract of George," 81.
148 Yúdice, *The Expediency of Culture*, 311 (emphasis added).

Chapter 6: Changing Narratives of Free Trade in Video Art

1 *Trade Winds (Canada) Ltd* was written and directed by Clive Robertson and narrated by Frances Leeming and Clive Robertson. All subsequent description of this work, unless otherwise noted, comes from the video itself.
2 Diamond and Kibbins, "Total Recall," 268. Note that Diamond and Kibbins categorize Lisa Steele and Kim Tomczak's 1988 video *White Dawn*, discussed below, as an example of new documentary.
3 Diamond and Kibbins, "Total Recall," 268.
4 Diamond and Kibbins, "Total Recall," 269.
5 The Massey Commission remains a touchstone for arts and cultural policy in Canada. For a detailed analysis of the commission and its report see Litt, *The Muses*. For

more on the history of the Canada Council, see Gattinger, *The Roots of Culture*. In *The Origins of the Arts Council Movement,* Anna Rosser Upchurch also discusses the origins of the Canada Council, placing it in a larger global context with the formation of arts councils in Britain and the United States.

6 Marisol J. D'Andrea explores the ambiguous relationship between government and artists under arm's-length funding structures. Assessing government priorities and arts funding distributed via peer review, she argues that such funding models are vulnerable to symbolic power and may support government agendas. See D'Andrea, "Symbolic Power," 245–58.

7 For instance, as a federal Crown corporation the Canada Council receives funding from the government but distributes awards largely via peer assessment, which provides a measure of independence and protection for artistic agency. See Canada Council for the Arts, "Decision-Making Process."

8 I see video art as a broad category encompassing contemporary productions intended for any manner of screening and/or display in a gallery. For a short overview of some of the difficulties in characterizing video art, see Westgeest, "Introduction," 5–7. In "Flaming Creatures," 46, artist and scholar Gary Kibbins comments on how video "trades on its 'alternative' status."

9 Gale, *Videotexts*, 1.

10 In the 1970s, Canadian artists established a range of centres through which to circulate video. One of the first was Art Metropole in Toronto, which emerged around the same time as Video Inn. Other significant distribution centres followed, including Vtape. See AA Bronson and Theodore Kerr, "Oral History Interview with AA Bronson, 2017 March 3, 5, and 6," Smithsonian Archives of American Art, https://www.aaa.si.edu/download_pdf_transcript/ajax?record_id=edanmdm-AAADCD_oh_387819.

11 Erin Morton, "Introduction: Unsettling Canadian Art History," in Morton, *Unsettling,* 4–5, 23.

12 Recent scholarship has sought to address this topic, with an emphasis on Mexico and the US-Mexico borderlands. See Carroll, *REMEX.*

13 Gale, *Videotexts,* 4.

14 This reuse of editorial content allowed American magazines such as *Sports Illustrated* to avoid tariffs that targeted foreign-produced magazines, since the split-run periodicals were printed in Canada. Additionally, split-run periodicals allowed American magazines to claim a larger portion of the Canadian advertising market than Canadian magazines, which meant lost revenue for these domestic periodicals. In the mid-1990s, Canada introduced legislation (Bill C-103) to apply an excise tax to split-run periodicals. In response, the United States brought a complaint against Canada to the World Trade Organization (WTO), alleging that government restrictions set

up to protect Canadian periodicals contravened the General Agreement on Tariffs and Trade. The WTO ruled in favour of the United States in 1997, and Canada withdrew these protectionist measures. See World Trade Organization, "Canada – Certain Measures"; World Trade Organization, "Canada – Periodicals," https://www.wto.org/english/tratop_e/dispu_e/cases_e/1pagesum_e/ds31sum_e.pdf; and Green, "The Great Cultural Divide."

15 Although Canadian broadcasting is not addressed in this book, the issue of cultural protection is prominent in this area as well. Broadcasting policy was initially implemented because of a scarcity of radio bands, but it also protected Canadian cultural production, thus advancing Canadian content. For content requirements and the Canadian Radio-Television and Telecommunications Commission, see Armstrong, *Broadcasting Policy,* 7–8. The dominance of US media was extensively discussed during the late twentieth century, including in arts periodicals such as *Fuse.* See "Special Supplement Br-r-r-roadcasting: The Winter of Our Discontent," *Fuse* 43 (Winter 1986–87). I thank Bryan Gee for bringing this special issue to my attention.

16 Roberts, *Discrepant Parallels,* 19.

17 Curnoe's work was critiqued and censored for its anti-Americanism, leading to a great deal of notoriety. See Roger, *Greg Curnoe.*

18 Crean, *Who's Afraid?,* 277.

19 Crean, *Who's Afraid?,* 278.

20 An earlier version of the arguments presented in this section appears in Smith, "The Permeable Border," 91–106; and in Smith, "Clive Robertson," 78–79.

21 The title *White Dawn* invokes reference to a popular commercial film from the same decade: *Red Dawn* (1984). Produced during the Cold War, *Red Dawn* fictionalized a Soviet invasion of the United States.

22 Steele and Tomczak, "White Dawn."

23 Steele and Tomczak, "White Dawn." All subsequent description of this work, unless otherwise noted, comes from the video itself.

24 The voiceover is integral to advancing the narrative. Throughout the work, the protagonist remains unnamed and never speaks directly to the viewer.

25 All subsequent description of this work, unless otherwise noted, comes from the video itself.

26 Manly, "The Winning of the North."

27 Manly, "The Winning."

28 Manly, "The Winning."

29 Moreton-Robinson, *The White Possessive,* xi.

30 Tuck and Yang, "Decolonization Is Not," 6.

31 Tuck and Yang, "Decolonization Is Not," 9.

32 Mills, *The Empire Within*, 60.
33 "Why do we *need to* represent ourselves as naive? What is the point of making room for the other *if not* as a metaphor for the self? What is the function of erasure? What is made possible by the idea that 'diversity' is always new? *Who* does denial benefit? To answer these questions is to begin to understand why the road to change is strewn with pitfalls." Nicolas, "Maîtres," 43–44 (emphasis in original).
34 "We are erasing centuries of political, militant and intellectual contributions by Indigenous and racialised women, while consolidating the myth of an 'old stock' and homogeneous Quebec, where ethnic diversity is something new and therefore alien, or even destined for successful 'integration' into Quebec." Nicolas, "Maîtres," 43.
35 Tuck and Yang, "Decolonization Is Not," 10.
36 Tuck and Yang, "Decolonization Is Not," 17.
37 Manly, "The Winning."
38 Tuck and Yang, "Decolonization Is Not," 3.
39 Here, Robertson alludes to the attempt to amend the Canadian Constitution through the Charlottetown Accord, which was defeated by referendum in 1992, following on the earlier failure of the Meech Lake Accord in the late 1980s.
40 Clive Robertson, "Trade Winds."
41 See J. Keri Cronin and Kirsty Robertson, "Imagining Resistance: An Introduction," in *Imagining Resistance: Visual Culture and Activism in Canada*, ed. J. Keri Cronin and Kirsty Robertson (Waterloo: Wilfrid Laurier University Press, 2011), 17, 21.
42 Cronin and Robertson, "Anarchy," 215–16.
43 Cronin and Robertson, "Anarchy," 216. The authors suggest that a plethora of film and video projects emerged from the FTAA protests in 2001.
44 Cronin and Robertson, "Anarchy," 216.
45 Fiske, "Videotech," 391.
46 All subsequent description of these works, unless otherwise noted, comes from the videos.
47 The compilation is titled *Blah Blah Blah: (Re)viewing Quebec*. The Toronto-based collective comprised David Best, Karma Clarke-Davis, Michael Connolly, Christopher Donaldson, Julie Fox, Gisèle Gordon, John Greyson, Ali Kazimi, Kevin McMahon, Lyndsay Moffatt, Charles Officer, Malcolm Rogge, Jody Shapiro, and b.h. Yael. See Allen and Marks, "Biographical Notes," 51–52.
48 Quoted in Jan Allen, "Better Worlds," in *Better Worlds: Activist and Utopian Projects by Artists*, ed. Jan Allen and Laura U. Marks (Kingston: Agnes Etherington Art Centre, 2002), 24.
49 Allen, "Better Worlds," 26.
50 John Greyson, "Packin,'" Vtape online catalogue, https://www.vtape.org/video?vi=5116.
51 Allen, "Better Worlds," 24.

52 Allen, "Better Worlds," 26.
53 Marks, "Plunging," 42.
54 Marks, "Plunging," 42.
55 Fiske, "Videotech," 391.
56 All description of this work, unless otherwise noted, comes from the video itself.
57 I acknowledge that norms of circulation differ between documentary, which is not typically produced for gallery and museum display, and video art, which is. By choosing to include *The Original Summit* in my discussion in this chapter I am approaching video as a broad category that encompasses a range of production from experimental art to feature-length documentary.
58 Ward Churchill is also interviewed, though his claim to Indigenous identity is disputed. See Cook-Lynn, "Scandal," 85–89.
59 Rebeka Tabobondung and Adrian Kahgee, "The Original Summit: Journey to the Sacred Uprising," 2002, Vtape online catalogue, https://www.vtape.org/video?vi=5123.
60 All description of this work, unless otherwise noted, comes from the video itself.
61 Benedict Anderson, "Staging Antimodernism," 98.
62 Heather Anderson, "Antonia Hirsch," 70.
63 Heather Anderson, "Antonia Hirsch," 70.
64 Heather Anderson, "Antonia Hirsch," 70.
65 Hirsch, "Tacet."
66 Heather Anderson, "Antonia Hirsch," 70.
67 Heather Anderson, "Antonia Hirsch," 103.
68 Hirsch, "Tacet," accessed June 27, 2013. Website was subsequently revised.
69 Hirsch, "Tacet," accessed June 27, 2013. Website was subsequently revised.
70 Tuck and Yang, "Decolonization Is Not," 7.
71 Peter Dykhuis, "State Dinner," artist's website, http://www.dykhuis.ca/art/state-dinner/state-dinner.php.
72 Peter Dykhuis to Sarah E.K. Smith, personal correspondence, 17 April 2024.
73 Dykhuis to Smith, 17 April 2024.
74 Dykhuis to Smith, 17 April 2024.

Epilogue: Art and the Invention of North America

1 Adams, *Continental Divides,* 17.
2 Adams, *Continental Divides,* 14.
3 Drache, "Big Picture Realities," 1.
4 Dosman, "Brazil and Mexico," 221.
5 Dosman, "Brazil and Mexico," 226.
6 Dosman, "Brazil and Mexico," 227.
7 Wallis, "Selling Nations," 266.

8 Quoted in Gómez-Peña, *The New World,* 10, 11.

9 For a history of the IAU, see de Peuter and Cohen, "The Art of Collective," 333–46; and Smith, "Condé and Beveridge's Art," 45–55. My discussion of the IAU draws from a larger and ongoing collaborative research project with scholar Greig de Peuter.

10 General Meeting, 8 August 1986, Queen's University Archives (QUA), Artists Union: General, Carole Condé and Karl Beveridge fonds, 1965–2010, F2665.

11 *Living Culture/Living Wage,* flyer, n.d., QUA, Member records file, Carole Condé and Karl Beveridge fonds, 1965–2010, F2665.

12 *Adopt an Artist?,* pamphlet, n.d., QUA, New Members - Info Package, Carole Condé and Karl Beveridge fonds, 1965–2010, F2665.

13 *Adopt an Artist?*

14 Letter from Lynn McDonald, 8 October 1985, QUA, NDP Reports and Policy Papers, Carole Condé and Karl Beveridge fonds, 1965–2010, F2665.

15 *Public Forum: Free Trade and the Arts,* poster/ad, n.d., QUA, Carole Condé and Karl Beveridge fonds, 1965–2010, F2665.

16 Karl Beveridge, Arts Watcher, Lynn McDonald, M.P., NDP Arts and Culture Critic, 12 November 1985, QUA, Carole Condé and Karl Beveridge fonds, 1965–2010, F2665.

17 Robertson made these remarks at the Strategies for Success conference organized by the Vancouver Artists League. Stephen Godfrey, "Artists Paint Bleak Picture but Cheer Guaranteed Income," *Globe and Mail,* 14 June 1986, QUA, Posters, Pamphlets (Archives), Press Clipping, Carole Condé and Karl Beveridge fonds, 1965–2010, F2665.

18 Jim Miller, "Artists Union Writes Back," letter to the *Ottawa Citizen,* n.d., QUA, Carole Condé and Karl Beveridge fonds, 1965–2010, F2665.

19 IAU newsletter, n.d., QUA, Posters, Pamphlets (Archives), Carole Condé and Karl Beveridge fonds, 1965–2010, F2665.

20 General Meeting, 8 August 1986.

21 Coalition Against Free Trade to Marjorie Cohen, 19 May 1987, QUA, Carole Condé and Karl Beveridge fonds, 1965–2010, F2665.

22 IAU newsletter, n.d., QUA, Artists Union: General, Carole Condé and Karl Beveridge fonds, 1965–2010, F2665.

23 January newsletter [IAU], n.d., QUA, Artists Union: General, Carole Condé and Karl Beveridge fonds, 1965–2010, F2665.

24 IAU newsletter, September 1986, QUA, Posters, Pamphlets, Carole Condé and Karl Beveridge fonds, 1965–2010, F2665.

25 Drache, "Big Picture Realities," 1.

26 FOCAL, "Our History."

27 The Conservative Party came to power as a minority government in the 2006 election. Jennifer Ditchburn, "Cuts Belie Harper's Commitment to Building Democracy Abroad," *Globe and Mail,* 4 April 2012.

28 Quoted in Lee Berthiaume, "Latin America, Caribbean Remain a Top Priority for Conservatives, John Baird Says," *Postmedia News*, 25 July 2013.

29 Berthiaume, "Latin America."

30 Waning interest in public diplomacy was evidenced by the government's abolishment of the Understanding Canada program in 2012. Run by DFAIT since 1977, Understanding Canada provided key funding for Canadian studies programs abroad. Its cancellation was widely decried by academic communities. M. Blanchfield, "Canada Axes Foreign Studies Program Despite Being Told of Economic Spinoffs," *Globe and Mail*, 16 May 2012; Paul Martin, "Canada's Image Abroad: Fade to Black," *University Affairs/Affaires universitaires*, 6 June 2012, http://www.universityaffairs.ca/opinion/in-my-opinion/canadas-image-abroad-fade-to-black.

31 For instance, see Canadian Dance Assembly/L'Assemblée canadienne de la dance, "End of Trade Routes and Promart Cultural Funding Programs Threatens End of Canada Abroad," press release, 13 August 2008. See also Greg Quill and Richard Brennan, "Torys Cut Five More Arts Programs," *Toronto Star*, 16 August 2008, https://www.thestar.com/news/canada/2008/08/16/tories_cut_five_more_arts_programs.html.

32 Carlo Dade to Sarah E.K. Smith, personal correspondence, 25 September 2011.

33 Dade to Smith, 25 September 2011.

34 See Canada, Standing Senate Committee on Foreign Affairs and International Trade, "Cultural Diplomacy."

35 Government of Canada, "The Canada-United States-Mexico Agreement (CUSMA)," last modified 11 November 2024, https://www.international.gc.ca/trade-commerce/trade-agreements-accords-commerciaux/agr-acc/cusma-aceum/index.aspx?lang=eng.

Bibliography

Archive Collections

Canadian Heritage (CH)

Virtual Museum of Canada (VMC), Executive Produced Exhibitions – Panoramas: The North American Landscape in Art

Canadian Museum of History Archives (CMHA)

Ancient Peoples of Canada: Treasures from the Collections of the Canadian Museum of Civilization, 2010-I0020

Nicholette Prince fonds, E2011.2

inSite Archive

IN/SITE92

inSITE94

inSITE97

inSITE2000

inSite_05

McMichael Canadian Art Collection Archives (MCACA)

McMichael Documents, *Carr, O'Keeffe, Kahlo: Places of Their Own*

Montreal Museum of Fine Arts Archives (MMFAA)

L'arte Moderne Mexicain, 1999, 610-86

National Gallery of Canada Archives (NGCA)

Exhibitions – Mexican Art Ex. (Proposed), 1948–1954

Exhibitions – Mexican Art Today, 1943

Exhibitions – Mexican Exchange Exhibition
Exhibitions – Mexican Modern Art, 1998
Exhibitions – Mexico as Muse, 1999
49th Parallel fonds

National Museum of Women in the Arts Archives
Curatorial Exhibition Design and Exhibition Files, *Carr, O'Keeffe, Kahlo: Places of Their Own*

Queen's University Archives (QUA)
Carole Condé and Karl Beveridge fonds, 1965–2010, F2665

Smithsonian American Art Museum (SAAM)
Curatorial Office, Exhibition Records, 1981–2001

Winnipeg Art Gallery Archives (WAGA)
Exhibition Files, Panoramas: The North American Landscape in Art

Other Sources

Abaroa, Eduardo. "Mobility." In *Moi et ma circonstance: mobilité dans l'art contemporain Mexicain,* 26–33. Montreal: Musée des beaux-arts, 1999.

Adams, Rachel. *Continental Divides: Remapping the Cultures of North America.* Chicago: University of Chicago Press, 2009.

"Alfredo Jaar, La Nube/The Cloud." In *inSITE2000–2001: Parajes fugitivos/Fugitive Sites,* ed. Osvaldo Sánchez and Cecilia Garza, 242–45. San Diego: Installation Gallery, 2002.

Allen, Jan. "Better Worlds." In *Better Worlds: Activist and Utopian Projects by Artists,* ed. Jan Allen and Laura U. Marks, 9–34. Kingston: Agnes Etherington Art Centre, 2002.

Allen, Jan, and Laura U. Marks. "Biographical Notes." In *Better Worlds: Activist and Utopian Projects by Artists,* ed. Jan Allen and Laura U. Marks, 51–52. Kingston: Agnes Etherington Art Centre, 2002.

Amihat-Szary, Anne-Laure. "The Geopolitical Meaning of a Contemporary Visual Arts Upsurge on the Canada-US Border." *International Journal* 67, 4 (Autumn 2012): 951–62.

Anderson, Benedict. *Imagined Communities: Reflections on the Origin and Spread of Nationalism.* London: Verso, 2006.

–. "Staging Antimodernism in the Age of High Capitalist Nationalism." In *Antimodernism and Artistic Experience: Policing the Boundaries of Modernity,* ed. Lynda Jessup, 87–103. Toronto: University of Toronto Press, 2001.

Anderson, Heather. "Antonia Hirsch." In *It Is What It Is: Recent Acquisitions of New Canadian Art,* 70–71. Ottawa: National Gallery of Canada, 2011.

Aragon, Alba F. "Uninhabited Dresses: Frida Kahlo, from Icon of Mexico to Fashion Muse." *Fashion Theory* 18, 5 (2014): 517–49.

Arce, José Manuel Valenzuela. "Forms of Resistance, Corridors of Power: Public Art on the Mexico-U.S. Border." In *Over Here: International Perspectives on Art and Culture,* ed. Gerardo Mosquera and Jean Fisher, 154–81. New York: New Museum of Contemporary Art, 2004.

Argonza, Mariza Rosales, ed. *Vues transversales: panorama de le la scène artistique latino-québécoise.* Montreal: Les éditions du CIDIHCA/La Fondation LatineArte, 2018.

Armony, Victor. "Latin American Communities in Canada: Trends in Diversity and Integration." *Canadian Ethnic Studies* 46, 3 (2014): 7–34.

Armstrong, Robert. *Broadcasting Policy in Canada.* 2nd ed. Toronto: University of Toronto Press, 2016.

Aronczyk, Melissa, and Miranda J. Brady. "Branding History at the Canadian Museum of Civilization." *Canadian Journal of Communication* 40, 2 (2015): 165–84. https://doi.org/10.22230/cjc.2015v40n2a2812.

Art Gallery of Ontario. "Are We Past the Age of an Aboriginal Art Show?" 23 August 2009. https://ago.ca/events/are-we-past-age-aboriginal-art-show.

Art Gallery of Windsor. "Border Cultures: Part One (Homes, Land)." https://www.agw.ca/exhibition/369.

Augaitis, Daina. "Stan Douglas." In *Baja to Vancouver: The West Coast and Contemporary Art,* ed. Ralph Rugoff, 44–47. San Francisco: CCA Wattis Institute for Contemporary Arts, 2003.

Avalos, David. "A Wag Dogging a Tale." In *La Frontera/The Border: Art about the Mexico/United States Border Experience,* ed. Natasha Bonilla Martinez, 59–75. San Diego: Centro Cultural de la Raza and Museum of Contemporary Art, San Diego, 1993.

Azzi, Stephen. *Reconcilable Differences: A History of Canada-US Relations.* Oxford: Oxford University Press, 2014.

Baker, Joe. "Interventions: Making a New Space for Indigenous Art." In *Remix: New Modernities in a Post-Indian World,* ed. Joe Baker and Gerald McMaster, 15–35. Phoenix: National Museum of the American Indian, Smithsonian Institution, and the Heard Museum, 2007.

Balfe, Judith Huggins "Artworks as Symbols in International Politics." *International Journal of Politics, Culture, and Society* 1, 2 (1987): 5–27.

Bartra, Roger. "I and My Circumstances/ My Circumstances and I: Melancholy and Mobility." In *Moi et ma circonstance: mobilité dans l'art contemporain Mexicain,* 102–6. Montreal: Musée des beaux-arts, 1999.

Baza, Larry T., and Hugh M. Davies. "Foreword." In *La Frontera/The Border: Art about the Mexico/United States Border Experience,* ed. Natasha Bonilla Martinez, ix–xi. San Diego: Centro Cultural de la Raza and Museum of Contemporary Art, San Diego, 1993.

Berelowitz, Jo-Anne. "Border Art since 1965." In *Postborder City: Cultural Spaces of Bajalta California,* ed. Michael Dear and Gustavo Leclerc, 143–81. New York: Routledge, 2003.

Berger, Dina. "Goodwill Ambassadors on Holiday: Tourism, Diplomacy, and Mexico-U.S. Relations." In *Holiday in Mexico: Critical Reflections on Tourism and Tourist Encounters,* ed. Dina Berger and Andrew G. Wood, 107–29. Durham: Duke University Press, 2010.

Bishop, Claire. "Antagonism and Relational Aesthetics." *October* 110 (2004): 51–79.

–. *Artificial Hells: Participatory Art and the Politics of Spectatorship.* London: Verso, 2012.

–. "The Social Turn: Collaboration and Its Discontents." *Artforum* 44, 6 (2006): 178–83.

Bothwell, Robert. *Your Country, My Country: A Unified History of the United States and Canada.* Oxford: Oxford University Press, 2015.

Bourriaud, Nicolas. *Relational Aesthetics.* Dijon: Les Presses du Réel, 2002.

Bradley, Jessica, Olivier Debroise, Ivo Mesquita, and Sally Yard. "Private Time in Public Space: A Dialogue/Tiempo privado en espacio público: un diálogo." In *inSITE97: Private Time in Public Space,* ed. Sally Yard, 50–63. San Diego: Installation Gallery, 1998.

Brison, Jeffrey, and Lynda Jessup. "*Terre Sauvage:* Globalizing Landscapes and the Group of Seven." *Journal of Canadian Studies* 56, 3 (2022): 495–535.

Brison, Jeffrey, and Sarah E.K. Smith, eds. "The Global Engagement of Museums in Canada: Report 2021." https://doi.org/10.5206/VDJM2980.

Bronson, A.A. "The Humiliation of the Bureaucrat: Artist-Run Centres as Museums by Artists." In *Museums by Artists,* ed. Peggy Gale and A.A. Bronson, 29–37. Toronto: Art Metropole, 1983.

Canada. Standing Senate Committee on Foreign Affairs and International Trade. "Cultural Diplomacy at the Front Stage of Canada's Foreign Policy." 1st sess., 43rd Parliament, June 2019. https://sencanada.ca/content/sen/committee/421/AEFA/Reports/Report_CulturalDiplomacy_e.pdf.

–. "North American Neighbours: Canada and Mexico, Cooperation in Uncertain Times." June 2017. https://sencanada.ca/content/sen/committee/421/AEFA/reports/Report-Canada-MexicoRelations_e.pdf.

–. "Studies and Bills – Study on the Impact and Utilization of Canadian Culture and Arts in Canadian Foreign Policy and Diplomacy, and Other Related Matters."

1st sess., 42nd Parliament, 31 May 2018. https://sencanada.ca/en/committees/aefa/studiesandbills/42-1.

Canada Council for the Arts. "Decision-Making Process." https://canadacouncil.ca/funding/funding-decisions/decision-making-process.

"The Canada-U.S. Free Trade Agreement." 1987. https://www.international.gc.ca/trade-commerce/assets/pdfs/agreements-accords/cusfta-e.pdf.

Canadian Museum of Civilization. "Museums on the Move." September 2009. Accessed 31 July 2013. http://www.civilization.ca/newsletter/archive/museums-on-the-move.

–. "Treasures from China." Accessed 31 July 2013. http://www.civilization.ca/cmc/exhibitions/cmc/china/chine02e.shtml.

Canadian Museum of Civilization Corporation. "Summary of the Corporate Plan (2009–2010 to 2013–2014)." https://www.warmuseum.ca/wp-content/uploads/2015/10/corp2009e.pdf.

Canadian Museum of History. "About." https://www.historymuseum.ca/about/history-timeline/#tabs.

–. "About – Mandate, Vision and Values." https://www.historymuseum.ca/about/#tabs.

Cárdenas, Micha, Amy Sara Carroll, Ricardo Dominguez, Elle Mehrmand, and Brett Stahlbaum. "Transborder Immigrant Tool." Net Art Anthology. Rhizome. 2007. https://anthology.rhizome.org/transborder-immigrant-tool.

Carr, Emily. *Klee Wyck*. Vancouver: Douglas and McIntyre, 2003.

Carroll, Amy Sara. *REMEX: Toward an Art History of the NAFTA Era*. Austin: University of Texas Press, 2017.

Center on Public Diplomacy. "PD & Advocacy for Effective Results." University of Southern California. n.d. https://uscpublicdiplomacy.org/event/pd-advocacy-effective-results.

Chasteen, John Charles. *Born in Flood and Fire: A Concise History of Latin America*. New York: W.W. Norton, 2001.

Chávez, Patricio. "Multi-Correct Politically Cultural." In *La Frontera/The Border: Art about the Mexico/United States Border Experience*, ed. Natasha Bonilla Martinez, 3–11. San Diego: Centro Cultural de la Raza and Museum of Contemporary Art, San Diego, 1993.

Cheran, Joanna Garcia. "An Indigenous Perspective on Frida Kahlo." *Hyperallergic*, 4 July 2021. https://hyperallergic.com/660471/indigenous-perspective-frida-kahlo.

Christ, R. "Michael Snow." *Arts Canada*, March/April 1981, n.p.

Clarkson, Stephen. *Does North America Exist?* Toronto: University of Toronto Press, 2008.

Clifford, Henry. "Introduction." In *Mexican Art Today*, 7–8. Philadelphia: Philadelphia Museum of Art, 1943.

Cogeval, Guy, and Stéphane Aquin. Untitled. In *Moi et ma circonstance: mobilité dans l'art contemporain mexicain*, n.p. Montreal: Musée des beaux-arts, 1999.

Cook-Lynn, Elizabeth. "Scandal." *Wicazo Sa Review* 22, 1 (2007): 85–89. https://doi.org/10.1353/wic.2007.0005.

Cooper, Andrew F. "Introduction." In *Canadian Culture: International Dimensions*, ed. Andrew F. Cooper, 3–26. Waterloo: Centre on Foreign Policy and Federalism, University of Waterloo/Wilfrid Laurier University, 1985.

Cooper, Andrew F., Jorge Heine, and Ramesh Thakur. "Introduction: The Challenges of 21st Century Diplomacy." In *The Oxford Handbook of Modern Diplomacy*, ed. Andrew F. Cooper, Jorge Heine, and Ramesh Thakur, 1–31. Oxford: Oxford University Press, 2013.

Coulthard, Glen. *Red Skin, White Masks: Rejecting the Colonial Politics of Recognition.* Minneapolis: University of Minnesota Press, 2014.

Courchene, Thomas J. "FTA at 15, NAFTA at 10: A Canadian Perspective on North American Integration." In *The Art of the State*. Vol. 2, *Thinking North America*, ed. Thomas J. Courchene, Donald Savoie, and Daniel Schwanen, 3–33. Montreal: Institute for Research on Public Policy, 2004.

Crean, Susan. *Who's Afraid of Canadian Culture?* Toronto: General, 1976.

Crean, Susan, Laurie Edwards, and Maria D. Hebb. "Intellectual Property and International Trade." Paper prepared for the Canada Council, March 1999. https://publications.gc.ca/collections/Collection/K23-39-2004E.pdf.

Cronin, J. Keri, and Kirsty Robertson. "Anarchy." In *Imagining Resistance: Visual Culture and Activism in Canada*, ed. J. Keri Cronin and Kirsty Robertson, 215–18. Waterloo: Wilfrid Laurier University Press, 2011.

Crosby, Marcia. "The Construction of the Imaginary Indian." In *Vancouver Anthology: The Institutional Politics of Art*, ed. Stan Douglas, 267–94. Vancouver: Talon Books, 1991.

Cruz, Teddy. "Border Postcards: Chronicles from the Edge." In *A Dynamic Equilibrium: In Pursuit of Public Terrain*, ed. Sally Yard, 68–91. San Diego: Installation Gallery, 2007.

Cuenca, Carmen, and Michael Krichman. "Foreword/inSite." In *Farsites/Sitios distantes*, eds. Adriano Pedrosa and Julie Dunn, 6–8. San Diego: Installation Gallery, 2005.

Cull, Nicholas J. *Public Diplomacy: Foundations for Global Engagement in the Digital Age.* Cambridge: Polity Press, 2019.

–. *Public Diplomacy: Lessons from the Past.* Los Angeles: Figueroa Press, 2009.

Cunningham, Ellen. "Taking a Bite out of 'the Big Apple': The 49th Parallel: Centre for Contemporary Canadian Art, 1981–1992." Master's thesis, Carleton University, 2001.

Cusack, Tricia. "Introduction: Art, Nation and Gender." In *Art, Nation and Gender: Ethnic Landscapes, Myths and Mother-Figures,* ed. Tricia Cusack and Síghle Bhreathnach-Lynch, 1–11. Aldershot, UK: Ashgate, 2003.

Daigle, Michelle. "The Spectacle of Reconciliation: On (the) Unsettling Responsibilities to Indigenous Peoples in the Academy," *Environment and Planning D: Society and Space* 37, 4 (2019): 703–21.

D'Andrea, Marisol J. "Symbolic Power: Impact of Government Priorities for Arts Funding in Canada." *Journal of Arts Management, Law, and Society* 47, 4 (2017): 245–58. https://doi.org/10.1080/10632921.2017.1340209.

Davis, Ann. "The Wembley Controversy in Canadian Art." *Canadian Historical Review* 54, 1 (1973): 48–74. https://doi.org/10.3138/CHR-054-01-03.

Dawn, Leslie. *National Visions, National Blindness: Canadian Art and Identities in the 1920s.* Vancouver: UBC Press, 2006.

de Peuter, Greig, and Nicole S. Cohen. "The Art of Collective Bargaining: An Interview with Carole Condé and Karl Beveridge." *Canadian Journal of Communication* 40, 2 (2015): 333–46.

Dear, Michael, and Gustavo Leclerc. "Introduction." In *Postborder City: Cultural Spaces of Bajalta California,* ed. Michael Dear and Gustavo Leclerc, 1–30. New York: Routledge, 2003.

Debroise, Olivier. "Mexican Art on Display." In *The Effects of the Nation: Mexican Art in an Age of Globalization,* trans. James Oles, ed. Carl Good and John V. Waldron, 20–36. Philadelphia: Temple University Press, 2001.

Diamond, Sara, and Gary Kibbins. "Total Recall: History, Memory and New Documentary." In *Video re/View: The (Best) Source for Critical Writings on Canadian Artist's Video,* ed. Peggy Gale and Lisa Steele, 265–69. Toronto: Art Metropole and Vtape, 1996.

Digital Museums Canada. "Digital Museums Canada Decommissions the Virtual Museum of Canada Website." https://www.digitalmuseums.ca/vmc-decommissioned/.

Dosman, Edgar J. "Brazil and Mexico: The Politics of Continental Drift." In *Big Picture Realities: Canada and Mexico at the Crossroads,* ed. Daniel Drache, 219–33. Waterloo: Wilfrid Laurier University Press, 2008.

Drache, Daniel. "Big Picture Realities in a Post-NAFTA Era." In *Big Picture Realities: Canada and Mexico at the Crossroads,* ed. Daniel Drache, 1–31. Waterloo: Wilfrid Laurier University Press, 2008.

Duchamp, L. Timmel. "What's the Story? Viewing *Carr, O'Keeffe, Kahlo: Places of Their Own.*" http://ltimmelduchamp.com/criticism/exhibit.html.

Dymond, W.A., and Michael M. Hart. "Abundant Paradox: The Trade and Culture Debate." *Canadian Foreign Policy Journal* 9, 2 (2002): 15–33. https://doi.org/10.1080/11926422.2002.9673281.

Estrada, Gerardo, and Eloisa Haudenschild. "Forewords/Prólogos." In *inSITE97: Private Time in Public Space,* ed. Sally Yard, 6. San Diego: Installation Gallery, 1998.

Evans, Paul. "China Choices: The Harper Era and Its Legacy." In *Harper's World: The Politicization of Canadian Foreign Policy, 2006–2015,* ed. Peter McKenna, 256–75. Toronto: University of Toronto Press, 2022.

"First Peoples of Canada Canadian Museum of Civilization." Online exhibition. Accessed 29 June 2020. https://www.historymuseum.ca/cmc/exhibitions/aborig/fp/fpint01e.html.

Fiske, John. "Videotech." In *The Visual Culture Reader,* ed. Nicholas Mirzoeff, 383–94. 2nd ed. London: Routledge, 2002.

FOCAL. "Our History." Accessed 28 July 2013. http://www.focal.ca/en/about-us.

Forsha, Lynda. "Foreword." In *inSITE94,* trans. Sandra del Castillo, ed. Sally Yard, 7–8. San Diego: Installation Gallery, 1995.

Fox, Claire. *The Fence and the River: Culture and Politics at the U.S.-Mexico Border.* Minneapolis: University of Minnesota Press, 1999.

"Francis Alÿs, the Loop." In *inSITE97: Private Time in Public Space,* ed. Sally Yard, 66–67. San Diego: Installation Gallery, 1998.

Fusco, Coco. *The Bodies That Were Not Ours.* London: Routledge and Institute of International Visual Arts, 2001.

Gagné, Gilbert. "The Evolution of Canada's Cultural Exemption in Preferential Trade Agreements." *Canadian Foreign Policy Journal* 26, 3 (2020): 298–312.

–. "L'identité québécoise et l'intégration continentale." *Politique et sociétés* 23, 2–3 (2004): 45–68.

Gale, Peggy. *Videotexts.* Waterloo: Wilfrid Laurier University Press for the Power Plant – Contemporary Art Gallery, 1995.

Galperin, Hernan. "Cultural Industries in the Age of Free-Trade Agreements." *Canadian Journal of Communication* 24, 1 (1999). https://cjc.utpjournals.press/doi/full/10.22230/cjc.1999v24n1a1082.

García Canclini, Néstor. "North Americans or Latin Americans? The Redefinition of Mexican Identity and the Free Trade Agreements." In *Mass Media and Free Trade: NAFTA and the Cultural Industries,* ed. Emile G. McAnany and Kenton T. Wilkinson, 142–56. Austin: University of Texas Press, 1996.

–. "Redefinitions: Art and Identity in the Era of Post-National Cultures." In *American Visions/Visiones de las Américas: Artistic and Cultural Identity in the Western Hemisphere,* ed. Noreen Tomassi, Mary Jan Jacob, and Ivo Mesquita, 160–73. New York: Arts International/Institute of International Education, 1994.

–. "A Re-Imagined Public Art on the Border." *Intromisiones compartidas: Arte y Sociedad en la frontera México/Estados Unidos,* 101–10. San Diego: Programa de

Fomento a Proyectos y Coinversiones Culturales del Fondo Nacional para la Cultura y las Artes y la Coedición de inSITE 97, 2000.

Gattinger, Monica. *The Roots of Culture, the Power of Art: The First Sixty Years of the Canada Council for the Arts.* Montreal and Kingston: McGill-Queen's University Press, 2017.

"George Yúdice." In *inSITE2000–2001: Parajes fugitivos/Fugitive Sites,* ed. Osvaldo Sánchez and Cecilia Garza, 78–85. San Diego: Installation Gallery, 2002.

Globerman, Steven, and Paul Storer. "Canada-U.S. Free Trade and Price Convergence in North America." *American Review of Canadian Studies* 35, 3 (2005): 423–52.

Goff, Patricia M. "Canada's Cultural Exemption." *International Journal of Cultural Policy* 25, 5 (2019): 552–67.

–. "Cultural Diplomacy." In *Oxford Handbook of Modern Diplomacy,* ed. Andrew F. Cooper, Jorge Heine, and Ramesh Thakur, 419–35. Oxford: Oxford University Press, 2013.

–. *Limits to Liberalization: Local Culture in a Global Marketplace.* Ithaca: Cornell University Press, 2007.

–. "NAFTA 2.0: Whither the Cultural Exemption?" *International Journal* 72, 4 (2017): 563–71.

–. "Trade and Culture: The Ongoing Debate." *International Journal of Cultural Policy* 25, 5 (2019): 547–51.

Goldman, Shifra M. *Contemporary Mexican Painting in a Time of Change.* Austin: University of Texas Press, 1977.

–. "Metropolitan Splendors: The Buying and Selling of Mexico." *Third Text* 5, 14 (Spring 1991): 17–26.

Gómez, Tania. "Presentan sin México exposición." *Reforma,* 4 April 2001, 3C.

Gómez-Peña, Guillermo. "The Multicultural Paradigm: An Open Letter to the National Arts Community." In *Beyond the Fantastic: Contemporary Art Criticism from Latin America,* ed. Gerardo Mosquera, 183–215. London: Institute of International Visual Arts, 1995.

–. *The New World Border: Prophecies, Poems and Loqueras for the End of the Century.* San Francisco: City Lights Books, 1996.

Good, Carl. "Introduction." In *The Effects of the Nation: Mexican Art in an Age of Globalization,* ed. Carl Good and John V. Waldron, 1–19. Philadelphia: Temple University Press, 2001.

Goodyear, Frank H., Jr. "Directors' Forewords: The Challenge of This Moment." In *Remix: New Modernities in a Post-Indian World,* ed. Joe Baker and Gerald McMaster, 7–8. Phoenix: National Museum of the American Indian, Smithsonian Institution, and the Heard Museum, 2007.

Government of Canada. *Canada in the World: Government Statement.* Ottawa: Her Majesty the Queen, 1995.

–. "Canada-Mexico First Peoples Dialogue at the National Museum of Cultures." Accessed 28 May 2020. https://www.canadainternational.gc.ca/mexico-mexique/cultr/firstpeoplesdialogue-dialoguepremierspeuples.aspx?lang=eng.

–. "The Canada-United States-Mexico Agreement (CUSMA)." https://www.international.gc.ca/trade-commerce/trade-agreements-accords-commerciaux/agr-acc/cusma-aceum/index.aspx?lang=eng.

–. "The Canada-US Free Trade Agreement." https://www.international.gc.ca/trade-commerce/assets/pdfs/agreements-accords/cusfta-e.pdf.

–. "First Peoples of Canada: Masterworks from the Canadian Museum of Civilization." Accessed 28 July 2013. http://www.canadainternational.gc.ca/mexico-mexique/cultr/firstpeoples-premierspeuples.aspx?lang=eng.

Government of Canada, Canadian Heritage. "2008–10 Canadian Heritage Cultural Activities in China." Accessed 31 July 2013. http://www.pch.gc.ca/eng/1332858451860/1332859644704.

Green, Christina F. "The Great Cultural Divide: Split-run Magazines in the 1990's." Master's thesis, Queen's University, 1999.

Gregson, Sandra. "Carr, O'Keeffe, Kahlo: Places of Their Own." *Lola* 11 (Winter 2001–02): 65.

Greyson, John, dir. *Packin.'* DVD. 2001.

Grincheva, Natalia. *Global Trends in Museum Diplomacy: Post-Guggenheim Developments.* Abingdon and New York: Routledge, 2020.

Grussani, Linda, and Ruth B. Phillips. "For We Have Waited a Hundred Thousand Years: The Indians of Canada Pavilion and Indigenous Curatorial Practices." In *Expo 67 and Its World,* ed. Craig Moyes and Steven Palmer, 115–49. Montreal and Kingston: McGill-Queen's University Press, 2022.

Grynsztejn, Madeleine. "La Frontera/The Border: Art about the Mexico/United States Border Experience." In *La Frontera/The Border: Art about the Mexico/United States Border Experience,* 23–39. San Diego: Centro Cultural de la Raza and Museum of Contemporary Art, San Diego, 1993.

Gutiérrez Haces, María Teresa. "Mexico-Canada Relations and the Impact of the NAFTA Renegotiations." In *Canada's Past and Future in Latin America,* ed. Pablo Heidrich and Laura Macdonald, 197–226. Toronto: University of Toronto Press, 2022.

Hain, Robert. "Message from the Sponsor." In *Mexican Modern Art, 1900–1950,* ed. Mayo Graham, 5. Ottawa: National Gallery of Canada, 1999.

Harvey, David. *A Brief History of Neoliberalism.* Oxford: Oxford University Press, 2005.

Haskell, Francis. *The Ephemeral Museum: Old Master Paintings and the Rise of the Art Exhibition.* New Haven: Yale University Press, 2000.

Haworth, John. "Intersections: Broadway and Central." In *Remix: New Modernities in a Post-Indian World,* ed. Joe Baker and Gerald McMaster, 91–93. Phoenix: National Museum of the American Indian, Smithsonian Institution, and the Heard Museum, 2007.

Heartney, Eleanor. "Native Identity in an Age of Hybridity." In *Remix: New Modernities in a Post-Indian World,* ed. Joe Baker and Gerald McMaster, 37–53. Phoenix: National Museum of the American Indian, Smithsonian Institution, and the Heard Museum, 2007.

Heidrich, Pablo, and Laura Macdonald, eds. *Canada's Past and Future in Latin America.* Toronto: University of Toronto Press, 2022.

–. "Introduction: Canada's Past and Future in the Americas: Beyond the 'Americas Strategy.'" In *Canada's Past and Future in Latin America,* ed. Pablo Heidrich and Laura Macdonald, 3–28. Toronto: University of Toronto Press, 2022.

Hernandez, Analays Alvarez, and Alena Robin. "Introduction to the Dialogues on Latin American Art(ists) from/in Canada: Expanding Narratives, Territories, and Perspectives." *Latin American and Latinx Visual Culture* 4, 1 (2022): 75–79.

Herzog, Lawrence A. "Global Tijuana: The Seven Ecologies of the Border." In *Postborder City: Cultural Spaces of Bajalta California,* ed. Michael Dear and Gustavo Leclerc, 119–42. New York: Routledge, 2003.

Hillmer, Norman, and J.L. Granatstein. *For Better or for Worse: Canada and the United States into the Twenty-First Century.* Toronto: Copp Clark Pitman, 1991.

Hinsley, Curtis. "The World as Marketplace: Commodification of the Exotic at the World's Columbian Exposition, Chicago, 1893." In *Exhibiting Cultures: The Poetics and Politics of Museum Display,* ed. Ivan Karp and Steven D. Lavine, 344–65. Washington: Smithsonian Press, 1991.

Hirsch, Antonia. "Tacet." Video installation. https://antoniahirsch.com/works/tacet-anthems-of-the-member-states-of-the-north-american-free-trade-agreement-mexican-united-states-united-states-of-america-canada/.

Hobsbawm, Eric. "Inventing Traditions." In *The Invention of Tradition,* ed. Eric Hobsbawm and Terence Ranger, 1–14. Cambridge: Cambridge University Press, 1983.

Indych-López, Anna. *Muralism without Walls: Rivera, Orozco and Siqueiros in the United States, 1927–1940.* Pittsburgh: University of Pittsburgh Press, 2009.

Insite. "Louis Hock." Closeup. https://insiteart.org/multimedia/closeup-louis-hock.

Institute of Ethnology and Anthropology, Chinese Academy of Social Sciences. "Canadian First Peoples' Masterworks Exhibited in Beijing." Accessed 27 July 2013. http://iea.cass.cn/content-BA0840-2011030211245851553.htm.

"Javier Téllez, One Flew over the Void (Bala perdida)." In *[Situational] Public,* ed. Osvaldo Sánchez and Donna Conwell, 72–83. San Diego: Installation Gallery, 2006.

Jessup, Lynda. "Art for a Nation?" In *Beyond Wilderness: The Group of Seven, Canadian Identity, and Contemporary Art,* ed. John O'Brian and Peter White, 187–92. Montreal and Kingston: McGill-Queen's University Press, 2007.

Jessup, Lynda, Erin Morton, and Kirsty Robertson, eds. *Negotiations in a Vacant Lot: Studying the Visual in Canada.* Montreal and Kingston: McGill-Queen's University Press, 2014.

"Jordan Crandall, Heat-Seeking." In *inSITE2000–2001: Parajes fugitivos/Fugitive Sites,* ed. Osvaldo Sánchez and Cecilia Garza, 48–51. San Diego: Installation Gallery, 2002.

Jowett, Garth S., and Victoria O'Donnell. *Propaganda and Persuasion.* 7th ed. Thousand Oaks: Sage, 2019.

"Judi Werthein, Brinco." In *[Situational] Public,* ed. Osvaldo Sánchez and Donna Conwell, 162–71. San Diego: Installation Gallery, 2006.

Kalant, Amelia. *National Identity and the Conflict at Oka: Native Belonging and Myths of Postcolonial Nationhood in Canada.* New York: Routledge, 2004.

Kamps, Toby. "Torolab." In *Baja to Vancouver: The West Coast and Contemporary Art,* ed. Ralph Rugoff, 112–13. San Francisco: CCA Wattis Institute for Contemporary Arts, 2003.

Kaplan, Rachel. "Mexican Art Today: Inés Amor, Henry Clifford and the Shifting Practices of Exhibiting Modern Mexican Art." *Journal of Curatorial Studies* 3, 2–3 (2014): 264–88.

Kester, Grant H. "Another Turn: A Response to Claire Bishop." *Artforum* 44, 9 (2006): 22–23.

–. *Conversation Pieces: Community and Communication in Modern Art.* Berkeley: University of California Press, 2004.

–. *The One and the Many: Contemporary Collaborative Art in a Global Context.* Durham: Duke University Press, 2011.

Kibbins, Gary. "Flaming Creatures: New Tendencies in Canadian Video." In *LUX: A Decade of Artists' Film and Video,* ed. Steve Reinke and Tom Taylor, 45–54. Toronto: YYZ Books, 2000.

Klein, Jennie. "Performance, Post-Border Art, and Urban Geography." *PAJ: A Journal of Performance and Art* 29, 2 (2007): 31–39.

Kong, Da. *Museums, International Exhibitions and China's Cultural Diplomacy.* London: Routledge/Taylor and Francis Group, 2021.

Konrad, Victor, and Heather Nicol. *Beyond Walls: Re-inventing the Canada-United States Borderland.* Aldershot, UK: Ashgate, 2008.

Krichman, Michael, and Carmen Cuenca. "Directors' Statement/Palabras de los directores." In *inSITE2000–2001: Parajes fugitivos/Fugitive Sites,* ed. Osvaldo Sánchez and Cecilia Garza, 14–19. San Diego: Installation Gallery, 2002.

–. "Preface/Prefacio." In *inSITE97: Private Time in Public Space,* ed. Sally Yard, 8–10. San Diego: Installation Gallery, 1998.

Krichman, Michael, Lynda Forsha, Hugh M. Davies, Ernesto Ruffo Appel, Héctor G. Osuna Jaime, Rafael Tovar, Gerardo Estrada Rodríguez, and Alfredo Álvarez Cárdenas. "Acknowledgements." In *inSITE94,* trans. Sandra del Castillo, ed. Sally Yard, 9–11. San Diego: Installation Gallery, 1995.

Kropp, Phoebe S., and Michael Dear. "Peopling Alta California." In *Postborder City: Cultural Spaces of Bajalta California,* ed. Michael Dear and Gustavo Leclerc, 47–82. New York: Routledge, 2003.

"Krzysztof Wodiczko, Proyección en Tijuana/Tijuana Projection." In *inSITE2000–2001: Parajes fugitivos/Fugitive Sites,* ed. Osvaldo Sánchez and Cecilia Garza, 74–75. San Diego: Installation Gallery, 2002.

Langford, Martha. *Michael Snow: Life and Work.* Toronto: Art Canada Institute, 2014.

–. *Narratives Unfolding: National Art Histories in an Unfinished World.* Montreal and Kingston: McGill-Queen's University Press, 2017.

Lennox, Patrick. *At Home and Abroad: The Canada-US Relationship and Canada's Place in the World.* Vancouver: UBC Press, 2010.

Levander, Caroline Field, and Robert S. Levine, eds. *Hemispheric American Studies.* New Brunswick, NJ: Rutgers University Press, 2007.

Levy, Evonne. "Art History in Canada: 1933–Present." Accessed 29 June 2020. https://arthistoryincanada.ca.

Lindauer, Margaret A. *Devouring Frida: The Art History and Popular Celebrity of Frida Kahlo.* Hanover: Wesleyan University Press, 1999.

Litt, Paul. *The Muses, the Masses and the Massey Commission.* Toronto: University of Toronto Press, 1992.

"Louis Hock, International Waters/Aguas Internacionales." In *inSITE97: Private Time in Public Space,* ed. Sally Yard, 78–79. San Diego: Installation Gallery, 1998.

Lozano, Luis-Martín. "Mexican Modern Art: Rendezvous with the Avant-garde." In *Mexican Modern Art, 1900–1950,* ed. Mayo Graham, 11–27. Ottawa: National Gallery of Canada, 1999.

Lu Zhangshen, and Victor Rabinovitch. "Foreword." In *Timeless Splendour: Treasures from the National Museum of China,* 5. Gatineau: Canada Museum of Civilization, 2007.

Mackey, Eva. *The House of Difference: Cultural Politics and National Identity in Canada.* Toronto: University of Toronto Press, 2002.

Manly, Eva. "The Winning of the North." Vtape online catalogue. https://vtape.org/video?vi=2003.

Mark, Simon L. "Rethinking Cultural Diplomacy: The Cultural Diplomacy of New Zealand, the Canadian Federation and Quebec." *Political Science* 62, 1 (2010): 62–83.

Marks, Laura U. "Plunging into the Event: Political Struggle between Language and the Earth." In *Better Worlds: Activist and Utopian Projects by Artists,* ed. Jan Allen and Laura U. Marks, 37–46. Kingston: Agnes Etherington Art Centre, 2002.

Marsh, Charity. "Bits and Pieces of Truth: Storytelling, Identity, and Hip Hop in Saskatchewan." In *Aboriginal Music in Contemporary Canada: Echoes and Exchanges,* ed. Anna Hoefnagels and Beverley Diamond, 346–71. Montreal and Kingston: McGill-Queen's University Press, 2012.

Martin, Lee-Ann. "Anger and Reconciliation: A Very Brief History of Exhibiting Contemporary Indigenous Art in Canada." *Afterall* 43 (2017): 108–15. https://www.journals.uchicago.edu/doi/pdf/10.1086/692560.

"Mauricio Dias and Walter Riedweg." In *inSITE2000–2001: Parajes fugitivos/Fugitive Sites,* ed. Osvaldo Sánchez and Cecilia Garza, 98–99. San Diego: Installation Gallery, 2002.

McAlear, Donna. "WAG Chosen for International Internet Exhibition." *Tableau,* November-December 2000, 3.

McKercher, Asa. *Camelot and Canada: Canadian-American Relations in the Kennedy Era.* Oxford: Oxford University Press, 2016.

–. "Locating Latin America: Geography, Identity, and the Americas in Canadian Foreign Policy." In *Canada's Past and Future in Latin America,* ed. Pablo Heidrich and Laura Macdonald, 29–56. Toronto: University of Toronto Press, 2022.

McMaster, Gerald. "Anna Tsouhlarakis." In *Remix: New Modernities in a Post-Indian World,* ed. Joe Baker and Gerald McMaster, 82–83. Phoenix: National Museum of the American Indian, Smithsonian Institution, and the Heard Museum, 2007.

–. "Hector Ruiz." In *Remix: New Modernities in a Post-Indian World,* ed. Joe Baker and Gerald McMaster, 80–81. Phoenix: National Museum of the American Indian, Smithsonian Institution, and the Heard Museum, 2007.

–. "Introductions: Mixing It Up." In *Remix: New Modernities in a Post-Indian World,* ed. Joe Baker and Gerald McMaster, 55–57. Phoenix: National Museum of the American Indian, Smithsonian Institution, and the Heard Museum, 2007.

–. "Kent Monkman." In *Remix: New Modernities in a Post-Indian World,* ed. Joe Baker and Gerald McMaster, 74–75. Phoenix: National Museum of the American Indian, Smithsonian Institution, and the Heard Museum, 2007.

–. "Steven Yazzie." In *Remix: New Modernities in a Post-Indian World,* ed. Joe Baker and Gerald McMaster, 88–89. Phoenix: National Museum of the American Indian, Smithsonian Institution, and the Heard Museum, 2007.

McMichael Canadian Art Collection. "Carr, O'Keeffe, Kahlo: Places of Their Own." Accessed 20 July 2013. http://mcmichael.com/exhibitions/efg/indexpast.cfm.

Medina, Cuauhtémoc. "A Line Is a Central Point with Two Sides ..." In *inSITE94*, trans. Sandra del Castillo, ed. Sally Yard, 54–63. San Diego: Installation Gallery, 1995.

Michelson, Alan. "Third Bank of the River." https://www.alanmichelson.com/third-bank-of-the-river/rso2rximdn6dna0eiabhsn620egyax.

Mills, Sean. *The Empire Within: Postcolonial Thought and Anti-Colonial Activism in Sixties Montreal.* Montreal and Kingston: McGill-Queen's University Press, 2010.

Mitchell, W.J.T. "Imperial Landscape." In *Landscape and Power*, ed. W.J.T. Mitchell, 5–34. Chicago: University of Chicago Press, 1994.

"Mônica Nador, Acción en Maclovio Rojas/Project at Maclovio Rojas." In *inSITE2000–2001: Parajes fugitivos/Fugitive Sites*, ed. Osvaldo Sánchez and Cecilia Garza, 87–88. San Diego: Installation Gallery, 2002.

Moray, Gerta. "Emily Carr: Modernism, Cultural Identity and Ethnocultural Art History." In *The Visual Arts in Canada: The Twentieth Century*, ed. Brian Foss, Sandra Paikowsky, and Anne Whitelaw, 59–77. Oxford: Oxford University Press, 2010.

Moreton-Robinson, Aileen. *The White Possessive: Property, Power, and Indigenous Sovereignty.* Minneapolis: University of Minnesota Press, 2015.

Morton, Erin, ed. *Unsettling Canadian Art History.* Montreal and Kingston: McGill-Queen's University Press, 2022.

Moser, Gabrielle. "Every Building on 100 West Hastings (2001)." In CanadARThistories: Reimagining the Canadian Art History Survey. eCampus Ontario, 2022. https://ecampusontario.pressbooks.pub/canadarthistories/chapter/every-building-on-100-west-hastings-2001/.

Mousseau, Heather. "Panoramas Extends to School Project." *Tableau*, May-June 2001, 4.

Muirhead, Bruce. "From Special Relationship to Third Option: Canada, the U.S., and the Nixon Shock." *American Review of Canadian Studies* 34, 3 (2004): 439–62.

Mulcahy, Kevin V. "Cultural Imperialism and Cultural Sovereignty: U.S.-Canadian Cultural Relations." *American Review of Canadian Studies* 30, 2 (2000): 181–206. https://doi.org/10.1080/02722010009481050.

–. "Cultural Patronage in Comparative Perspective: Public Support for the Arts in France, Germany, Norway, and Canada." *Journal of Arts Management, Law, and Society* 27, 4 (1998): 247–63. https://doi.org/10.1080/10632929809597270.

Myre, Nadia. *Rethinking Anthem*, 2008. http://www.nadiamyre.net/time-based#/rethinking-anthem-2008/.

National Gallery of Canada. "Sol y Vida – Mexican Modern Art: 1900–1950." https://www.gallery.ca/whats-on/exhibitions-and-galleries/sol-y-vida-mexican-modern-art-1900-1950.

National Inquiry into Missing and Murdered Indigenous Women and Girls. "Reclaiming Power and Place: The Final Report of the National Inquiry into Missing and Murdered Indigenous Women and Girls." Vols. 1a and 1b. 2019. https://www.mmiwg-ffada.ca/final-report/.

Neathery-Castro, Jody. "Canada as Multilateral Player: Trade in Cultural Products." *Canadian Foreign Policy Journal* 18, 1 (2012): 76–91. https://doi.org/10.1080/11926422.2012.674377.

Nelson, Marcel. *A History of the FTAA: From Hegemony to Fragmentation in the Americas.* New York: Palgrave Macmillan, 2015.

"New York's 49th Parallel." *Visual Arts Ontario,* 1981, 3.

Nicolas, Emilie. "Maîtres chez l'autre." *Liberté* 326 (Winter 2020): 43–44. Accessed 21 October 2001. https://www.sodep.qc.ca/wp-content/uploads/2020/03/PrixExcellence2020_Liberte_326_EmilieNicolas.pdf.

NoiseCat, Julian Brave. "How Canada Uses Indigenous Art to Market Itself to the World." *The Walrus,* 17 November 2019. https://thewalrus.ca/how-canada-uses-indigenous-art-to-market-itself-to-the-world.

North American Cultural Diplomacy Initiative. "Cultural Diplomacy and Trade: Making Connections." Kingston and Ottawa, Queen's University/Canadian Heritage, March 2018. https://culturaldiplomacyinitiative.com/wp-content/uploads/2021/06/Cultural-Diplomacy-and-Trade_NACDI-Report.pdf.

Nossal, Kim Richard, and Leah Sarson. "About Face: Explaining Changes in Canada's China Policy, 2006–2012." *Canadian Foreign Policy Journal* 20, 2 (2014): 146–62. https://doi.org/10.1080/11926422.2014.934864.

"A Note on Context/Nota sobre el context." In *A Dynamic Equilibrium: In Pursuit of Public Terrain,* ed. Sally Yard, 6–7. San Diego: Installation Gallery, 2007.

Ochoa Bilbao, Luis, and Jorge A. Schiavon. "Is Mexico a North American or Latin American Country? An Analysis of Public Opinion." *Latin American Policy* 9, 1 (2018): 113–38. https://doi.org/10.1111/lamp.12137.

"October 2003/Residencies." In *[Situational] Public,* ed. Osvaldo Sánchez and Donna Conwell, 24–27. San Diego: Installation Gallery, 2006.

Orme, William A., Jr. *Understanding NAFTA: Mexico, Free Trade, and the New North America.* Austin: University of Texas Press, 1996.

Palumbo-Liu, David. "Hybridities and Histories: Imaging the Rim." In *Postborder City: Cultural Spaces of Bajalta California,* ed. Michael Dear and Guatavo Leclerc, 249–75. New York: Routledge, 2003.

Paschalidis, Gregory. "Exporting National Culture: Histories of Cultural Institutes Abroad." *International Journal of Cultural Policy* 15, 3 (2009): 275–89.

Paz, Octavio. "Will for Form." *Mexico: Splendors of Thirty Centuries,* 3–38. New York/Boston: Metropolitan Museum of Art/Little, Brown, 1990.

Pedrosa, Adriano. "Farsites." In *Farsites/Sitios distantes,* ed. Adriano Pedrosa and Julie Dunn, 22–36. San Diego: Installation Gallery, 2005.

Phillips, Ruth B. "Disrupting Past Paradigms: The National Museum of the American Indian and the First Peoples Hall at the Canadian Museum of Civilization." *Public Historian* 28, 2 (2006): 75–80. https://doi.org/10.1525/tph.2006.28.2.75.

–. *Museums Pieces.* Montreal and Kingston: McGill-Queen's University Press, 2011.

–. "Show Times: De-celebrating the Canadian Nation, De-colonizing the Canadian Museum, 1967–92." In *Rethinking Settler Colonialism: History and Memory in Australia, Canada, Aotearoa New Zealand and South Africa,* ed. Annie E. Coobes, 121–39. Manchester: Manchester University Press, 2006.

Poitras, Guy. *Inventing North America: Canada, Mexico, and the United States.* Boulder: Lynne Rienner, 2001.

"Preface." In *Mexican Art: From Pre-Columbian Times to the Present Day,* compiled by Donald W. Buchanan and Jorge Olvera, n.p. Vancouver: Keystone Press, 1960.

Priewe, Sascha. *Museum Diplomacy: Parsing the Global Engagement of Museums.* Los Angeles: Figueroa Press, 2021.

Ramírez, Mari Carmen. "Beyond 'the Fantastic': Framing Identity in US Exhibitions of Latin American Art." In *Beyond the Fantastic: Contemporary Art Criticism from Latin America,* ed. Gerardo Mosquera, 229–46. London: Institute of International Visual Arts, 1995.

Randall, Stephen J., and Herman W. Konrad. "Introduction." In *NAFTA in Transition,* ed. Stephen J. Randall and Herman W. Konrad, 1–11. Calgary: University of Calgary Press, 1995.

Rankin, Monica A. "A Revolutionary Mural of Propaganda." In *Mexico, La Patria: Propaganda and Production during World War II,* 104–58. Lincoln: University of Nebraska Press, 2009.

Ravensbergen, Lisa C. "Potluck Protocols." SpiderWebShow Performance, 26 January 2016. https://spiderwebshow.ca/potluck-protocols.

Reid, Dennis. "Introduction to the Group of Seven." In *Beyond Wilderness: The Group of Seven, Canadian Identity and Contemporary Art,* ed. John O'Brian and Peter White, 101–8. Montreal and Kingston: McGill-Queen's University Press, 2007.

"Residencies/Residencias." In *inSITE2000–2001: Parajes fugitivos/Fugitive Sites,* edited by Osvaldo Sánchez and Cecilia Garza, 60–61. San Diego: Installation Gallery, 2002.

Rice, Ryan. "Rethinking Anthem." Artist's website. Accessed 28 July 2013. http://www.nadiamyre.com/Nadia_Myre/video/Pages/Rethinking_Anthem.html.

Rickard, Jolene. "Rebecca Belmore: Performing Power." In *Rebecca Belmore: Fountain,* 68–76. Vancouver: Morris and Helen Belkin Art Gallery, 2005.

Roberts, Gillian. *Discrepant Parallels: Cultural Implications of the Canada-US Border.* Montreal and Kingston: McGill-Queen's University Press, 2015.

Robertson, Clive. *Policy Matters: Administrations of Art and Culture.* Toronto: YYZBooks, 2006.

–. "Trade Winds (Canada) Ltd." Vtape online catalogue. https://vtape.org/video?vi=1349.

Robertson, Kirsty. "Crude Culture: The Creative Industries in Canada." *Fuse* 31, 2 (Spring 2008): 12–21.

–. *Tear Gas Epiphanies: Protest, Culture, Museums.* Montreal and Kingston: McGill-Queen's University Press, 2019.

Robertson, Kirsty, Stephanie Anderson, Elizabeth Diggon, Ahlia Moussa, and Sarah E.K. Smith. "'More a Diplomatic than an Esthetic Event': Canada, Brazil, and Cultural Brokering in the São Paulo Biennial and 'Isumavut.'" *Journal of Canadian Studies* 47, 2 (2013): 60–88.

Robertson, Kirsty, and J. Keri Cronin. "Imagining Resistance: An Introduction." In *Imagining Resistance: Visual Culture and Activism in Canada,* ed. J. Keri Cronin and Kirsty Robertson, 1–21. Waterloo: Wilfrid Laurier University Press, 2011.

Robin, Alena. "Colores de Latinoamérica: Teaching Latin American Art in London (Ontario, Canada)." *International Journal of Education and the Arts* 21, 16 (June 2020). http://doi.org/10.26209/ijea21n16.

–. "Mapping the Presence of Latin American Art in Canadian Museums and Universities." *Latin American and Latinx Visual Culture* 1, 2 (2019): 33–57.

Robin, Alena, and Maria del Carmen Suescun Pozas, eds. *Latin America Made in Canada.* Ottawa: Lugar Común Editorial, 2022.

Robinson, Dylan. *Hungry Listening: Resonant Theory for Indigenous Sound Studies.* Minneapolis: University of Minnesota Press, 2020.

–. "Public Writing, Sovereign Reading: Indigenous Language Art in Public Space." *Art Journal* 76, 2 (2017): 85–99. https://doi.org/10.1080/00043249.2017.1367195.

Roger, Judith. *Greg Curnoe: Life and Work.* Toronto: Art Canada Institute, 2016.

Rogge, Malcolm, dir. *Like a Nice Rubber Gas Mask.* DVD. 2001.

Roth, Michael S., Hugh M. Davies, Mimi Gates, and Kathleen S. Bartels. "Foreword." In *Baja to Vancouver: The West Coast and Contemporary Art,* ed. Ralph Rugoff, 6–7. San Francisco: CCA Wattis Institute for Contemporary Arts, 2003.

Rugoff, Ralph. "Baja to Vancouver: The West Coast and Contemporary Art." In *Baja to Vancouver: The West Coast and Contemporary Art,* ed. Ralph Rugoff, 13–19. San Francisco: CCA Wattis Institute for Contemporary Arts, 2003.

Sadowski-Smith, Claudia, and Claire F. Fox. "Theorizing the Hemisphere: Inter-Americas Work at the Intersection of American, Canadian, and Latin American Studies." *Comparative American Studies* 2, 1 (2004): 5–38.

Salvatore, Ricardo D. "On Knowledge Asymmetries and Cognitive Maps: Reconsidering Hemispheric American Studies." *MLN* 130, 2 (2015): 362–89.

"Scenarios." In *[Situational] Public,* ed. Osvaldo Sánchez and Donna Conwell, 372–73. San Diego: Installation Gallery, 2006.

Schneider, C.P. "Cultural Diplomacy: Hard to Define but You'd Know It If You Saw It." *Brown Journal of World Affairs* 8, 1 (Fall-Winter 2006): 191–203.

Siemerling, Winfried, and Sarah Phillips Casteel. *Canada and Its Americas: Transnational Navigations.* Montreal and Kingston: McGill-Queen's University Press, 2010.

Simpson, Audra. *Mohawk Interruptus: Political Life across the Borders of Settler States.* Durham: Duke University Press, 2014.

Skoggard, R. "The 49th Parallel." *Art in America* 6 (Summer 1981): 17–18.

–. "The 49th Parallel: After Two Years." *artmagazine* 14, 63–64 (Summer 1983): 32–33.

Smith, Sarah E.K. "Bridging the 49th Parallel." In *Canada's Public Diplomacy,* ed. Nicholas J. Cull and Michael K. Hawes, 95–125. Basingstoke, UK: Palgrave Macmillan, 2021.

–. "Clive Robertson." In *Trans-Pacific Transmissions: Video Art across the Pacific,* ed. Haema Sivanesan, 78–79. Victoria: Art Gallery of Greater Victoria, 2016.

–. "Condé and Beveridge's Art Activism." *Prefix Photo* 33 (May 2016): 45–55.

–. "Cross-Border Identifications and Dislocations: Visual Art and the Construction of Identity in North America." In *Parallel Encounters: Culture at the Canada-US Border,* ed. D.F. Stirrup and Gillian Roberts, 187–205. Kitchener: Wilfrid Laurier University Press, 2013.

–. "Exhibiting Mexican Art in Canada: Histories of Cultural Exchange and Diplomacy in the Mid-Twentieth Century." *Latin America Made in Canada,* ed. Alena Robin and Maria del Carmen Suescun Pozas, 67–84. Ottawa: Lugar Común Editorial, 2022.

–. "The Permeable Border: Examining Responses to North American Integration in Video Art." *Comparative American Studies* 13, 1–2 (2015): 91–106.

–. "Visualizing the 'New' North American Landscape." In *Negotiations in a Vacant Lot: Studying the Visual in Canada,* ed. Lynda Jessup, Erin Morton, and Kirsty Robertson, 130–49. Montreal and Kingston: McGill-Queen's University Press, 2014.

Smith, Sarah E.K., and Sascha Priewe, eds. *Museum Diplomacy: How Cultural Institutions Shape Global Engagement.* Lanham: Rowman and Littlefield, 2023.

Smithsonian American Art Museum. "Museum History." https://americanart.si.edu/about/history.

Springer, José. "Birds of a Feather: Canada, Mexico, NAFTA and Culture." *Fuse* 19, 3 (1996): 31–38.

Steele, Lisa, and Kim Tomczak. "White Dawn." 1988. Artists' website. http://s133370137.onlinehome.us/2020/06/04/white-dawn/.

Stein, Sally. "Looking Backward and Forward: A Preliminary Historical Conversation about inSite." In *[Situational] Public,* ed. Osvaldo Sánchez and Donna Conwell, 417–25. San Diego: Installation Gallery, 2006.

Sterbak, Jana. "Testimony before the Standing Senate Committee on Foreign Affairs and International Trade." 1st sess., 42nd Parliament, 31 May 2018. Accessed 21 October 2001. http://senparlvu.parl.gc.ca.

Stewart, Janice. "Cultural Appropriations and Identificatory Practices in Emily Carr's 'Indian Stories.'" *Frontiers: A Journal of Women Studies* 26, 2 (2005): 59–72.

Steyerl, Hito. *Duty Free Art in the Age of Planetary Civil War.* London: Verso, 2017.

Stirrup, David. "Bridging the Third Bank: Indigeneity and Installation Art at the Canada-US Border." In *Parallel Encounters: Culture at the Canada-US Border,* ed. D.F. Stirrup and Gillian Roberts, 163–85. Kitchener: Wilfrid Laurier University Press, 2013.

Stirrup, David, and Jan Clarke. "Straddling Boundaries: Culture and the Canada-US Border." *Comparative American Studies: An International Journal* 13, 1–2 (2015): 1–15.

Sutherland, Camilla. "Indigenismo and the Limits of Cultural Appropriation: Frida Kahlo and Marina Núñez Del Prado." *Angelaki: Journal of Theoretical Humanities* 27, 3–4 (2022): 75–90.

Tabobondung, Rebeka, and Adrian Kahgee. *The Original Summit: Journey to the Sacred Uprising.* VHS. 2002.

Théberge, Pierre, and Guy Cogeval. "Foreword." In *Mexican Modern Art, 1900–1950,* ed. Mayo Graham, 7. Ottawa: National Gallery of Canada, 1999.

Thompson, John Herd, and Stephen J. Randall. *Canada and the United States: Ambivalent Allies.* 4th ed. Montreal and Kingston: McGill-Queen's University Press, 2008.

Tsouhlarakis, Anna. "About." https://www.naveeks.com/about.

Tuck, Eve, and K. Wayne Yang. "Decolonization Is Not a Metaphor." *Decolonization: Indigeneity, Education and Society* 1, 1 (2012): 1–40.

Udall, Sharyn Rohlfsen. *Carr, O'Keeffe, Kahlo: Places of Their Own.* New Haven: Yale University Press, 2000.

–. "Carr, O'Keeffe, Kahlo: Places of Their Own." *Sketches* 1, 7 (Spring-Summer 2001): 2–3.

UNESCO. "Background Document." UNESCO World Conference on Cultural Policies and Sustainable Development MONDIACULT 2022, 28–30 September 2022, Mexico City. https://www.unesco.org/sites/default/files/medias/fichiers/2022/09/4.MONDIACULT_EN_BACKGROUND%20DOCUMENT.pdf.

–. "The Convention on the Protection and Promotion of the Diversity of Cultural Expressions." UNESCO, n.d. https://webarchive.unesco.org/20230614143248/http://en.unesco.org/creativity/convention.

"Unfolding Process; Summaries of Key Moments during the Projects' Development." In *[Situational] Public,* ed. Osvaldo Sánchez and Donna Conwell, 50–65. San Diego: Installation Gallery, 2006.

Upchurch, Anna Rosser. "Keynes's Legacy: An Intellectual's Influence Reflected in Arts Policy." *International Journal of Cultural Policy* 17, 1 (2011): 69–80. https://doi.org/10.1080/10286630903456851.

–. *The Origins of the Arts Council Movement: Philanthropy and Policy.* London: Palgrave Macmillan, 2016.

Varga, Vincent. "Untitled." *Vernissage,* Spring 2002, 42.

Veracini, Lorenzo. *Settler Colonialism: A Theoretical Overview.* New York: Palgrave Macmillan, 2010.

Virtual Museum of Canada. "About Us." http://www.virtualmuseum.ca/about-vmc.

–. "Perspectives: Women Artists in North America, About." Accessed 20 July 2013. http://www.museevirtuel-virtualmuseum.ca/edu/ViewLoitCollection.do;jsessionid=EB8CECCB63CE1D5A72D6F106D02E313D?method=previewAbout&lang=EN&id=12740.

Virtual Museum of Canada, Canadian Heritage Information Network. "Panoramas: The North American Landscape in Art – Virtual Tours and Media Exhibition." Accessed 20 December 2018. http://www.museevirtuel-virtualmuseum.ca/edu/ViewLoitCollection.do?method=preview&lang=EN&id=4783.

–. "Suggested Activities." Accessed 20 December 2018. http://www.virtualmuseum.ca/edu/ViewLoitLo.do?method=preview&lang=EN&id=5034.

Virtue, John. *Leonard and Reva Brooks: Artists in Exile in San Miguel de Allende.* Montreal and Kingston: McGill-Queen's University Press, 2001.

Vizenor, Gerald. "Native Cosmototemic Art." In *Sakahàn: International Indigenous Art,* 41–52. Ottawa: National Gallery of Canada, 2013.

Vucetic, Srdjan. *The Anglosphere: A Genealogy of a Racialized Identity in International Relations.* Stanford: Stanford University Press, 2011.

Wakefield, Sarina. "Arts and the Super-Rich: Emerging Relations in the Gulf and the East." In *Cities and the Super-Rich: Real Estate, Elite Practices, and Urban Political Economics,* ed. Ray Forrest, Sin Yee Koh, and Bart Wissink, 167–86. New York: Palgrave Macmillan, 2017.

Wallen, Ruth. "Barrier or Bridge: Photojournalism of the San Diego/Tijuana Border Region." *Communication Review* 6, 2 (2003): 137–64.

Wallis, Brian. "Selling Nations: International Exhibitions and Cultural Diplomacy." In *Museum Culture: Histories, Discourses, Spectacles,* ed. Daniel J. Sherman and Irit Rogoff, 265–81. Minneapolis: University of Minnesota Press, 1994.

Wasney, Tricia. "Panoramas: The North American Landscape in Art." *Tableau* 7 (2001): 1.

Watson, Scott, and Rebecca Belmore. "Interview." In *Rebecca Belmore: Fountain,* 24–28. Vancouver: Morris and Helen Belkin Art Gallery, 2005.

Wayne, Joyce. "Does Canada Have a Cultural Foreign Policy?" *Canadian Art* 2, 2 (1985): 34–36, 38–39, 62–63.

West, W. Richard, Jr. "Directors' Forewords: On the Edge." In *Remix: New Modernities in a Post-Indian World,* 11–12. Phoenix: National Museum of the American Indian, Smithsonian Institution, and the Heard Museum, 2007.

Westgeest, Helen. "Introduction." In *Video Art Theory: A Comparative Approach,* 1–19. Chichester, UK: Wiley Blackwell, 2016.

Williams, Raymond. "The Analysis of Culture." In *Cultural Theory and Popular Culture: A Reader,* ed. John Storey, 48–56. Athens: University of Georgia Press, 1998.

Wolfe, Patrick. "Settler Colonialism and the Elimination of the Native." *Journal of Genocide Research* 8, 4 (2006): 387–409.

"Works in the Exhibition." In *Mexican Modern Art, 1900–1950,* ed. Mayo Graham, 162–90. Ottawa: National Gallery of Canada, 1999.

World Trade Organization. "Canada – Certain Measures concerning Periodicals." 14 March 1996. https://docs.wto.org/dol2fe/Pages/SS/directdoc.aspx?filename=Q:/G/L/66.pdf&Open=True.

Yard, Sally. "A Dynamic Equilibrium: In Pursuit of Public Terrain/Equilibrio dinámico: En busca de un terreno público." In *A Dynamic Equilibrium: In Pursuit of Public Terrain,* ed. Sally Yard, 12–25. San Diego: Installation Gallery, 2007.

–. "Tagged Turf in the Public Sphere." In *inSITE94,* trans. Sandra del Castillo, ed. Sally Yard, 34–53. San Diego: Installation Gallery, 1995.

Yúdice, George. *The Expediency of Culture: Uses of Culture in the Global Era.* Durham: Duke University Press, 2003.

–. "Extract of George Yúdice's Participation in *Conversation IV: Image Power: Cultural Interventions as Public Memory in Post-modern Spaces,* February 25, 2001. In(fo) SITE, Centro Cultural Tijuana." In *inSITE2000-2001: Parajes fugitivos/Fugitive Sites,* ed. Osvaldo Sánchez and Cecilia Garza, 78–84. San Diego: Installation Gallery, 2002.

Zorbas, Jason Gregory. "Diefenbaker, Latin America and the Caribbean: The Pursuit of Canadian Autonomy." PhD diss., University of Saskatchewan, 2009.

Index

Note: "(f)" after a page number indicates an illustration; "(t)" after a page number indicates a table; CUSFTA stands for Canada-US Free Trade Agreement; CUSMA stands for Canada-United States-Mexico Agreement; FTAA stands for Free Trade Area of the Americas; NAFTA stands for North American Free Trade Agreement

Printed and bound in Canada by Friesens

Set in Zurich Condensed and Minion by Artegraphica Design Co.

Copy editor: Deborah Kerr

Proofreader: Helen Godolphin

Indexer: Timothy Pearson

Cover designer: George Kirkpatrick

Cover image: Peter Dykhuis, *State Dinner*, detail, 2005

Authorized Representative:
Easy Access System Europe -
Mustamäe tee 50, 10621 Tallinn, Estonia,
gpsr.requests@easproject.com